体育英语专业系列教材

总主编　田　慧

综合英语教程
AN INTEGRATED ENGLISH COURSE

（第四册）

主　　编：李　晶
副 主 编：柳莉蕊　王　严

编　　委：（按姓氏笔画排名）
　　　　　王　严　李　晶　陈　杰
　　　　　陈翩翩（美）　柳莉蕊　赵　雪
审　　校：田　慧　Vera Lee

北京大学出版社
PEKING UNIVERSITY PRESS

图书在版编目（CIP）数据

综合英语教程.4/ 田慧总主编. —北京：北京大学出版社，2010.4
（体育英语专业系列教材）
ISBN 978-7-301-17066-3

Ⅰ. 综… Ⅱ. 田… Ⅲ. 体育 – 英语 – 高等学校 – 教材 Ⅳ. H31

中国版本图书馆CIP数据核字(2010) 第 047995 号

书　　名	综合英语教程（第四册）
	ZONGHE YINGYU JIAOCHENG (DI-SI CE)
著作责任者	田　慧　总主编
责任编辑	徐万丽
标准书号	ISBN 978-7-301-17066-3
出版发行	北京大学出版社
地　　址	北京市海淀区成府路205号　100871
网　　址	http://www.pup.cn
电　　话	邮购部 010-62752015　发行部 010-62750672　编辑部 010-62759634
电子信箱	zln0120@163.com
印刷者	北京虎彩文化传播有限公司
经销者	新华书店
	787 毫米 × 1092 毫米　16 开本　14.75 印张　295 千字
	2010 年 4 月第 1 版　2020 年 9 月第 3 次印刷
定　　价	33.00 元（配有光盘）

未经许可，不得以任何方式复制或抄袭本书之部分或全部内容。
版权所有，侵权必究
举报电话：010-62752024　电子信箱：fd@pup.pku.edu.cn
图书如有印装质量问题，请与出版部联系，电话：010-62756370

前　言

　　从 2002 年开始，国内的体育院校纷纷开设了体育英语专业，培养在体育领域从事对外交流工作的国际体育人才。经过近 7 年发展，体育英语专业既显示出强大的生机和活力，又面临着诸多困难，首要的问题就是教材问题。目前，体育英语专业大多在技能类课程，特别是基础阶段课程中沿用了全国统编英语专业教材。这些教材选材精当、设计合理，对夯实学生语言基本功起到巨大作用，但针对性不强，未能体现出本专业特色。因此，从 2004 年开始，我们就着手策划编写一套供体育英语专业学生使用的系列教材，并于 2007 年获得北京高等教育精品教材立项。系列教材包括基础阶段的《综合英语教程》、《英语听说教程》、《英语阅读教程》和高级阶段的《体育英语阅读》等，首批推出的是基础阶段的《综合英语教程》和《英语听说教程》。

　　经教育部批准的《高等学校英语专业英语教学大纲》指出：英语专业学生应具有扎实的语言基本功、宽广的知识面、一定的相关专业知识、较强的能力和较高素质。基础阶段各教程正是按照这一培养目标编写，立足于加强学生语言基本功，在培养语言基本功的同时渗透体育元素、人文精神，以提高学生的体育知识水平和人文素养，并在设计中力图培养学生的跨文化交际能力和独立思维能力。同时，本系列教材的一个突出特点是将各门课程的同一单元统一于一个话题，学生在综合英语、英语阅读、英语听说中同步围绕一个话题进行不同的技能训练，也使得他们能从不同角度认识同一问题。

　　《综合英语教程》是为第一、二学年的专业基础教学配备的课本，训练听说读写译等各方面技能。教程没有将语法和语言功能作为编写主线，而是以课文的主题和内容作为编写的基础；每一单元围绕同一主题选编了两篇文章，并将有关的体育内容穿插其中。随着学生语言技能、思维能力和人文素养的提高及文化知识的丰富，从第三册开始，除沿袭前两册教材的编写体例，教程还增加了一些内容，并对原有的设计进行了更新，融入了一些新的教学思想和理念。在突出体育特色

方面,教材不仅通过课文本身渗透体育元素,同时在词汇练习及完形填空设计中尽可能选用一些体育类语篇,让学生在了解体育知识的同时逐步熟悉体育类文本(包括体育类新闻报道)的语言表达方式及特点。在写作练习中,编者结合课文主题设计了丰富多样的体育类话题,将体育和人文相结合,引导学生关注体育文化并进行广泛深入的思考。

  Text I 作为主课文,教师课堂精讲,并处理与课文相关的课文理解、词汇、翻译等练习。从第三册开始,课文理解部分丰富了练习题型,更加注重引导学生抓住关键信息,培养他们的归纳能力。词汇练习更加注重在语境中全面理解词义,练习所用语料均选自国外报纸杂志或图书的原句,有相对完整的语境,学生在做练习的同时可以进一步学习原汁原味的语言表达。翻译练习除保留本单元出现的重要生词、词组及习惯表达进行单句操练外,还增加了汉译英和英译汉的段落翻译。汉译英段落选取了与本单元话题相关且难度不大的语篇,英译汉段落则是选取了 Text I 中比较重要的语篇。这些段落翻译旨在引导学生在丰富的语境中提高语言综合运用的能力。

  为了让学生在增强语言技能的同时进一步感知和领悟语言的特点并体验语言的魅力,第三、四册增加了"语言欣赏"这一环节。该环节分三部分,第一部分通过摘录课文中的精妙词句引导学生关注英语母语使用者经常使用的句式、词汇和表达方式,并逐步运用到自己的写作中;第二部分选取课文中描写优美、分析清晰、说理有力的段落供学生朗读并背诵,以增强语感;第三部分以文体学主要理论为切入点,结合课文内容引导学生用文体学知识分析语言特点,兼谈翻译、汉英语言的比较以及修辞,引导体验语言奥妙。该部分重在实践和体验,理论介绍和讲解不多,主要通过语篇(句子)实例,设计相关问题以引导学生,激活以往语言知识,主动思考,归纳特点,深刻体味,从而增强语感,将语言学习作为生活中的愉悦体验。

  Text II 是对本单元话题的扩展和深化,只配课文理解练习和话题讨论,目的在于开拓学生思路,就相关问题提出自己的观点和见解,从而培养学生分析问题和解决问题的能力。课文后设计了综合能力训练和口语活动及写作练习,进一步巩固本单元的知识,加强语言应用能力,同时为参加全国英语专业四级考试做准备。从第三册开始,口语活动的设计在强调趣味性基础上,着重加强了对学生思维能力及跨文化交际能力的培养；写作练习多在背景介绍中引入名言警句，鼓励学生在写作中进行深入思考，引导他们观察社会，感悟生活，形成自己的观点，培养批判性思维的能力，避免人云亦云。

通过每个单元两篇课文的学习和各种练习，学生可对每单元话题的认识加深，在掌握语言知识、加强语言技能的基础上，还能就话题进行口头、笔头交流，陈述观点，发表意见。

本教程课文大都选自英美原文，为了方便教学个别地方做了删节和微小的改动。选材注重体育专业与人文通识并重，注重内容的专业性和人文性，在英语学习中既学到体育知识，又增加人文知识，提高人文素养。有关体育方面的课文均选自国外的体育教科书及权威杂志，有极强的针对性。

《综合英语教程(第四册)》共12个单元，供体育英语专业二年级第二学期教学使用。按照综合英语课程每学期96个学时的教学时数，每单元需用8个学时完成教学，各校在使用时也可以根据需要进行调整。

教程选材过程中，参阅了大量英美国家报纸杂志和有关教科书及网络资源，对一些文章进行了选编，在此谨向原著者致以谢意。

北京体育大学外语系承担了本系列教材的编写工作。由于经验和水平限制，书中不当之处在所难免，敬请使用本教程的师生批评指正。

我国已全面进入后奥运时期，国家的体育事业迎来了一个崭新的发展机遇期，对外交流日益扩大。随着全球化的不断深入，国际体育交往愈发凸显其重要性，中国亟需引进国外先进的体育科学理论、训练方法、休闲理念和健康的生活方式。我们期待，本套教程能对提高我国体育英语专业的建设水平，培养更多的国际体育人才，进而提高我国的体育发展水平贡献绵薄之力。

编者

2010年3月

TABLE OF CONTENTS

Unit 1　Civilization ·· 1
　　　　Text I　The Emergence of Civilization / 1
　　　　Text II　Ancient Western Civilizations and Leisure / 13

Unit 2　Peace and Conflicts ··· 21
　　　　Text I　The Power of Sport / 21
　　　　Text II　On War / 33

Unit 3　Prizes and Awards ·· 38
　　　　Text I　History of the Pulitzer Prizes / 38
　　　　Text II　Nobel Prize Acceptance Speech / 50

Unit 4　Universities ·· 56
　　　　Text I　Universities and Their Function / 56
　　　　Text II　"Illuminating One's Bright Virtue": Higher Education in a Changing World / 66

Unit 5　In a Lifetime ·· 74
　　　　Text I　It's Not About the Bike: My Journey Back to Life / 74
　　　　Text II　The Old Man and the Sea / 86

Unit 6　Nutrition ··· 91
　　　　Text I　Nutrition for Exercise and Health / 91
　　　　Text II　Combat Stress with Good Nutrition / 102

Unit 7　Success and Failure ·· 107
　　　　Text I　The Art of Turning Failure into Success / 107
　　　　Text II　Born to Win / 120

Unit 8   Aesthetics 126
Text I   The Beauty Industry / 126
Text II   Sport and Physical Education As a Means of Aesthetic
          Education / 140

Unit 9   Humor 147
Text I   On the Sense of Humor / 147
Text II   The Ransom of Red Chief / 160

Unit 10   Medicine 170
Text I   A Doctor's Vision of the Future of Medicine / 170
Text II   Use of Stimulants in Doping / 180

Unit 11   Communication 186
Text I   I Blog, Therefore I Am / 186
Text II   Oprah Talks to Nelson Mandela / 198

Unit 12   Nurturing 206
Text I   Take This Fish and Look at It / 206
Text II   My Mother's Promise / 219

References 226

Unit 1 Civilization

Warm-up Activities

1. If you could change any event in history, what would it be and why?
2. "Those who forget history are doomed to repeat it." Do you agree or disagree with this statement? Why?

Text I

The Emergence of Civilization

Pre-reading Questions

1. In your own words, describe and define "civilization".
2. Based on your previous knowledge, why is Egypt such a well-appreciated "civilization"?

1 *Civilization* is derived from the Latin *citatas*, meaning "commonwealth," or "city". The first civilizations, beginning in Mesopotamia and Egypt between 3500 and 3000 B.C, did indeed contain the first cities. What differentiated them from their Neolithic predecessors, however, was not so much size (a city versus a town) as complexity. Civilization allowed human beings to think big. With a sufficiently large and specialized labor force and with a sufficiently strong government, it became possible to expand control over nature, to pursue advances in technology, to trade and compete over ever widening areas, to free an elite for ever more ambitious projects in art and to invent writing. In short, the advent of civilization in the fourth millennium B.C. marked a major turning point, when the human horizon expanded forever.

2   Civilization arose in southern Iraq, in the valley between the Tigris and Euphrates Rivers, a region that the Greeks called "Mesopotamia" (literally, "between the rivers"). At around the same time or shortly afterward, civilization also began in the valley of the Nile River in Egypt. A perennial topic of debate among scholars is whether different civilizations develop independently or whether one culture spreads to other locations from an original source. As we shall see, early civilizations are characterized by a combination of contacts and independent developments.

3   Both Mesopotamia and Egypt are home to valleys containing alluvial land—that is, a relatively flat tract where fertile soil is deposited by a river. Otherwise, the two regions are quite different. Although the Nile Valley is easy to farm, the Tigris-Euphrates plain had to be tamed by would-be farmers. Every summer the Nile flooded in a relatively regular and predictable manner, bringing north to Egypt the waters of the monsoon rains of the Ethiopian highlands, where one branch of the river rises. The spring deluges of the Tigris and Euphrates were more sudden and less predictable. Moreover, the Nile's waters spread so broadly that it took little human effort to irrigate most of the available farmland in the Nile Valley. In southern Mesopotamia, by contrast, most of the soil was alternately so dry or so marshy that agriculture would not have been possible without irrigation and drainage—that is, the use of channels, dikes or dams to control floodwaters and improve the fertility of the land. One Mesopotamian text describes a farmer as "the man of dike, ditch, and plow." Some scholars argue that the very hostility of Mesopotamia's environment generated the cooperation and control that civilization represents.

4   The first cities emerged in Mesopotamia through a slow, incremental process of action and reaction. Labor became more specialized and agricultural production was maximized. When part of the population moves to a city, those who remain on the land must work harder or use better farming techniques or increase the amount of land under cultivation. In fourth- and third-millennium B.C. Mesopotamia, farmers did all three. Meanwhile, both the number and vari-

Unit 1　Civilization

ety of settlements increased. Urban populations required the support of people in smaller units—towns, villages, and hamlets—clustered around a city.

5　　In short, river-valley society became more complex, which in turn created a need for cooperation and central direction. By the end of the fourth millennium B.C., Mesopotamia consisted of numerous city-states—that is, independent political units that each contained a rural countryside with villages controlled by a capital city. The urban landscape's most visible sign of centralized authority was the temple.

6　　Along with the growth of cities came the development of writing. Mesopotamia was the first civilization to leave a written record, having invented writing about 3500–3000 B.C. Writing was the child of recordkeeping, so a plausible theory argues, since complex economy required records and inventories. Before they invented writing, Mesopotamian people used tiny clay or stone tokens to represent objects being counted or traded. By 3500 B.C., with 250 different types of tokens, the system had grown unwieldy enough for people to start using signs to indicate tokens. It was a short step to dispensing with the tokens and placing the signs on a clay tablet, using a reed stylus with a triangular point: the first writing. New words were soon added through pictographs. In time the pictographs evolved into ideograms—that is, abstract symbols that are no longer recognizable as specific objects and thus can be used to denote ideas as well as things.

7　　An adaptable system, cuneiform became the standard script of various languages of western Asia for several thousand years. Compared to a modern alphabet, in which a small number of letters stand for the sounds of speech, cuneiform is clumsy, but alphabets were not invented before about 4000 B.C., and they took nearly a thousand years to displace cuneiform. Clumsy it may have been, but cuneiform was writing, and writing is both a catalyst for change and the historian's best friend. Mesopotamia after 3000 B.C. was dynamic, sophisticated, and, best of all, intelligible to us.

8　　The people of Mesopotamia after 3000 B.C. flourished and experimented: in government, in cooperation and conflict among different ethnic groups, in law, and in the working out of class and gender relations. Their quest for divine justice laid the foundations on which the Hebrews later built. Their engineering skill, mathematics, and astronomy set ancient science on a grand trajectory. A keen and often bitter awareness of human limitations and vanity, moreover, gives Mesopotamian civilization a sympathetic quality.

9 Archaeologists sometimes refer to the third and second millennia in the eastern Mediterranean and western Asia as the "Bronze Age." In this period people mastered the technology of making bronze, an alloy of copper and tin. As a result, bronze frequently replaces stone as a primary material for everyday use.

10 The formative era of Mesopotamian civilization is called the Uruk Period (ca. 3800–3200 B.C.) after one of its major archaeological sites. The Uruk Period encompassed a series of major technological breakthroughs, including the wheel and the plow, the first orchards—of dates, figs, or olives—and the first sophisticated metal-casting processes. It witnessed the emergence of the first cities, for example, Uruk. Moreover, it marked a dramatic increase in the extent of territory and population, in warfare and political centralization, in social complexity, and in institutional formality. Finally, as if to cap a period of remarkable change, the end of the Uruk Period witnessed the invention of writing.

11 Mesopotamian cities flourished in this era. By the period that scholars have named the "Early Dynastic Period" (2800–2350 B.C.), named for the first royal dynasties (ruling families), a large Mesopotamian city had grown to the point where it might cover a thousand acres surrounded by more than five miles of walls, within which lived about fifty thousand people. Such a city with its monumental temples and palaces, was not only larger and more impressive than a Çatal Hüyük or Jericho, it was also part of a network of thirty such city-states with a common culture, commerce, and propensity to make war on each other. Hence the city-states of Mesopotamia may be called the first civilization.

12 The dominant inhabitants of that civilization are called Sumerians. Present in southern Mesopotamia by 3200 B.C. and probably earlier, the Sumerians entered their great age in the third millennium B.C., when their city-states enjoyed a proud independence. Conscious of the unique achievement represented by their way of living, their economy, politics, art and architecture, language, thought, and literature—in short, by Sumerian culture—the Sumerians called southern Mesopotamia simply "the land."

13 From Babylon to the valley of the Nile River, the distance was about 750 miles by way of the caravan routes through Syria and Palestine: close enough to exchange customs, goods, and, if necessary, blows, but far enough for a distinct

Unit 1　Civilization

Egyptian civilization to emerge. As in Sumer, so too in Egypt developed writing around 3100 B.C., slightly after Mesopotamia (and possibly under Mesopotamian influence), but was much earlier than Mesopotamia in becoming a unified kingdom under one ruler.

14　　With its unique contributions in religion, politics, the arts, and the science, and with its wealth of huge, surviving stone monuments, Egypt has impressed both scholars and lay people as few other ancient civilizations have. In the ancient world, Egyptian culture was distinct but influential, from the spread of such Egyptian notions as a Last Judgment in the afterlife to Egyptian techniques in architecture and sculpture.

15　　Mesopotamia and Egypt are the first and best remembered of the early civilizations. Their extraordinary achievements, later built on by the Greeks and Hebrews, laid the foundation for important Western concepts in government, religion, technology, art and literature. It is hard to avoid the appearance of exaggeration when listing the inventions of Mesopotamia and Egypt, among them the first cities, kingdoms, and multi-ethnic empires; the first monumental architecture; the first advances in agriculture sweeping enough to support a large urban population; the first writing, and with it the first written attempts to explore the most profound subjects of life and death.

By Thomas F.X. Noble (abridged)
(1,487 words)

Words and Expressions

differentiate	/ˌdɪfəˈrenʃɪeɪt/	vt.	to be the quality, feature etc. that makes one thing or person clearly different from another 区别,辨别
Neolithic	/ˌniːəˈlɪθɪk/	adj.	relating to the last period of the Stone Age, about 10,000 years ago, when people began to live together in small groups and make stone tools and weapons 新石器时代的
predecessor	/ˈpriːdɪsesə/	n.	one who precedes you in time 前辈,前任
literally	/ˈlɪtərəlɪ/	adv.	according to the most basic or original meaning of a word or expression 根据字面意思,按照原义
perennial	/pəˈrenɪəl/	adj.	continuing or existing for a long time, or happening again and again 长期存在的,不断发生的

alluvial	/əˈluːvɪəl/	adj.	made of soil left by rivers, lakes, floods etc. 冲积的,淤积的
tract	/trækt/	n.	a large area of land (土地的)一大片
tame	/teɪm/	vt.	to reduce the power or strength of something and prevent it from causing trouble 制服,控制
monsoon	/mɒnˈsuːn/	n.	the season, from about April to October, when it rains a lot in India and other southern Asian countries 季风季节,雨季
deluge	/ˈdeljuːdʒ/	n.	a large flood, or period when there is a lot of rain 使……泛滥,淹没
irrigate	/ˈɪrɪɡeɪt/	vt.	to supply land or crops with water 灌溉
marsh	/mɑːʃ/	n.	an area of low flat ground that is always wet and soft 沼泽,湿地 **marshy** adj. 沼泽的,湿地的
dike	/daɪk/	n.	a narrow passage to carry water away 堤,堰,坝
fertility	/fɜːˈtɪlɪtɪ/	n.	the ability of the land or soil to produce good crops 肥力,肥沃
ditch	/dɪtʃ/	n.	a long narrow hole dug at the side of a field, road etc. to hold or remove unwanted water 沟,渠
incremental	/ˌɪnkrɪˈmentl/	adj.	happening gradually over time 增加的,增值的
hamlet	/ˈhæmlɪt/	n.	a very small village 村庄,村落
cluster	/ˈklʌstə/	vi.	to form a small group in a place 群集,(使)丛生
plausible	/ˈplɔːzɪbəl/	adj.	being reasonable and seems likely to be true 似乎是真的,有道理的
inventory	/ˈɪnventrɪ/	n.	list of all the things in a place 详细目录,清单
token	/ˈtəʊkən/	n.	a round piece of metal that is used instead of money 金属代币
unwieldy	/ʌnˈwiːldɪ/	adj.	being difficult to control or manage because it is too complicated 难操纵的,难控制的
dispense with			not to use or do something that people usually use or do, because it is not necessary 省掉,不用
reed	/riːd/	n.	a type of tall plant like grass that grows in wet places 芦苇
stylus	/ˈstaɪləs/	n.	an ancient writing implement, consisting of a small rod with a pointed end for scratching letters on wax-covered tablets, and a blunt end for obliterating them (古时在蜡版上刻写用的)尖笔
ideogram	/ˈɪdɪəɡræm/	n.	a written sign that represents an idea or thing rather than the sound of a word 表意文字,表意符号

Unit 1   Civilization

denote	/dɪˈnəʊt/	vt.	to represent or mean something 表示,意为
cuneiform	/ˈkjuːnɪfɔːm/	n.	relating to the writing used by the people of ancient Mesopotamia 楔形文字
displace	/dɪsˈpleɪs/	vt.	to take the place or position of something or someone 取代,替代
catalyst	/ˈkætəlɪst/	n.	something or someone that causes an important change or event to happen 促进因素
trajectory	/trəˈdʒektərɪ/	n.	the curved path of an object that has been fired or thrown through the air 轨道,轨迹
archaeology	/ˌɑːkɪˈɒlədʒɪ/	n.	the study of ancient societies by examining what remains of their buildings, graves, tools etc. 考古学 **archaeologist** n. 考古学家 **archaeological** adj. 考古学的
alloy	/ˈælɔɪ/	n.	a metal that consists of two or more metals mixed together 合金
tin	/tɪn/	n.	a soft silver-white metal 锡
formative	/ˈfɔːmətɪv/	adj.	having an important influence on the way someone or something develops 形成的,塑造性的
propensity	/prəˈpensɪtɪ/	n.	a natural tendency to behave in a particular way 倾向,习性
caravan	/ˈkærəvæn/	n.	a group of people with animals or vehicles who travel together for safety, especially through a desert 旅行队,商队

Notes:

1. **Mesopotamia**   is an area in western Asia around the River Tigris and the River uphrates in Iraq, where, in ancient times, the world's first cities were built and several important ancient civilizations developed.
2. **Ethiopian highlands**   are a rugged mass of mountains in Ethiopia.
3. **Palestine**   is a conventional name used, among others, to describe a geographic region between the Mediterranean Sea and the Jordan River, and various adjoining lands.
4. **Sumer**   is the southern part of ancient Mesopotamia (modern Iraq), where people called the Sumerians lived from about 3500 B.C., in one of the world's earliest societies.

Reading Comprehension

I. Summarize the similarities and differences of Mesopotamia and Egypt in their civilization development according to the text.

Similarities	Differences

II. Answer the following questions.

1. How did the cities emerge in Mesopotamia?
2. What is cuneiform? What is the significance of the cuneiform system in ancient civilization?
3. Why do archaeologists sometimes refer to the third and second millennia in the eastern Mediterranean and western Asia as the "Bronze Age?"
4. Why are the city-states of Mesopotamia often called the first civilization?
5. What are the scholars' and lay people's impression toward Egypt? Explain.

III. Paraphrase the following sentences within the context of the reading passage.

1. (Para. 1) What differentiated them from their Neolithic predecessors, however, was not so much size (a city versus a town) as complexity.
2. (Para. 3) Both Mesopotamia and Egypt are home to valleys containing alluvial land—that is, a relatively flat tract where fertile soil is deposited by a river.
3. (Para. 6) It was a short step to dispensing with the tokens and placing the signs on a clay tablet, using a reed stylus with a triangular point: the first writing.
4. (Para. 7) Clumsy it may have been, but cuneiform was writing, and writing is both a catalyst for change and the historian's best friend.
5. (Para. 10) Finally, as if to cap a period of remarkable change, the end of the Uruk Period witnessed the invention of writing.

Unit 1 Civilization

IV. **Based on the text, decide whether the following statements are true or false. For false statements, write the facts in parentheses.**

1. At around the fourth millennium B.C., civilization began in the valley of the Nile River in Egypt.
   (   )
2. By the end of the fourth millennium B.C., the rural landscape's most visible sign of centralized authority was the temple.
   (   )
3. Alphabets took nearly a thousand years to displace cuneiform.
   (   )
4. The Sumerians were the dominant inhabitants of Northern Mesopotamia.
   (   )
5. The achievements of Mesopotamia and Egypt laid the foundation for important Western concepts.
   (   )

Vocabulary Exercises

I. **Fill in the blank in each sentence with a word or phrase from the box below. Make sure the appropriate form of the word is used.**

| tame | quest | inventory | elite |
| alternately | warfare | predecessor | fertile |

1. My first visit to San Francisco was to see his first "Swan Lake" in 1988; last year he presented this new one, which is entirely inferior to its _____.
2. In other sports, like tennis, doubles players who play on the regular tour with a partner from another nation can easily find a partner from their own country for the Olympics. But pairs and ice dance teams generally require years of training together to reach the _____ level.
3. He could still remember a time when his land had been _____ enough not only to feed a family, but also to provide a healthy income.
4. With the right mix of spending, regulation and interest rates, they believed, the business cycle could be _____ and unemployment largely eliminated.
5. It can also help them acquire higher-order thinking skills, like generating testable hypotheses, imagining situations from someone else's perspective and thinking of _____ solutions.

6. Figures released Thursday showed that retailers, by keeping tight control over their _____, were able to avoid deep discounting.
7. Those whose _____ for happiness involves regular purchases of lottery tickets may want to consider another strategy.
8. After 30 years of incessant _____, many of the traditional societal networks in this country have been weakened or destroyed.

II. Fill in the blanks with the appropriate forms of the given words.
   1. Since the implementing of a new federal tax law, many people have struggled with the _____ (complex) of the tax forms.
   2. These diplomatic efforts have also strengthened our hand in dealing with those nations that insist on violating international agreements in _____ (pursue) of nuclear weapons.
   3. In part because of global warming, the glacier is retreating perhaps as much as 100 feet a year. Even from the visitor center you can see the kinds of rock and soil it _____ (deposit) as it moved inland.
   4. He said his supporters are not _____ (hostility) to security forces and are only seeking reforms.
   5. Moscow has long asserted that the Soviet Union allowed Germany to _____ (unified) only in return for a pledge from Washington never to expand the Atlantic alliance.

III. Replace the italicized words or phrases with simple, everyday words.
   1. ...the *advent* of civilization in the fourth millennium B.C. marked a major turning point, ...
      (   )
   2. A *perennial* topic of debate among scholars is whether different civilizations develop independently or whether one culture spreads to other locations from an original source.
      (   )
   3. The spring *deluges* of the Tigris and Euphrates were more sudden and less predictable.
      (   )
   4. ...through a slow, *incremental* process of action and reaction. (   )
   5. ...it was also part of a net work of thirty such city-states with a common culture, commerce, and *propensity* to make war on each other. (   )

IV. Choose the word or phrase that best completes each of the following sentences.
   1. People should strive to be "strict ethical vegans", avoiding all products derived _____ animals, including wool and silk. Killing animals for human food and finery is nothing less than "outright murder."
      A. in   B. to   C. of   D. from

Unit 1 Civilization

2. Many Americans are concerned about this Administration's efforts to exert greater control _____ car companies, banks, energy and health care.
   A. over   B. to   C. at   D. for

3. Mr. Christie's speech offered more determination than inspiration, even when he called on legislators and citizens alike to dispense _____ cynicism and lend a hand.
   A. with   B. at   C. on   D. over

4. Americans often assume newer, smaller companies are the engines of innovation and job creation — _____ President Obama's decision to make a $30 billion program to encourage small-business loans a centerpiece of his jobs plan.
   A. while   B. still   C. yet   D. hence

Translation Exercises

I. **Translate each of the following sentences into English, using the word or phrase given in the brackets.**

1. 如何区别这两个历史时期一直是个难题。(differentiate...from)

2. 他倾注毕生心血撰写了一部研究中国古代科学技术和文明成就的鸿篇巨制。(monumental)

3. Ann建议在她的婚礼上摒弃大办酒席的陋习。(dispense with)

4. 这些研究极具前瞻性,将来可能发展为被大家所认可的治疗手段。(evolve into)

5. 他的被捕成为独立运动的催化剂并导致了一场武装冲突。(catalyst)

6. "装饰艺术"这一名词包含20世纪二三十年代三个截然不同,但相互关联的设计趋势。(encompass)

II. **Translate the following paragraph into English.**

历史书上最常见、最风光的人物大多为伟大的征服者、将军和士兵,而真正推动人类文明发展的人却很少提及。我们不知道是谁第一个医好一条断腿,谁第一个发动适于航海的船只,谁第一个计算出了一年的长度,又是谁第一个去开垦农田;相反,我们对那些屠杀者和毁灭者却了如指掌。在世界上一些大城市里所有最高柱石上,你常常会发现这些征服者、将军或士兵的雕像。

III. Translate the following paragraph into Chinese.

Civilization allowed human beings to think big. With a sufficiently large and specialized labor force and with a sufficiently strong government, it became possible to expand control over nature, to pursue advances in technology, to trade and compete over ever widening areas, to free an elite for ever more ambitious projects in art and to invent writing.

Language Appreciation

I. Read the text carefully, then pick out the sentences that you think are well-written. Pay close attention to the italicized words or phrases of the following sentences. Try to appreciate the way in which the author expresses his/her ideas. Learn how to use them in your own writing.

1. With a sufficiently large and specialized labor force and with a sufficiently strong government, it became possible to *expand control over nature, to pursue advances in technology, to trade and compete over ever widening areas, to free an elite for ever more ambitious projects in art and to invent writing.*
2. In southern Mesopotamia, *by contrast*, most of the soil was alternately so dry or so marshy that agriculture would not have been possible without irrigation and drainage—that is, the use of channels, dikes or dams to control floodwaters and improve the fertility of the land.
3. *Along with the growth of cities* came the development of writing.
4. Writing was the *child* of recordkeeping...
5. *Clumsy it may have been*, but cuneiform was writing, and writing is both a catalyst for change and the historian's best friend.

II. Read aloud and recite paragraphs 15 and 16.

III. Stylistics Study

Inversion—A Technique to Convey Emphasis

Examples: 1) <u>Along with the growth of cities</u> came the development of writing.
—From Text I of Unit 1

2) <u>Clumsy</u> it may have been, but cuneiform was writing, and writing is both a catalyst for change and the historian's best friend.
—From Text I of Unit 1

3) *He clasps the crag with crooked hands;*
Close to the sun in lonely lands,
Ring'd with the azure world, he stands.
The wrinkled sea beneath him crawls;

> *He watches from his mountain walls,*
> *<u>And like a thunderbolt</u> he falls.*
> —From Alfred Tennyson, *The Eagle*
>
> 4) *As fair art thou, my bonie lass,*
> *So deep in luve am I,*
> *And I will luve thee still, my dear,*
> *Till a' the seas gang dry.*
> —From Robert Burns, *A Red, Red Rose*

Questions: 1) What special characteristic does the underlined portion have on each sentence?

2) What effect does the writer intend to achieve in the underlined portion of the text?

3) Why does inversion frequently appear in poetry?

4) Pick more examples in the texts you have previously read. Have you ever used inversion in your own writing? In what context would you use this technique?

Text II

Ancient Western Civilizations and Leisure

> *Pre-reading Questions*
>
> 1. What are some well-known accomplishments left by the Greek and Roman civilizations?
> 2. What are some Greek and Roman traditions that exist today? Why do you think they've lasted throughout the centuries?

1 The great games were invented by the classical Greeks as a celebration of human life dedicated to Zeus, the king of their many gods. "Strip or retire" was the admonition over the gate to the Olympic Games stadium in Olympus. The Greeks competed in the nude, and only men were allowed in. Spectators were unwelcome. One either participated (stripped) or had to leave (retired). This reflected the Greek philosophy of citizen participation, whether in athletic contests, military expeditions, or government.

2 The Greek contribution to civilization was both mental and spiritual. Deeply embedded in its ideals of heroism, satire, education, political awareness,

and aesthetics were the need for and use of leisure. Most Greek men spent time in the gymnasium each afternoon as well as attending the tragedies, comedies, and satires of the greatest writers and thinkers. Leisure brought happiness.

3   Despite powerful goddesses and oracles, women were excluded from citizenship and, in some instances, could neither inherit nor own property. Except for those married to wealthy men, women lived lives of drudgery and seclusion. Entertainers and prostitutes were the only women who could routinely expect a public life. In classical Greece, girls were thought to be unworthy of education. A respectable woman's leisure was regulated by the strict social taboos that were placed on her. She might engage in art, crafts, writing, or other practical outlets, but usually in the privacy of her home.

4   Sitting in the Colosseum in Rome, the spectator could look down on 60,000 screaming fans as an entire naval battle was staged on the water-covered floor of the arena. When that spectacle was over, the area was cleared and wild animals were released to attack one another. This was the heyday of bread and circuses.

5   Rome had begun as a small hill town that grew and annexed land and peoples. At first a republic, then a military dictatorship, it finally evolved into an empire. All roads led to Rome because, along with everything else, the Romans built and maintained the best road system in the world.

6   Although Rome bequeathed structural and practical capacities to the world, it still set aside time for games, races, gladiatorial contests, and other amusements. The leisure of Rome permeated the known world. Its decadence produced antagonism among the early Church fathers that reverberated for centuries. Leisure and culture are the story of ancient Western civilizations.

7   Parallel with the ancient Near Eastern civilizations, another culture arose on the island of Crete. Remains at its capital of Knossos indicate an advanced civilization, much of which is now submerged beneath the Mediterranean. This island civilization is at least as old as that of Sumer, but political unification did not occur until about 2500 B.C. For the next thousand years, the Cretans lived in peace, prosperity, and safety. They developed commerce with every civilized nation in the known world.

8   Secure in their island citadel and immune from invasion for more than 3000 years, the Cretans were free to perfect their leisure habits. Their artisans produced sophisticated textiles, sculpture, painting, and jewelry. They enjoyed

amenities quite similar to those of our modern life. Excavations show that the people of Crete devoted much time to the leisure arts and participated in a variety of recreational activities, such as shows, festivals, bullfights, gymnastics exhibitions, dance, swimming, wrestling, and other sports.

9   Crete presents a vibrant, unrestrained, exuberant picture of the good life, illustrated by the luxurious conditions surrounding the aristocrats—at the expense of the enslaved masses. The slaves were too busy trying to survive to have much leisure, but their masters enjoyed a great deal of it. Clearly, security encourages leisure. Wherever humans have been safe for any length of time, they have been able to develop their arts, standards of living, and other cultural benefits to an amazing degree. It is not surprising, therefore, that the Cretans achieved such a society in light of their immunity to invasion and comparative freedom from want.

10   Cretans played a type of chess at home, patronized pugilistic exhibitions, and attended the theater in towns. Music and dance combined to provide entertainment for those fortunate enough to have spare time. Of all recreational activities, hunting seems to have had the dominant role during the leisure of Crete's soldier class and aristocracy. Many drawings and paintings of hunting scenes, especially boar hunting, have been discovered.

11   The art of Crete captured the life and times of those who were privileged and those who served them. Whether frescoed on palace walls or some merchant's house, stamped on cups, embossed on shields, fans, lamps, or seals, sculpted as little figures, or molded in bas-relief, these artworks reveal a civilization with order and wealth, free time, and an appreciation for such experiences and ornamentation.

12   The Greek national character was molded by the history of its culture, beginning in the aristocratic arena of early Greece, where human perfection was a coveted ideal toward which the upper class was steadily trained and educated.

13   To discuss the influence of Greek thought on Western leisure theory and philosophy, we must first survey the structure of the Greek mind, which conceived and directed such intellectual pursuits as ethics, morality, and education. To do

this, we must be aware of the effect the ideal of acrétè had on all Greek achievements, including recreation. Acrétè combines the idea of what is best in all things and is worthy of emulation and adoration—complete mastery. To the Greeks, a thing had acrétè if performed not just efficiently but excellently in the manner for which it was created. This view applied to people as well. As Werner Jaeger puts it:

We can find a more natural clue to the history of Greek culture in the history of the ideal of acrétè, which goes back to the earliest times. There is no complete equivalent for the word acrétè in modern English—its oldest meaning is a combination of proud and courtly morality with warlike valour. But the idea of acrétè is the quintessence of early Greek aristocratic education.

14   The ancient tradition of heroic power was not enough to satisfy the chroniclers of a younger era. Their concept of acrétè combined noble actions and noble thoughts. Human perfection was the ideal that joined exalted deeds with nobility of mind. This concept of unity forced its way into the very foundation of the Greek code of life that has been handed down to us in the modern meaning of recreation.

15   Unity and wholeness seem to be the salient features of the Greek psyche. They are best described by Kitto, who states:

The sharp distinction which the Christian and the oriental world has normally drawn between the body and the soul, the physical and the spiritual, was foreign to the Greek—at least until the time of Socrates and Plato. To him there was simply the whole man. The Greek made physical training an important part of education...because it could never occur to him to train anything but the whole man.

16   Although slavery was already an institution in early Greece, it was no shame for aristocrats to handle a plow and farm their own land. Noblewomen performed a variety of craft activities, including sewing, weaving, and spinning. Artisans and crafters were never slaves and were accorded the respect due to their skill. Since each household was essential self-sufficient in its production of needed goods and articles, as well as homegrown staples, crafts were specialty trades and were performed to order. Even though they might work long hours on a given project, the artisans worked in a leisurely manner without the compulsion of a competitive market economy.

17   **The Games**. Even war did not diminish the Greek passion for games. Children and adults engaged in contests of skill. For example, Penelope's suitors played at draughts and threw the javelin and discus. When Odysseus landed at Phaeacia, his hosts played at quoits and danced for his entertainment.

18   But more important were the athletic games that were held to celebrate religious rites, commemorate the lives of heroes, or entertain a guest—or just for the pleasure of playing. When games were held, other affairs were halted so that participants could come together and compete peacefully. The leisure that was then insured by oath was used to satisfy the competitive urge as well as produce a spectacle for entertainment (as it still does). The funeral games described by Homer were the forerunner to the great Olympics.

19   The Panhellenic Games were organized to honor the gods and were an intrinsic part of the Greeks' pantheistic religion. Every town had its own place of worship or sacred grove. Eventually, local games graduated from their original commemorative purpose to a more encompassing scope and became the Pythian, Nemean, and Isthmian Games. The greatest games were given in honor of the Olympian deities; they are still held every four years, after being revived in 1896 by Baron de Coubertin of France. Although 776 B.C. is the date of the earliest Olympic victor on record, the Olympic Games probably began much earlier and may originally have been held every year. The games were gradually secularized until only the athletic events held significance.

20   Over a period of several centuries, the Achaean civilization slowly lost its vitality, and northern outsiders noticed its weakness. By immigration or invasion the northern hordes all but destroyed the Mycenaean civilization in the Dorian conquest. Hundreds of years after the Dorians invaded the Peloponnesus and disrupted social, political, and economic life, the synthesis of invaders and indigenous populations produced a people of vigorous abilities and intellectual acumen.

21   **Cultural Diversity**. After centuries of interbreeding, the Greeks retained some vestiges of the Mycenaean culture. Preserved were social institutions for government, religious rites, craft skills, technology, commercial forms and trade routes, elements of art and architecture, poetry, literature, and song. The impact of diverse cultures (Cretan, Mycenaean, Achaean, and Dorian) gave new impetus to a dying civilization.

22　　　In the Greece of 400 B.C., there were two reasons for the leisure that gave rise to great intellectual, artistic, creative, and philosophical achievements. One was the owning of domestic, factory, and mine-working slaves upon whose shoulder the leisure of the well-to-do rested. The other was the simplicity of life. The standard of living was far removed from what we consider the bare necessities of life today. Then, too, the Greeks saved time by not having to travel to work and back home, and there were no conventional hours of work. Kitto has put it quite well:

Again, the daily round was ordered not by the clock but by the sun, since there was no effective artificial light. Activity began at dawn. We envy, perhaps, ordinary Athenians who seem to spend a couple of hours in the afternoon at the baths or a gymnasium (a spacious athletic and cultural center provided by the public for itself). The Greek got up as soon as it was light, shook out the blanket in which he had slept, draped it elegantly around himself as a suit, had a beard and no breakfast, and was ready to face the world in five minutes. The afternoon, in fact, was not the middle of his day, but very near the end of it.

23　　　It is significant that leisure to the Greeks, especially the Athenians, was not conceived as many of us see it today. Leisure was put to practical use in learning (education) or in participation in government, or it was directed to the contemplation of philosophy, civic service, rhetoric, or artistic creativity. Free time was used to benefit the society in which the Greek citizen (that is, the nonslave) lived.

By Jay S. Shivers & Lee J. Lisle (abridged)

(1,931 words)

Reading Comprehension

I. **Answer the following questions with the information you read from the passage.**
  1. What did "strip or retire" mean in the ancient Olympic Games?
  2. How do you interpret the sentence "The Greek contribution to civilization was both mental and spiritual" (Para. 2)?
  3. What was the Colosseum in Rome used for?
  4. How could the island of Crete enjoy a civilization which was as old as that of Sumer?
  5. What does the author say about the Cretan civilization?

Unit 1 Civilization

II. **Topics for discussion and reflection.**
 1. Why are some groups labeled uncivilized?
 2. What would you attribute to the transformations within a great civilization? Discuss your opinion with examples.

Exercises for Integrated Skills

I. **Dictation**

   Listen to the following passage. The passage will be read to you four times. During the first reading, which will be read at normal speed, listen and try to understand the meaning. For the second and third readings, the passage will be read sentence by sentence, or phrase by phrase, with intervals of 15 to 20 seconds. The last reading will be done at normal speed again and during this time check your work. You will then be given 2 minutes to check through your work a second time.

_____

_____

_____

_____

_____

II. **Cloze**

   ____1____ Western civilization ____2____ during the Middle Ages, its position in the world changed gradually as well. Many European leaders have wished they could project the power in the world that Rome had conveyed for several centuries. How active this ____3____ was as a motive ____4____ aggressive action is hard to assess. Interestingly, a similar desire to emulate Rome has been ____5____ to the Russian tsars as they ____6____ a process of expansion from about 1450 onward, and again it is not easy to say how much the Roman example was window dressing, how much real impulse. ____7____ when greater control returned, Western Europe remained visibly backward compared to its relevant neighbors. Its technology was ____8____, its cities far smaller, its nobility far less polished. Even as Western Europe ____9____ become wealthier, more capable of trade and more urban, its inferiority remained obvious to anyone with a (n) ____10____ for comparison.

   1. A. With   B. As   C. While   D. During
   2. A. rose   B. formed   C. took shape   D. originated
   3. A. sense   B. sentiment   C. emotion   D. feeling

4. A. for	B. to	C. of	D. on
5. A. contributed	B. lead	C. due	D. attributed
6. A. launched	B. originated	C. waged	D. carried on
7. A. Still	B. Then	C. Even	D. But
8. A. bad	B. inferior	C. lower	D. lesser
9. A. /	B. has	C. had	D. did
10. A. knowledge	B. awareness	C. basis	D. sense

Oral Activities

1. Events in history have often created prejudice among different races or groups of people. List 3–5 historical events and explain how specific prejudices came about from them.
2. In groups of 3–4, choose one of the 7 Wonders of the World and argue your case for why your wonder is the most wondrous.

Writing Practice

Composition Writing

In 1988, 75 Nobel Prize laureates made a statement in Paris that if humankind were to survive in the 21st century, they must seek the wisdom of Confucius. Write a composition of about 200 words on the topic: **The Influence of Confucianism on World Civilization**.

Unit 2 Peace and Conflicts

Warm-up Activities

1. Brainstorm reasons why conflicts arise. What are some strategies to resolve them?
2. Choose a major conflict that has happened in the world recently and list reasons why such a conflict has occurred.

Text I

The Power of Sport

Pre-reading Questions

1. Why do you think there is a universal appeal for sports?
2. What is sportsmanship and why is it important?

1   The Olympic Truce has a strategically important alliance with sport. While the Truce and its relationship with the Olympic Movement provide much needed inspiration broadcast from a stage of unparalleled magnitude, two dangers remain: firstly that interest wanes as the athletes leave the stadium, and secondly that the spectacle of the Games becomes a barrier that prevents the individual spectator from understanding the relevance and application of the Truce for them. Sport is a constant force in most people's lives—either as a participant, spectator or unwilling observer. Sport has a rich network that inhabits all levels of the pyramid of conflict, and so can offer a potential architecture for peace. If the Olympic Movement is able to harness this potential, the Olympic Truce could come alive on street corners and in playgrounds the

world over.

2   The universal appeal of sport enables it to move with ease between the political and the personal. Proof of the influence of sport is found in the fact that politicians regularly use it as a domestic political tool. Individuals use sport to make political statements, too. But perhaps most importantly, the values that sport teaches participants and spectators alike—of fair play, accepting mediation, respect for rules and self-discipline, for example—help to tackle the factor that contribute to the perpetuation of the culture of violence that underpins the pyramid of conflict and which causes disharmony and tension at all levels, from downtown Los Angeles to the battlefields of Sierra Leone.

3   Sport also has what Joseph Nye would call *soft power*, or the ability to "influence events through persuasion and attraction rather than by military or financial coercion." September 11 was a stark reminder of the cultural gulf that has opened up between East and West. Governments—mainly in the West—have woken up to the need to operate beyond their state counterparts and appeal directly to the "hearts and minds" of overseas populations. Public diplomacy—attempts by governments to understand, inform, influence and build relationships with foreign publics in order to achieve policy goals—and other tools for soft power now sit alongside traditional diplomatic efforts. Sport, like branches of the arts and culture, is an established public diplomacy tool and remains one of the few activities that can bridge cultural, political and social gaps and schisms.

4   Politicians have been quick to utilize the power of sport to influence the "mood of the nation." Indeed, popular mythology puts the 1970 general election defeat for the British Labour Party down to the fact that England lost a quarter-final World Cup match against West Germany. While this is cultural legend, there is no denying the fact that Wilson had a reservation about the date of the election because England's match was scheduled to take place just before. It is not surprising, then, that competition between President Chirac and Prime Minister Lionel Jospin to prove their support for the French side *les Bleus*

almost eclipsed battles that were taking place on the pitch during the 1998 football World Cup in France.

5   Sport is a leveller that can bridge even unlikely gaps. From the English and German soldiers who convened a game of football on Christmas Day in no man's land during the First World War to more contemporary cases, such as the game between the allies and the locals in Sarajevo after the Bosnian conflict and Nelson Mandela awarding the rugby world cup to the winning South African team in 1995, examples can be found from right around the world. As Pakistani tennis player Aisam ul-Haq Qureshi commented of his pairing with Israeli Amir Hadad at the U.S. Open in 2002, "I don't believe to bring religion or politics to tennis. Everyone gets together, people from all religions, backgrounds. That's the best part of being a sportsman."

6   Peaceful societies are not created overnight, but are advanced towards slowly through taking many small steps that make peaceful outcomes more likely. Sports-based initiatives are so important because they are able to bridge the political and the personal. Conflict starts and finishes in the minds of individuals and the only hope of a lasting, sustainable peace lies in unpicking the culture of violence that exists at all levels in our societies. The values that underpin sport—discipline, accepting mediation, positive competition, fair play and equality—help individuals to develop the types of skills that remove the desire for conflict and find peaceful means of resolving their disagreements.

7   As the U.N. Special Adviser on Sport for Development and Peace has argued:

Sport through play and fun teaches young people essential values such as respect for opponents, for rules and for referees' decisions. Sport also teaches the temporary nature of victory, the need for regular training to reach the top and that defeat can be overcome. Team sports also teach integration and the need for confidence between team members, and reliability. However, sport also teaches that it doesn't take much to enjoy the benefits of physical activity. These qualities are essential to citizens in all societies and situations of life. They may make a difference in favour of a peaceful world.

8   Discovering tools which enable de-freezing processes in conflict zones all over the world is the challenge that faces us today. The task might seem immense—from development and democratization across troubled regions, to building the sort of global institutions which can act with legitimacy. It might be that the

most appropriate measure of success is not the resolution of absolute peace, but relative gains in terms of individuals' quality of life. This is particularly the case in chaotic states where the traditional diplomatic channels have even less chance than usual of making a difference. As Cooper observes, "in the pre-modern world victory is not a relevant objective...they will be goals of relatives and not absolutes: more lives saved, lower levels of violence among the local populations." Relative gains of this sort provide opportunities to kick-start periods of transition, as took place in the case of the Cold War during the 1970s and 1980s. As Mient Jan Faber argues, the "de-freezing" process which began with detente moved a state of confrontation on the brink of war through successive stages in which relations stabilized and finally normalized through peaceful means. The Olympic Truce, through a strengthened partnership with sport, can be an important part of this solution.

9   It is therefore not surprising that sport is frequently used as a way of helping to tackle conflict across many different layers of the pyramid of conflict, most notably in breaking down the forces that maintain a culture of violence. The United Nations Inter-Agency Taskforce for Sport for Development and Peace has created an inventory of sports initiatives that work to promote peace and development. Over 120 initiatives have been identified so far, with examples from almost every country, and both developed and developing worlds. These include "Right to Play," an NGO working towards improving the lives of the most disadvantaged children and their communities through sport for development; "Kick," an initiative for cooperation between Berlin's police, social workers and sports organizations to benefit juvenile delinquents aged 12–20 from eight problematic and low-income neighbourhoods; and "Futbol Futur" in Argentina, a programme which uses sports such as football, netball and basketball to address crime, delinquency and drugs.

10   The wider values and mechanisms of sport offer many opportunities for the Olympic Movement to enhance the scope and impact of the Olympic Truce. The reach of sport makes it a more constant presence in our lives, which would help to keep the Olympic Flame burning between Olympic Games. Also, the myriad of sports networks offers rich potential for sustaining work from the political to the personal level.

By Rachel Briggs (abridged)

(1,283 words)

Unit 2 Peace and Conflicts

Words and Expressions

wane	/weɪn/	vi.	to become gradually less strong or less important 逐渐减弱(变小)
harness	/ˈhɑːnɪs/	vt.	to control and use the natural force or power of something 治理利用(自然力等)
come alive			to become interesting and seems real 变得有生气(逼真,有趣)
mediation	/ˌmediˈteɪʃən/	n.	negotiation to resolve differences conducted by some impartial party 调解,斡旋
self-discipline	/ˌself-ˈdɪsɪplɪn/	n.	the ability to make yourself do the things you know you ought to do, without someone making you do them 自我约束,自律
tackle	/ˈtækəl/	vt.	to try to deal with a difficult problem 处理,对付
perpetuation	/pəˌpetʃʊˈeɪʃən/	n.	the act of prolonging something 永存,不朽
underpin	/ˌʌndəˈpɪn/	vt.	to give strength or support to something and to help it succeed 巩固,支持
disharmony	/ˌdɪsˈhɑːməni/	n.	disagreement about important things which makes people be unfriendly to each other (在重要事情上的)分歧,不一致,不和谐
coercion	/kəʊˈɜːʃən/	n.	the use of threats or orders to make someone do something they do not want to do 强迫,胁迫,迫使
stark	/stɑːk/	adj.	unpleasantly clear and impossible to avoid 显而易见的,无法掩饰的
gulf	/gʌlf/	n.	a great difference and lack of understanding between two groups of people, especially in their beliefs, opinions, and way of life (尤指信仰、观念和生活方式之间的)鸿沟,分歧,隔阂
schism	/ˈskɪzəm/	n.	the separation of a group into two groups, caused by a disagreement about its aims and beliefs, especially in the Christian church 分裂;教会分裂
quarter-final		n.	one of the four games near the end of a competition, whose winners play in the two semi-finals 四分之一决赛
leveller	/ˈlevələ/	n.	something that makes people of all classes and ranks seem equal 使众人平等的事物

convene	/kən'viːn/	vt.	to come together, especially for a formal meeting 聚集，集合，开会
Pakistani	/ˌpɑːkɪ'stɑːnɪ/	adj.	relating to Pakistan or its people 巴基斯坦的
unpick	/ʌn'pɪk/	vt.	to examine the different parts of a subject, deal etc., especially in order to find faults 仔细分析
integration	/ˌɪntɪ'greɪʃən/	n.	the acceptance of someone or something into a group or society 融入（团体或社会）
immense	/ɪ'mens/	adj.	extremely large 巨大的，极大的
democratize	/dɪ'mɒkrətaɪz/	vt.	to change the way in which a government, company etc. is organized so that it is more democratic 使民主化 **democratization** n. 民主化
legitimate	/lɪ'dʒɪtɪmɪt/	adj.	fair or reasonable 公正的，合理的 **legitimacy** n. 公正，合理
resolution	/ˌrezə'luːʃən/	n.	a formal decision or statement agreed on by a group of people, especially after a vote 决议，决定
kick-start		vt.	to do something to help a process or activity start or develop more quickly 启动，促进
détente	/'deɪtɒnt/	n.	a time or situation in which two countries that are not friendly towards each other agree to behave in a more friendly way（国家间紧张关系的）缓和
brink	/brɪŋk/	n.	a crucial or critical point, esp. of a situation or state beyond which success or catastrophe occurs（尤指坏事的）边缘，关头
successive	/sək'sesɪv/	adj.	coming or following one after the other 连续的，接连的
normalize	/'nɔːməlaɪz/	vt.	(of two countries) behave in a normal way towards each other again（使）正常化，（使）变得正常
layer	/'leɪə/	n.	one of several different levels in a complicated organization, system, set of ideas etc.（组织、系统、思想等的）层次，构架
disadvantaged	/ˌdɪsəd'vɑːntɪdʒd/	adj.	having social problems, such as a lack of money or education, which make it difficult for someone to succeed 弱势的，社会地位低下的，处于不利地位的
juvenile delinquent			a child or young person who behaves in a criminal way 青少年罪犯
problematic	/ˌprɒblə'mætɪk/	adj.	involving problems and difficult to deal with 有很多问题的，成问题的，难对付的

Unit 2 Peace and Conflicts

netball	/ˈnetbɔːl/	n.	a game similar to basketball played in Britain, especially by girls 无挡板篮球
delinquency	/dɪˈlɪŋkwənsɪ/	n.	illegal or immoral behaviour or actions, especially by young people 违法(不道德)行为,(尤指)青少年犯罪
a myriad of			a very large number of things 数量极大的,无数的
sustain	/səˈsteɪm/	vt.	to make something continue to exist or happen for a period of time 使某事继续

Notes:

1. **Sierra Leone**   is a country in West Africa between Liberia and Guinea.
2. **Labour Party**   is a political party in Britain and some other countries that aims to improve social conditions for ordinary working people and lower-class people.
3. **Jacques Chirac**   served as the President of France from 17 May 1995 until 16 May 2007.
4. **Lionel Jospin**   is a French politician who served as Prime Minister of France from 1997 to 2002, during the third "cohabitation," under Jacques Chirac.
5. **les Bleus**   is often used in a French sporting context, and in particular may refer to the French national football team and national rugby union team.
6. **Sarajevo**   is the capital city of Bosnia Herzegovina. Many battles between Serbs and Bosnian Muslims were fought in Sarajevo in the 1990s during the Bosnian War. It is also the place where the Archduke Franz Ferdinand was murdered in 1914, an event which led to the start of World War I.
7. **Bosnian conflict**   was an international armed conflict that took place between March 1992 and November 1995.
8. **Nelson Mandela (1918–   )**   was the leader of South Africa's ANC party since 1994, and the First black President of South Africa. In 1993 he shared the Nobel Prize for Peace with President F.W. de Klerk after they had worked together to end the system of apartheid.
9. **S. Open (tennis)**   formally the United States Open tennis championships, is a tennis tournament which is the modern incarnation of one of the oldest tennis championships in the world.
10. **Cold War**   (1945–1991) was the continuing state of political conflict, military tension, and economic competition existing after World War II, primarily between the USSR and its Eastern Bloc allies, and the powers of the Western world, especially the United States.
11. **Olympic Flame**   is a symbol of the Olympic Games. Its origins lie in ancient Greece, where a fire was kept burning throughout the celebration of the ancient Olympics. The fire was reintroduced at the 1928 Summer Olympics in Amsterdam, and it has been part of the modern Olympic Games ever since.

Reading Comprehension

I. Fill in the boxes according to the information taken from the text.

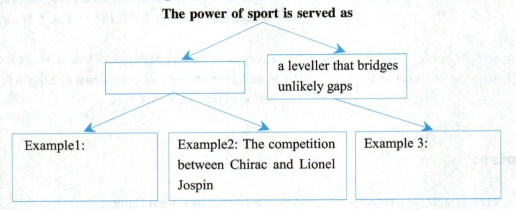

The power of sport is served as
- [ ]
- a leveller that bridges unlikely gaps

Example1:

Example2: The competition between Chirac and Lionel Jospin

Example 3:

II. Answer the following questions.

1. What values does sport teach participants and spectators?
2. According to Joseph Nye, what is the *soft power* of sport?
3. How did Pakistani tennis player Aisam ul-Haq Qureshi comment of his pairing with Israeli Amir Hadad at the U.S. Open in 2002?
4. What might be done to discover more tools to enable de-freezing processes in conflict zones?
5. What is the significance of the wider values and mechanisms of sport?

III. Paraphrase the following sentences within the context of the reading passage.

1. (Para.1) While the Truce and its relationship with the Olympic Movement provide much needed inspiration broadcast from a stage of unparalleled magnitude ...
2. (Para.4) It is not surprising, then, that competition between President Chirac and Prime Minister Lionel Jospin to prove their support for the French side les Bleus almost eclipsed battles that were taking place on the pitch during the 1998 football World Cup in France.
3. (Para.6) Conflict starts and finishes in the minds of individuals and the only hope of a lasting, sustainable peace lies in unpicking the culture of violence that exists at all levels in our societies.
4. (Para.8) This is particularly the case in chaotic states where the traditional diplomatic channels have even less chance than usual of making a difference.
5. (Para.8) As Mient Jan Faber argues, the "de-freezing" process which began with *detente* moved a state of confrontation on the brink of war through successive stages in which relations stabilized and finally normalized through peaceful means.

Unit 2 Peace and Conflicts

IV. Based on the text, decide whether the following statements are true or false. For false statements, write the facts in parentheses.

1. The charm of sport enables it to move between the political and the personal with ease.
   (   )
2. The reason for the 1970 general election defeat of the British Labour Party was due to England's loss of a quarter-final World Cup match against West Germany.
   (   )
3. Politicians have been quick to make use of the power of sport to influence their political campaign.
   (   )
4. The values underlying sport help individuals develop the skills that eliminate the inclinations for conflict.
   (   )
5. "Right to Play" works to benefit juvenile delinquents from eight problematic and low-income neighborhoods.
   (   )

Vocabulary Exercises

I. Fill in the blank in each sentence with a word or phrase from the box below. Make sure the appropriate form of the word is used.

| juvenile   delinquency   magnitude   underpin   wane   democratization |

1. To those who have suggested that the recovery ought to be moving more quickly, they underestimate the _____ of the problem.
2. Skiing was introduced to the county by the Swedes in the 1870s and became a major form of transportation in an area that receives more than eight feet of snow from November through April. That tradition _____ after the 1930s, when townspeople began plowing the roads between communities.
3. Foreign trade is the cornerstone of development strategies from China to Brazil. It is what links countries all over the world in a network of production that _____ global prosperity.
4. Ever since he was taken into custody, Mr. Muse's age has been in sharp dispute. His lawyers say he is under 18 and should be treated as a _____; However prosecutors allege that he is over 18.
5. During the campaign, Mr. Johnson boasted that he would create one million new jobs and

crack down on _____ and drug trafficking.
6. Canada, which last month froze most ties with Belarus to protest against the disputed March 19 presidential vote, said it had strong concerns about the country's commitment to _____ and human rights.

II. **Fill in the blanks with the appropriate forms of the given words.**
1. In Smith's vision, greed is socially beneficial only when properly _____ (harness) and channeled.
2. Wolff believed that the illness was caused by a _____ (harmony) between a person and his or her environment.
3. The Constitution is a way for the military to _____ (perpetuation) its control over the political and economic life of the country.
4. "We'll finally be able to make the case for investing in popular streetcar projects and other transit systems that people want," Mr. LaHood said to thousands of engineers, academics and transportation officials attending the annual _____ (convene) of the Transportation Research Board, a division of the National Research Council.
5. We are 100 percent sure that this election was _____ (legitimacy). All the international communities, and even more important, the Ukrainian public can accept this result.

III. **Replace the italicized words or phrases with simple, everyday words.**
1. If the Olympic Movement is able to *harness* this potential...( )
2. ...to "influence events through persuasion and attraction rather than by military or financial *coercion*." ( )
3. September 11 was a *stark* reminder of the cultural gulf that has opened up between East and West. ( )
4. ...to benefit juvenile *delinquents* aged 12–20... ( )

IV. **Choose the word or phrase that best completes each of the following sentences.**
1. Mr. Jackson was called "the cornerstone to the entire music business," who _____ the gap between rhythm and blues and pop music and made it into a global culture.
    A. went over   B. overcame   C. melted   D. bridged
2. Today the restaurants in Russia employ 25,000 people, a number far _____ by the businesses in McDonald's supply chain, which employ 100,000.
    A. swung   B. eclipsed   C. fallen   D. concealed
3. It is essential that the public _____ the information it needs to understand and be assured of the integrity of all our operations, including all aspects of our balance sheet and our financial controls.
    A. have   B. to have   C. has   D. had

30

Unit 2 Peace and Conflicts

4. Talks aimed at preventing the collapse of the power-sharing government in Northern Ireland appeared to be _____ the brink of failure on Wednesday when the British and Irish prime ministers withdrew after three days of talks and flew back to their respective capitals.
   A. to   B. in   C. on   D. at
5. Expand the range of professional options for graduate students. Most graduate students will never hold the kind of job for which they are being trained. It is, _____, necessary to help them prepare for work in fields other than higher education.
   A. though   B. however   C. then   D. therefore

Translation Exercises

I. **Translate each of the following sentences into English, using the word or phrase given in the brackets.**

1. 作为一种开发地球能源的方式,风车已被沿用了几百年。(harness)

2. 他刚才所阐述的是支撑管理体系和加强民主的基本原则。(underpin)

3. 简·奥斯汀是一位了不起的作家,她真正懂得如何使自己笔下的人物栩栩如生。(come alive)

4. 成百上千的公司在金融危机中债台高筑,处于破产边缘。(on the brink of)

5. 在相邻房间里使用截然不同的装饰设计会导致风格上不和谐、不一致。(disharmony)

II. **Translate the following paragraph into English.**

奥林匹克运动力图通过体育的教育价值,促使人类拥有一个和平的未来。奥运会使世界各国的运动员聚集在一起,共同参加这一最盛大的国际体育活动,藉此促进各个国家和人民之间的和平、相互了解和善意,这些目标也是联合国基本价值的组成部分。

III. **Translate the following paragraph into Chinese.**

The wider values and mechanisms of sport offer many opportunities for the Olympic Movement to enhance the scope and impact of the Olympic Truce. The reach of sport makes it a more constant presence in our lives, which would help to keep the Olympic Flame burning between Olympic Games. Also, the myriad of sports networks offers rich potential for sustaining work from the political to the personal level.

Language Appreciation

I. Read the text carefully, then pick out the sentences that you think are well-written. Pay close attention to the italicized words or phrases of the following sentences. Try to appreciate the way in which the author expresses his/her ideas. Learn how to use them in your own writing.

1. Sport has a rich network that *inhabits* all levels of the pyramid of conflict, and so can offer a potential architecture for peace.
2. While this is cultural legend, *there is no denying the fact that* Wilson had a reservation about the date of the election because England's match was scheduled to take place just before.

II. Read aloud and recite paragraphs 1 and 2.

III. Stylistics Study

Periodic Sentence vs. Loose Sentence—Art vs. Nature

Examples: 1) *The Olympic Truce, through a strengthened partnership with sport, can be an important part of this solution.*
—From Text I of Unit 2
2) *It is a truth universally acknowledged that a single man in possession of a fortune must be in want of a wife.*
—From J. Austin, *Pride and Prejudice*
3) *To believe your own thought, to believe that what is true for you in your private heart is true for all men—that is genius.*
—From Ralph Waldo Emerson

Questions: 1) What is the function of the underlined portion of each sentence?
2) Are these sentences usually used in colloquial English? Why or why not?
3) What is a periodic sentence and what is a loose sentence?

Unit 2 Peace and Conflicts

Text II

On War

> *Pre-reading Questions*
> 1. What are some motives behind conflicts among people? Countries? Groups? Organizations?
> 2. In your opinion, why do people choose war as a means to resolve conflicts?

1   To fight is a radical instinct; if men have nothing else to fight over they will fight over words, fancies, or women, or they will fight because they dislike each other's looks, or because they have met walking in opposite directions. To knock a thing down, especially if it is cocked at an arrogant angle, is a deep delight to the blood. To fight for a reason and in a calculating spirit is something your true warrior despises; even a coward might screw his courage up to such a reasonable conflict. The joy and glory of fighting lie in its pure spontaneity and consequent generosity; you are not fighting for gain, but for sport and for victory. Victory, no doubt, has its fruits for the victor. If fighting were not a possible means of livelihood the bellicose instinct could never have established itself in any long-lived race. A few men can live on plunder, just as there is room in the world for some beasts of prey; other men are reduced to living on industry, just as there are diligent bees, ants, and herbivorous kine. But victory need have no good fruits for the people whose army is victorious. That it sometimes does so is an ulterior and blessed circumstance hardly to be reckoned upon.

2   Since barbarism has its pleasures, it naturally has its apologists. There are panegyrists of war who say that without a periodical bleeding a race decays and loses its manhood. Experience is directly opposed to this shameless assertion. It is war that wastes a nation's wealth, chokes its industries, kills its flowers, narrows its sympathies, condemns it to be governed by adventurers, and leaves the puny, deformed, and unmanly to breed the next generation. Internecine war, foreign and civil, brought about the greatest set-back which the life of reason has ever suffered; it exterminated the Greek and Italian aristocracies. Instead of being descended from heroes, modern nations are descended from slaves; and it is not

their bodies only that show it. After a long peace, if the conditions of life are propitious, we observe a people's energies bursting their barriers; they become aggressive on the strength they have stored up in their remote and unchecked development. It is the unmutilated race, fresh from the struggle  with nature (in which the best survive, while in war it is often the best that perish), that descends victoriously into the arena of nations and conquers disciplined armies at the first blow, becomes the military aristocracy of the next epoch and is itself ultimately sapped and decimated by luxury and battle, and merged at last into the ignoble conglomerate beneath. Then, perhaps, in some other virgin country a genuine humanity is again found, capable of victory because unbled by the war. To call war the soil of courage and virtue is like calling debauchery the soil of love.

3   Blind courage is an animal virtue indispensable in a world full of dangers and evils where a certain insensibility and dash are requisite to skirt the precipice without vertigo. Such animal courage seems therefore beautiful rather than desperate or cruel, and being the lowest and most instinctive of virtues it is the one most widely and sincerely admired. In the form of steadiness under risks rationally taken, and perseverance so long as there is a chance of success, courage is a true virtue; but it ceases to be one when the love of danger, a useful passion when danger is unavoidable, begins to lead men into evils which it was unnecessary to face. Bravado, provocativeness, and a gambler's instinct, with a love of hitting hard for the sake of exercise, is a temper which ought already to be counted among the vices rather than the virtues of man. To delight in war is a merit in the soldier, a dangerous quality in the captain, and a positive crime in the statesman.

4   The panegyrist of war places himself on the lowest level on which a moralist or patriot can stand and shows as great a want of refined feeling as of right reason. For the glories of war are all blood-stained, delirious, and infected with crime; the combative instinct is a savage prompting by which one man's good is found in another's evil. The existence of such a contradiction in the moral world is the original sin of nature, whence flows every other wrong. He is

a willing accomplice of that perversity in things who delights in another's discomfiture or in his own, and craves the blind tension of plunging into danger without reason, or the idiot's pleasure in facing a pure chance. To find joy in another's trouble is, as man is constituted, not unnatural, though it is wicked; and to find joy in one's own trouble, though it be madness, is not yet impossible for man. These are the chaotic depths of that dreaming nature out of which humanity has to grow.

By George Santayana
(821 words)

Reading Comprehension

I. Answer the following questions with the information you read from the passage.
   1. What does the joy and glory of fighting lie in?
   2. What do panegyrists have to say about wars? Do you agree?
   3. What is the consequence of a war?
   4. How do you interpret the sentence: "To call war the soil of courage and virtue is like calling debauchery the soil of love (Para. 2)."?
   5. What does "delight in war" mean to the soldier, the captain, and the statesman respectively?

II. Topics for discussion and reflection.
   1. Conflicts often elicit a variety of emotions. Brainstorm a list of emotions that may result in or ensue from conflict.
   2. Brainstorm and discuss some ways other than war for countries to resolve conflicts.

Exercises for Integrated Skills

I. **Dictation**

   Listen to the following passage. The passage will be read to you four times. During the first reading, which will be read at normal speed, listen and try to understand the meaning. For the second and third readings, the passage will be read sentence by sentence, or phrase by phrase, with intervals of 15 to 20 seconds. The last reading will be done at normal speed again and during this time check your work. You will then be given 2 minutes to check through your work a second time.

II. **Cloze**

Since its re-emergence onto the global scene just over ten years ago, the Olympic Truce has played a role in tackling conflicts and the drivers of violence ___1___ all levels of the pyramid of conflict.

The ___2___ of the Truce is greatly enhanced by two ___3___: its home at the Olympic Games and its association with sport. The Games provide the Truce ___4___ the world's largest stage from which to project its message, a safe and prestigious forum for mediation and reconciliation, and a ___5___ window within which to focus efforts and resources— ___6___, a good excuse to ___7___ for progress and a forum steeped in the values essential to peace-building and conflict resolution. ___8___ sport offers a bridge between the political and the personal spheres and comes with a ready-made network of organisations, clubs and ___9___ that ___10___ it into the heart of almost every community around the world.

1. A. in   B. at   C. on   D. for
2. A. potential   B. fulfillment   C. accomplishment   D. embodiment
3. A. cases   B. terms   C. factors   D. points
4. A. with   B. of   C. /   D. for
5. A. common   B. regular   C. normal   D. conventional
6. A. in one word   B. in a word   C. in other words   D. in words
7. A. persuade   B. promote   C. advance   D. push
8. A. And   B. Then   C. Instead   D. Yet
9. A. establishments B. units   C. institutions   D. societies
10. A. embed   B. insert   C. embody   D. add

Oral Activities

1. Besides financial costs, what other costs are there to war? List at least three costs of war. Is war worth the price? Under what conditions is war worth the cost?
2. When given a wish, people often say that they wish for world peace. Unfortunately, achieving world peace is not that easy. In pairs, discuss some ways that world peace can occur. Give specific examples to support your answer.

Unit 2　Peace and Conflicts

Writing Practice

Composition Writing

　　Nowadays, more and more people believe that sports are essential to advance world peace. Popular events such as The FIFA World Cup and other international sporting occasions play an important role in easing international tensions and expressing patriotic emotions in a safe way. To what extent do you agree or disagree with this opinion? Write a composition of about 200 words to voice your opinion.

Unit 3 Prizes and Awards

Warm-up Activities

1. If you could win any award or receive any prize what would it be and why?
2. What criteria do you think are crucial to have for a scholarship program and why?

Text I

History of the Pulitzer Prizes

Pre-reading Questions

1. What criteria are needed to win a Pulitzer Prize?
2. In your opinion, what constitutes as good journalism?

1   In the latter years of the 19th century, Joseph Pulitzer stood out as the very embodiment of American journalism. Hungarian-born, an intense indomitable figure, Pulitzer was the most skillful of newspaper publishers, a passionate crusader against dishonest government, a fierce, hawklike competitor who did not shrink from sensationalism in circulation struggles, and a visionary who richly endowed his profession. His innovative *New York World* and *St. Louis Post-Dispatch* reshaped newspaper journalism.

2   Pulitzer was the first to call for the training of journalists at the university level in a school of journalism. And certainly, the lasting influence of the Pulitzer Prizes on journalism, literature, music, and drama is to be attributed to his visionary acumen. In writing his 1904 will, which made provision for the establishment of the Pulitzer Prizes as an incentive to excellence, Pulitzer

Unit 3 Prizes and Awards

specified solely four awards in journalism, four in letters and drama, one for education, and four traveling scholarships.

3 In letters, prizes were to go to an American novel, an original American play performed in New York, a book on the history of the United States, an American biography, and a history of public service by the press. But, sensitive to the dynamic progression of his society Pulitzer made provision for broad changes in the system of awards. He established an overseer advisory board and willed it "power in its discretion to suspend or to change any subject or subjects, substituting, however, others in their places, if in the judgment of the board such suspension, changes, or substitutions shall be conducive to the public good or rendered advisable by public necessities, or by reason of change of time." He also empowered the board to withhold any award where entries fell below its standards of excellence. The assignment of power to the board was such that it could also overrule the recommendations for awards made by the juries subsequently set up in each of the categories.

4 Since the inception of the prizes in 1917, the board, later renamed the Pulitzer Prize Board, has increased the number of awards to 21 and introduced poetry, music, and photography as subjects, while adhering to the spirit of the founder's will and its intent.

5 The board typically exercised its broad discretion in 1997, the 150th anniversary of Pulitzer's birth, in two fundamental respects. It took a significant step in recognition of the growing importance of work being done by newspapers in online journalism. Beginning with the 1999 competition, the board sanctioned the submission by newspapers of online presentations as supplements to print exhibits in the Public Service category. The board left open the distinct possibility of further inclusions in the Pulitzer process of online journalism as the electronic medium developed. Thus, with the 2006 competition, the Board allowed online content in all 14 of its journalism categories and said it will continue to monitor the field.

6 The other major change was in music, a category that was added to the Plan of Award for prizes in 1943. The prize always had gone to composers of

classical music. The definition and entry requirements of the music category beginning with the 1998 competition were broadened to attract a wider range of American music. In an indication of the trend toward bringing mainstream music into the Pulitzer process, the 1997 prize went to Wynton Marsalis's "Blood on the Fields," which has strong jazz elements, the first such award. In music, the board also took tacit note of the criticism leveled at its predecessors for failure to cite two of the country's foremost jazz composers. It bestowed a Special Citation on George Gershwin marking the 1998 centennial celebration of his birth and Duke Ellington on his 1999 centennial year. In 2004, the Board further broadened the definition of the prize and the makeup of its music juries, resulting in a greater diversity of entries. In 2006, the Board also awarded a posthumous Special Citation to jazz composer Thelonious Monk.

7   Over the years the Pulitzer board has at times been targeted by critics for awards made or not made. Controversies also have arisen over decisions made by the board counter to the advice of juries. Given the subjective nature of the award process, this was inevitable. The board has not been captive to popular inclinations. Many, if not most, of the honored books have not been on bestseller lists, and many of the winning plays have been staged off-Broadway or in regional theaters. In journalism the major newspapers, such as *The New York Times, The Wall Street Journal,* and *The Washington Post*, have harvested many of the awards, but the board also has often reached out to work done by small, little-known papers. The Public Service award in 1995 went to *The Virgin Islands Daily News, St. Thomas,* for its disclosure of the links between the region's rampant crime rate and corruption in the local criminal justice system.

8   In letters, the board has grown less conservative over the years in matters of taste. The board in 1941 denied the fiction prize to Ernest Hemingway's *For Whom the Bell Tolls*, but gave him the award in 1953 for *The Old Man and the Sea*, a lesser work. Notwithstanding these contretemps, from its earliest days, the board has in general stood firmly by a policy of secrecy in its deliberations and refusal to publicly debate or defend its decisions. The challenges have not lessened the reputation of the Pulitzer Prizes as the country's most prestigious awards and as the most sought-after accolades in journalism, letters, and music. The Prizes are perceived as a major incentive for high-quality journalism and have focused worldwide attention on American achievements in letters and music.

9   The formal announcement of the prizes, made each April, states that the awards are made by the president of Columbia University on the recommendation of the Pulitzer Prize board. This formulation is derived from the Pulitzer will, which established Columbia as the seat of the administration of the prizes. Today, in fact, the independent board makes all the decisions relative to the prizes. In his will Pulitzer bestowed an endowment on Columbia of $2,000,000 for the establishment of a School of Journalism, one-fourth of which was to be "applied to prizes or scholarships for the encouragement of public service, public morals, American literature, and the advancement of education." In doing so, he stated: "I am deeply interested in the progress and elevation of journalism, having spent my life in that profession, regarding it as a noble profession and one of unequaled importance for its influence upon the minds and morals of the people. I desire to assist in attracting to this profession young men of character and ability, also to help those already engaged in the profession to acquire the highest moral and intellectual training." In his ascent to the summit of American journalism, Pulitzer himself received little or no assistance. He prided himself on being a self-made man, but it may have been his struggles as a young journalist that imbued him with the desire to foster professional training.

By Seymour Topping (abridged)

(1,172 words)

Words and Expressions

crusade /kruːˈseɪd/ n. a determined attempt to change something because you think you are morally right 改革运动 **crusader** n. (某)改革的参与者

sensationalism /senˈseɪʃənəlɪzəm/ n. a way of reporting events or stories that makes them seem as strange, exciting, or shocking as possible—used in order to show disapproval 用追求轰动效应(耸人听闻)的手法

visionary /ˈvɪʒənəri/ n. someone who has clear ideas and strong feelings about the way something should be in the future 有远见的人,有预见的人

innovative	/'ɪnəveɪtɪv/	adj.	being new, different, and better than those that existed before 革新的，新颖的
acumen	/ə'kjuːmən/	n.	the ability to think quickly and make good judgments 敏锐，聪明，机智
progression	/prə'greʃən/	n.	a gradual process of change or development 进步，进展
overseer	/'əʊvəsɪə/	n.	someone who is in charge of a project, group of workers etc., and who makes sure that the job is done properly 监工，工头
advisory	/əd'vaɪzərɪ/	adj.	having the purpose of giving advice 提供意见（咨询）的
discretion	/dɪ'skreʃən/	n.	the ability and right to decide exactly what should be done in a particular situation 谨慎，慎重
substitution	/ˌsʌbstɪ'tjuːʃən/	n.	when someone or something is replaced by someone or something else 替换，代替
conducive	/kən'djuːsɪv/	adj.	providing the right conditions for something good to happen or exist 有益于某事，有助于某事
render	/'rendə/	vt.	to cause someone or something to be in a particular condition 使……成为，致使
empower	/ɪm'paʊə/	vt.	to give someone more control over their own life or situation 使自主，给(某人)权利 **empowerment** n. 激励自主，授权，赋权
overrule	/ˌəʊvə'ruːl/	vt.	to change an order or decision that you think is wrong, using your official power （用职权）改变，否决(认为是错误的命令或决定)
inception	/ɪn'sepʃən/	n.	the start of an organization or institution 开创，开端
photography	/fə'tɒgrəfɪ/	n.	the art, profession, or method of producing photographs or the scenes in films 摄影，摄影业，摄影术
adhere	/əd'hɪə/	vi.	to continue to behave according to a particular rule, agreement, or belief 坚守，信守
sanction	/'sæŋkʃən/	vt.	to officially accept or allow something 批准，准许
submission	/səb'mɪʃən/	n.	when you give or show something to someone in authority, for them to consider or approve 呈递，呈送，递交
distinct	/dɪs'tɪŋkt/	adj.	that certainly exists 确实存在的

Unit 3 Prizes and Awards

inclusion	/ɪnˈkluːʒən/	n.	the act of including someone or something in a larger group or set, or the fact of being included in one 包括，包含
indication	/ˌɪndɪˈkeɪʃən/	n.	a sign, remark, event etc. that shows what is happening, what someone is thinking or feeling, or what is true 迹象
tacit	/ˈtæsɪt/	adj.	understood without being expressed directly 默认的，心照不宣的
foremost	/ˈfɔːməʊst/	adj.	the best or most important 最杰出的，最著名的
bestow	/bɪˈstəʊ/	vt.	to give someone something of great value or importance 授予，赠给，给予
citation	/saɪˈteɪʃən/	n.	a formal statement or piece of writing publicly praising someone's actions or achievements 嘉奖状(令)
centennial	/senˈtenɪəl/	n.	the day or year exactly 100 years after a particular event 一百周年(纪念)
posthumous	/ˈpɒstjʊməs/	adj.	happening, printed etc. after someone's death 死后发生的，死后获得的，死后出版的
be captive to something			to be unable to think or speak freely, because of being influenced too much by something 受制于……
inclination	/ˌɪŋklɪˈneɪʃən/	n.	a feeling that makes you want to do something 意向，爱好
disclosure	/dɪsˈkləʊʒə/	n.	a secret that someone tells people, or the act of telling this secret 曝光，泄露，透露，被公开的秘密
rampant	/ˈræmpənt/	adj.	(of something bad) getting worse quickly and in an uncontrolled way 猖獗的，肆虐的，失控的
notwithstanding	/ˌnɒtwɪθˈstændɪŋ/	prep.	in spite of something 尽管
contretemps	/ˈkɒntrətɒŋ/	n.	an unlucky and unexpected event, especially an embarrassing one 令人困窘的意外事件，不幸的意外
secrecy	/ˈsiːkrəsɪ/	n.	the process of keeping something secret, or when something is kept a secret 保密，保密状态
deliberation	/dɪˌlɪbəˈreɪʃən/	n.	careful consideration or discussion of something 仔细考虑，商议，讨论
sought-after		adj.	wanted by a lot of people but rare or difficult to get 广受欢迎的，吃香的

accolade	/ˈækəleɪd/	n.	praise for someone who is greatly admired, or a prize given to them for their work 嘉奖，赞扬
elevation	/ˌelɪˈveɪʃən/	n.	an act of moving someone to a more important rank or position 提升，晋升
ascent	/əˈsent/	n.	the process of becoming more important, powerful, or successful than before（地位等的）升高，进步，前进
imbue with			to make someone or something have a quality, idea, or emotion very strongly 赋予（某物某种特质，尤指强烈感情）
foster	/ˈfɒstə/	vt.	to help a skill, feeling, idea, etc. develop over a period of time 促进，培养，助长

Notes:

1. **Seymour Topping** is a renowned journalist and former managing editor of the New York Times.
2. **New York World** was a newspaper published in New York from 1860 until 1931.
3. **St. Louis Post-Dispatch** is the major city-wide newspaper in St. Louis, Missouri.
4. **Wynton Marsalis (1961–)** is an American jazz and classical trumpeter and composer.
5. **George Gershwin (1898–1937)** was an American composer and pianist.
6. **Duke Ellington (1899–1974)** was an American composer, pianist, and big band leader.
7. **Thelonious Monk (1917–1982)** was an American jazz pianist and composer who, according to The Penguin Guide to Jazz, was "one of the giants of American music."
8. **Broadway** is a wide avenue in New York City, famous for the pinnacle of the American theater industry.
9. **The New York Times** is an American daily newspaper founded in 1851 and published in New York City. Nationally, The Times is third in circulation, and yet remains the largest metropolitan local newspaper in the United States. Although The Times is a local and regional paper, it is regarded within the industry as a national newspaper of record.
10. **The Wall Street Journal** is an international daily newspaper published by Dow Jones & Company with Asian and European editions. Its name derives from Wall Street in New York City, the heart of the financial district, and thus the paper primarily covers U.S. and international business, and financial news and issues. It has won the Pulitzer Prize thirty-three times.

Unit 3 Prizes and Awards

11. *Washington Post* is Washington, D.C.'s largest newspaper and its oldest, founded in 1877. Located in the nation's capital, the Post has a particular emphasis on national politics.
12. *Ernest Hemingway* (1899–1961) was an American writer and journalist. Hemingway's distinctive writing style characterized by economy and understatement had an enormous influence on 20th-century fiction, as did his apparent life of adventure and the public image he cultivated.
13. *For Whom the Bell Tolls* is a novel by Ernest Hemingway published in 1940. It is widely regarded to be among Hemingway's greatest works.
14. *The Old Man and the Sea* is a novella by Ernest Hemingway, written in Cuba in 1951 and published in 1952. It was the last major work of fiction to be produced by Hemingway and published in his lifetime.
15. *Columbia University* is a private university in the United States and a member of the Ivy League. It was founded in 1754 as King's College by royal charter of George II of Great Britain, and is one of the only two United States universities to have been founded under such authority.

Reading Comprehension

I. Fill in the table below according to the information you read from the text.

Year	Event
	Pulitzer in his will made provision for the establishment of the Pulitzer prize.
1917	
1943	
	The Old Man and the Sea by Hemingway won the prize.
1999	

II. Answer the following questions.
   1. What was Joseph Pulitzer like according to the text?
   2. What are the subjects of the Pulitzer Prizes?
   3. What are the most significant changes to the Pulitzer Prizes since 1997?
   4. Why didn't Ernest Hemingway win the Prize in 1941?
   5. How are the Pulitzer Prizes formulated? Who decides who will receive a Pulitzer Prize?

III. Paraphrase the following sentences within the context of the reading passage.

1. (Para. 3) But, sensitive to the dynamic progression of his society Pulitzer made provision for broad changes in the system of awards.
2. (Para. 3) The assignment of power to the board was such that it could also overrule the recommendations for awards made by the juries subsequently set up in each of the categories.
3. (Para. 7) The board has not been captive to popular inclinations.
4. (Para. 8) Notwithstanding these contretemps, from its earliest days, the board has in general stood firmly by a policy of secrecy in its deliberations and refusal to publicly debate or defend its decisions.
5. (Para. 9) He prided himself on being a self-made man, but it may have been his struggles as a young journalist that imbued him with the desire to foster professional training.

IV. Based on the text, decide whether the following statements are true or false. For false statements, write the facts in parentheses.

1. Pulitzer was among the pioneers who called for professional training of journalists.
   (   )
2. Many of the books that have won Pulitzer Prizes have become the most popular books.
   (   )
3. Pulitzer was born in 1847.
   (   )
4. Controversies over the Prizes are unavoidable because the board has become less conservative.
   (   )
5. The Board allowed online journalism in all of its journalism categories in the 2006 competition.
   (   )

Vocabulary Exercises

I. Fill in the blank in each sentence with a word or phrase from the box below. Make sure the appropriate form of the word is used.

| discretion | bestow | tacit | empower | indomitable | suspension |

1. When Winston Churchill rejected negotiations with the Nazis, France was on its knees. Hitler seemed _____, and there was no assurance that Britain could survive if it faced

German might alone.
2. It is up to local authorities to use their _____ in setting the charges.
3. The investigation led to the _____ of several officers.
4. They can see we just want to _____ Iraqi women in the educational and economic sectors. It's a very wide range of objectives, but I believe that Iraqi women need it.
5. No one actually claims this is how the brain works, but there is a _____ assumption that it might be.
6. The university said it had never _____ an award on an anonymous work before.

II. **Fill in the blanks with the appropriate forms of the given words.**
1. According to a Kenyan police report, Colin Bruce, the World Bank's country director for Kenya, who has _____ (crusader) against corruption, was approaching downtown Nairobi on Thursday afternoon when police officers stopped his driver for speeding.
2. His depth of experience and exceptional record as a university dean and legal scholar, his profound commitment to public service and _____ (vision) leadership make him the ideal person to lead the university at this remarkable time in the university's history.
3. In countries without adequate welfare _____ (provide) for the poor, unemployment may be very much more severe in its effects.
4. Mr. Putin and other senior Russian officials had warned in recent weeks that Ukraine would create another dispute by not _____ (adhere) to its contracts.
5. While the government has _____ (disclosure) more information about military spending in recent years, much of its spending remains secret.

III. **Choose the word or phrase that best completes each of the following sentences.**
1. This is a film above all about what it is like to take part in combat, though it does not shrink _____ showing an appalling number of civilian casualties.
   A. in   B. from   C. on   D. at
2. The book itself was _____ circulation for over two years in Malaysia before the minister decided to ban it.
   A. in   B. to   C. on   D. at
3. Western powers pressed for new sanctions against Iran on Thursday but China and Russia called _____ diplomatic negotiations as the best way to achieve a peaceful settlement of the dispute over Tehran's nuclear program.
   A. to   B. in   C. for   D. at
4. The car maker said earlier this month that it had had to _____ provision for possible losses of up to $260 million because of the possible currency fraud.
   A. make   B. do   C. prepare   D. take
5. He said he was "stunned by Robin's looks," but fell captive _____ her creative mind. "Robin has an incredible brain," he added. "There's no past, present and future—it's all

simultaneous."

   A. on   B. to   C. at   D. in

6. Although the hospital serves a large number of poor and uninsured patients, it is also perceived _____ a destination for middle-class Harlem residents.

   A. as   B. to   C. of   D. for

Translation Exercises

I. Translate each of the following sentences into English, using the word or phrase given in the brackets.

1. 这是一个非常艰巨的任务，但是她那大无畏的精神使她毫不畏惧地去追寻解决问题的方案。(shrink from)

2. 一些气象学家把飓风及其他灾难性天气归因为全球气候变暖。(attribute...to)

3. 许多游客在国外旅行时都遵循当地的传统和风俗。(adhere to)

4. 菲兹杰拉德(Fitzgerald)的小说世界是爵士时代精神的最佳体现。他的小说对上层社会，特别是上层社会的年轻人尤为关注。(embodiment)

5. 当地政府将扶持有利于高新技术发展的资本市场。(be conducive to)

6. 在我很小的时候，父母就给我灌输了有关家庭、信念和爱国主义的观念。(imbue... with)

7. 为了培养孩子的独立意识，Johnson先生在遗嘱中故意没有给他的独生女留下任何财产。(make provision for)

II. Translate the following paragraph into English.

    劳伦斯(Laureus)源于拉丁语，意为"桂冠"，是世界体坛胜利的象征。劳伦斯世界体育奖被公认为有史以来国际体育界的重大盛事，素有"体坛奥斯卡"之称。劳伦斯奖对每一年度世界上最杰出的男女运动员的运动成就予以奖励。此外，劳伦斯在全球范围内积极宣扬体育为世界人民大团结所发挥的有益作用。正如纳尔逊·曼德拉曾说过的那样："体育拥有改变世界的力量。……体育能够使原本陷入绝望的人们重新唤起希望。"

Unit 3　Prizes and Awards

III. **Translate the following paragraphs into Chinese.**

   In the latter years of the 19th century, Joseph Pulitzer stood out as the very embodiment of American journalism. Hungarian-born, an intense indomitable figure, Pulitzer was the most skillful of newspaper publishers, a passionate crusader against dishonest government, a fierce, hawklike competitor who did not shrink from sensationalism in circulation struggles, and a visionary who richly endowed his profession. His innovative *New York World* and *St. Louis Post-Dispatch* reshaped newspaper journalism.

Language Appreciation

I. **Read the text carefully, then pick out the sentences that you think are well-written. Pay close attention to the italicized words or phrases of the following sentences. Try to appreciate the way in which the author expresses his/her ideas. Learn how to use them in your own writing.**
   1. Hungarian-born, an intense indomitable figure, Pulitzer was *the most skillful of newspaper publishers, a passionate crusader against dishonest government, a fierce, hawklike competitor who did not shrink from sensationalism in circulation struggles, and a visionary who richly endowed his profession.*
   2. Many, *if not most*, of the honored books have not been on bestseller lists, and many of the winning plays have been staged off-Broadway or in regional theaters.
   3. This formulation is derived from the Pulitzer will, which established Columbia as the *seat* of the administration of the prizes.

II. **Read aloud and recite paragraph 9.**

III. **Stylistics Study**

   Parallelism—A Syntactic Form for Emphasis

   Examples: 1) *With a sufficiently large and specialized labor force and with a sufficiently strong government, it became possible to expand control over nature, to pursue advances in technology, to trade and compete over ever widening areas, to free an elite for ever more ambitious projects in art and to invent writing.*
   　　　　　　—From Text I of Unit 1
   　　　　2) *To spend too much time in studies is sloth; to use them too much for ornament is affection; to make judgment wholly by their rules, is the humour of a scholar.*

—From Francis Bacon, *Of Studies*

Questions:
1) Read the two sentences aloud. Pay attention to your volume and pitch, especially in the underlined portion, when reading. What is the feeling you get when reading the sentences, particularly for the underlined portion?
2) Make a grammatical analysis of the underlined portion. Are the underlined structures in both sentences similar in syntax?
3) Why do writers use parallelism in their writings? Have you ever used it in your own writing? Find an example in your own writing and recall why you used it when you wrote it.

Text II

Nobel Prize Acceptance Speech

Pre-reading Questions

1. What are some internationally recognized awards and what are they given for?
2. At many award shows people prepare a speech just in case they win. What is your opinion of this? Would you do the same, why or why not?

Your Majesty, Your Royal Highness, Mr. President, Excellencies, Ladies and Gentlemen:

1   I accept the Nobel Prize for Peace at a moment when 22 million Negroes of the United States of America are engaged in a creative battle to end the long night of racial injustice. I accept this award on behalf of a civil rights movement which is moving with determination and a majestic scorn for risk and danger to establish a reign of freedom and a rule of justice. I am mindful that only yesterday in Birmingham, Alabama, our children, crying out for brotherhood, were answered with fire hoses, snarling dogs and even death. I am mindful that only yesterday in Philadelphia, Mississippi, young people seeking to secure the right to vote were brutalized and murdered. And only yesterday more than 40 houses of worship in the State of Mississippi alone were bombed or burned because they offered a sanctuary to those who would not accept segregation. I am mindful that debilitating and grinding poverty afflicts my people and chains

them to the lowest rung of the economic ladder.

2   Therefore, I must ask why this prize is awarded to a movement which is beleaguered and committed to unrelenting struggle; to a movement which has not won the very peace and brotherhood which is the essence of the Nobel Prize.

3   After contemplation, I conclude that this award which I receive on behalf of that movement is a profound recognition that nonviolence is the answer to the crucial political and moral question of our time—the need for man to overcome oppression and violence without resorting to violence and oppression. Civilization and violence are antithetical concepts. Negroes of the United States, following the people of India, have demonstrated that nonviolence is not sterile passivity, but a powerful moral force which makes for social transformation. Sooner or later all the people of the world will have to discover a way to live together in peace, and thereby transform this pending cosmic elegy into a creative psalm of brotherhood. If this is to be achieved, man must evolve for all human conflict a method which rejects revenge, aggression and retaliation. The foundation of such a method is love.

4   The tortuous road which has led from Montgomery, Alabama to Oslo bears witness to this truth. This is a road over which millions of Negroes are travelling to find a new sense of dignity. This same road has opened for all Americans a new era of progress and hope. It has led to a new Civil Rights Bill, and it will, I am convinced, be widened and lengthened into a super highway of justice as Negro and white men in increasing numbers create alliances to overcome their common problems.

5   I accept this award today with an abiding faith in America and an audacious faith in the future of mankind. I refuse to accept despair as the final response to the ambiguities of history. I refuse to accept the idea that the "isness" of man's present nature makes him morally incapable of reaching up for the eternal "oughtness" that forever confronts him. I refuse to accept the idea that man is mere flotsam and jetsam in the river of life, unable to influence the unfolding events which surround him. I refuse to accept the view that mankind is so tragically bound to the starless midnight of racism and war that the bright

daybreak of peace and brotherhood can never become a reality.

6 I refuse to accept the cynical notion that nation after nation must spiral down a militaristic stairway into the hell of thermonuclear destruction. I believe that unarmed truth and unconditional love will have the final word in reality. This is why right temporarily defeated is stronger than evil triumphant. I believe that even amid today's mortar bursts and whining bullets, there is still hope for a brighter tomorrow. I believe that wounded justice, lying prostrate on the blood-flowing streets of our nations, can be lifted from this dust of shame to reign supreme among the children of men. I have the audacity to believe that peoples everywhere can have three meals a day for their bodies, education and culture for their minds, and dignity, equality and freedom for their spirits. I believe that what self-centered men have torn down men other-centered can build up. I still believe that one day mankind will bow before the altars of God and be crowned triumphant over war and bloodshed, and nonviolent redemptive good will proclaim the rule of the land. "And the lion and the lamb shall lie down together and every man shall sit under his own vine and fig tree and none shall be afraid." I still believe that We Shall overcome!

7 This faith can give us courage to face the uncertainties of the future. It will give our tired feet new strength as we continue our forward stride toward the city of freedom. When our days become dreary with low-hovering clouds and our nights become darker than a thousand midnights, we will know that we are living in the creative turmoil of a genuine civilization struggling to be born.

8 Today I come to Oslo as a trustee, inspired and with renewed dedication to humanity. I accept this prize on behalf of all men who love peace and brotherhood. I say I come as a trustee, for in the depths of my heart I am aware that this prize is much more than an honor to me personally.

9 Every time I take a flight, I am always mindful of the many people who make a successful journey possible—the known pilots and the unknown ground crew. So you honor the dedicated pilots of our struggle who have sat at the controls as the freedom movement soared into orbit. You honor, once again, Chief Lutuli of South Africa, whose struggles with and for his people, are still met with the most brutal expression of man's inhumanity to man. You honor the ground crew without whose labor and sacrifices the jet flights to freedom could never have left the earth. Most of these people will never make the headline and their names will not appear in Who's Who. Yet when years have

rolled past and when the blazing light of truth is focused on this marvelous age in which we live—men and women will know and children will be taught that we have a finer land, a better people, a more noble civilization—because these humble children of God were willing to suffer for righteousness' sake.

I think Alfred Nobel would know what I mean when I say that I accept this award in the spirit of a curator of some precious heirloom which he holds in trust for its true owners—all those to whom beauty is truth and truth beauty—and in whose eyes the beauty of genuine brotherhood and peace is more precious than diamonds or silver or gold.

By Martin Luther King Jr.
(1,162 words)

Reading Comprehension

I. **Answer the following questions with the information you read from the passage.**
   1. Why was Martin Luther King Jr. awarded the Nobel Prize for peace?
   2. What was Martin Luther King's attitude towards nonviolence?
   3. What did Martin Luther King refuse to accept?
   4. What did Martin Luther King believe?
   5. How do you interpret the sentence "I say I come as a trustee, for in the depths of my heart I am aware that this prize is much more than an honor to me personally (Para. 8)."?

II. **Topics for discussion and reflection.**
   1. What notable acceptance speeches do you remember? What did the winner say that made such a lasting impression?
   2. What criteria do you think are necessary for a well-written acceptance speech?

Exercises for Integrated Skills

I. **Dictation**

   Listen to the following passage. The passage will be read to you four times. During the first reading, which will be read at normal speed, listen and try to understand the meaning. For the second and third readings, the passage will be read sentence by sentence, or phrase by phrase, with intervals of 15 to 20 seconds. The last reading will be done at normal speed again and during this time check your work. You will then be given 2 minutes to check through your work a second time.

_____

_____

_____

_____

II. **Cloze**

The choice of Barack Obama as the ___1___ of the 2009 Nobel Peace Prize was an unexpected ___2___ that ___3___ praise and puzzlement around the globe. ___4___ the prize has been presented, ___5___ controversially, for accomplishment. This prize seemed a kind of prayer and encouragement by the Nobel ___6___ for future endeavor and more consensual American leadership. But the prize quickly loomed as a potential political liability—perhaps more burden than ___7___ —for Mr. Obama. Republicans ___8___ that he had won more for his star power and oratorical skills than for his actual ___9___, and even some Democrats privately questioned whether he ___10___ it.

1. A. receiver   B. acceptor   C. recipient   D. taker
2. A. prize   B. honor   C. award   D. reward
3. A. elicited   B. showed   C. conveyed   D. got
4. A. Normally   B. In fact   C. Actually   D. Mostly
5. A. still   B. but   C. while   D. even
6. A. foundation   B. committee   C. institute   D. organization
7. A. glory   B. prize   C. reputation   D. fame
8. A. convinced   B. agreed   C. contended   D. assumed
9. A. significance   B. achievements   C. success   D. fulfillments
10. A. worth   B. entitled   C. deserved   D. afforded

Oral Activities

1. Discuss your opinion of beauty contests. Debate whether or not they should be banned.
2. Discuss whether having a prize/award as a goal encourages or deters you from doing certain things.

Unit 3　Prizes and Awards

Writing Practice

Composition Writing

　　If you were honored with an internationally recognized prize or award (such as Nobel Prize in Literature, Pulitzer Prize for Photography, Oscar Awards for Best Actor/Actress, The Laureus World Sports Awards, etc.), what would you say to the world upon receiving the award/prize at the ceremony? Compose an acceptance speech of about 200 words to express your thoughts.

Unit 4 Universities

Warm-up Activities

1. Compare your university with the one you dreamt of. Your comparison may include, but is not limited to, the following aspects:
   Location:
   History:
   Faculty (teachers & staff):
   Research:
   Facilities / Services:
   Campus & Surrounding area:
   Student activities (e.g. clubs, societies, sports teams, etc.)
   Scholarship:
2. Peking University and Tsinghua University were once the primary choices for top students in mainland China. However, in recent years, this prominence has been challenged by overseas universities and Hong Kong universities. In your opinion, what is the main reason for the increasing number of students studying abroad? What should universities do to attract more outstanding students?

Text I

Universities and Their Function

Pre-reading Questions

1. As a college student, what do you think is the basic function that universities should perform for society?
2. What is imagination? Albert Einstein once said, "Imagination is more important than knowledge." What is your interpretation of this?

Unit 4 Universities

1. The universities are schools of education, and schools of research. But the primary reason for their existence is not to be found either in the mere knowledge conveyed to the students or in the mere opportunities for research afforded to the members of the faculty.

2. The justification for a university is that it preserves the connection between knowledge and the zest of life, by uniting the young and the old in the imaginative consideration of learning. The university imparts information, but it imparts it imaginatively. At least, this is the function which it should perform for society. A university which fails in this respect has no reason for existence. This atmosphere of excitement, arising from imaginative consideration, transforms knowledge. A fact is no longer a bare fact: it is invested with all its possibilities. It is no longer a burden on the memory: it is energizing as the poet of our dreams, and as the architect of our purposes.

3. Imagination is not to be divorced from the facts: it is a way of illuminating the facts. It works by eliciting the general principles which apply to the facts, as they exist, and then by an intellectual survey of alternative possibilities which are consistent with those principles. It enables men to construct an intellectual vision of a new world, and it preserves the zest of life by the suggestion of satisfying purposes.

4. Youth is imaginative, and if the imagination be strengthened by discipline, this energy of imagination can in great measure be preserved through life. The tragedy of the world is that those who are imaginative have but slight experience, and those who are experienced have feeble imaginations. Fools act on imagination without knowledge; pedants act on knowledge without imagination. The task of a university is to weld together imagination and experience.

5. These reflections upon the general functions of a university can be at once translated in terms of the particular functions of a business school. We need not flinch from the assertion that the main function of such a school is to produce men with a greater zest for business.

6   In a simpler world, business relations were simpler, being based on the immediate contact of man with man and on immediate confrontation with all relevant material circumstances. Today business organization requires an imaginative grasp of psychologies of populations engaged in differing modes of occupation; of populations scattered through cities, through mountains, through plains; of populations on the ocean, and of populations in mines, and of populations in forests. It requires an imaginative grasp of conditions in the tropics, and of conditions in temperate zones. It requires an imaginative grasp of the interlocking interests of great organizations, and of the reactions of the whole complex to any change in one of its elements. It requires an imaginative understanding of laws of political economy, not merely in the abstract, but also with the power to construe them in terms of the particular circumstances of a concrete business. It requires some knowledge of the habits of government, and of the variations of those habits under diverse conditions. It requires an imaginative vision of the binding forces of any human organization, a sympathetic vision of the limits of human nature and of the conditions which evoke loyalty of service. It requires some knowledge of the laws of health, and of the laws of fatigue, and of the conditions for sustained reliability. It requires an imaginative understanding of the social effects of the conditions of factories. It requires a sufficient conception of the role of applied science in modern society. It requires that discipline of character which can say "yes" and "no" to other men, not by reason of blind obstinacy, but with firmness derived from a conscious evaluation of relevant alternatives.

7   The universities have trained intellectual pioneers of our civilization—the priests, the lawyers, the statesmen, the doctors, the men of science, and the men of letters. The conduct of business now requires intellectual imagination of the same type as that which in former times has mainly passed into those other occupations.

8   There is one great difficulty which hampers all the higher types of human endeavor. In modern times this difficulty has even increased in its possibilities for evil. In any larger organization the younger men, who are novices, must be set to jobs which consist in carrying out fixed duties in obedience to orders. No president of a large corporation meets his youngest employee at his office door with the offer of the most responsible job which the work of that corporation

includes. The young men are set to work at a fixed routine, and only occasionally even see the president as he passes in and out of the building. Such work is a great discipline. It imparts knowledge, and it produces reliability of character; also it is the only work for which the young men, in that novice stage, are fit, and it is the work for which they are hired. There can be no criticism of the custom, but there may be an unfortunate effect—prolonged routine work dulls the imagination.

9   The way which a university should function in the preparation for an intellectual career, such as modern business or one of the older professions, is by promoting the imaginative consideration of the various general principles underlying that career. Its students thus pass into their period of technical apprenticeship with their imaginations already practiced in connecting details with general principles. The routine then receives its meaning, and also illuminates the principle which gives it that meaning. Hence, instead of a drudgery issuing in a blind rule of thumb, the properly trained man has some hope of obtaining an imagination disciplined by detailed facts and by necessary habits.

10   Thus the proper function of a university is the imaginative acquisition of knowledge. Apart from this importance of the imagination, there is no reason why businessmen, and other professional men, should not pick up their facts bit by bit as they want them for particular occasions. A university is imaginative or it is nothing—at least nothing useful.

By Alfred North Whitehead
(1,031 words)

Words and Expressions

justification	/ˌdʒʌstɪfɪˈkeɪʃən/	n.	a good and acceptable reason for doing something 正当理由，可接受的理由
zest	/zest/	n.	eager interest and enjoyment 热情
impart	/ɪmˈpɑːt/	vt.	to give information, knowledge, wisdom, etc. to someone 传授（知识，智慧等）
divorce	/dɪˈvɔːs/	vt.	to separate two ideas, subjects, etc. 把……完全分开
illuminate	/ɪˈluːmɪneɪt/	vt.	to make something much clearer and easier to understand 解释，阐明

elicit	/ɪˈlɪsɪt/	vt.	to draw (facts, etc.) from somebody, sometimes with difficulty 诱出，探出（事实等）
feeble	/ˈfiːbəl/	adj.	not very good or effective 蹩脚的，无效的
pedant	/ˈpednt/	n.	a person who is too interested in formal rules and small unimportant details 学究，迂夫子
weld	/weld/	vt.	to join things into a single strong group 使紧密结合
not flinch from (doing) something			to be willing to do something even though it is difficult or unpleasant 不回避（做）某事
assertion	/əˈsɜːʃn/	n.	action of claiming or stating forcefully 声言，陈词
confrontation	/ˌkɒnfrʌnˈteɪʃn/	n.	a situation in which there is a lot of angry disagreement between two people or groups 对抗，冲突
scatter	/ˈskætə/	vt.	to (cause to) move far apart in different directions 分散，驱散
interlocking	/ˌɪntəˈlɒkɪŋ/	adj.	firmly joined together; closely connected 连锁的
construe	/kənˈstruː/	vt.	to explain the meaning of (words, sentences, actions, etc.); to interpret something 理解
variation	/ˌveərɪˈeɪʃən/	n.	something that is done in a different way 变化，变更
sympathetic	/ˌsɪmpəˈθetɪk/	adj.	caring and feeling sorry about someone's problem 体谅的，同情的
evoke	/ɪˈvəʊk/	vt.	to produce a strong feeling or memory in someone 唤起，引起
loyalty	/ˈlɔɪəltɪ/	n.	a feeling of support for someone or something 忠诚
fatigue	/fəˈtiːg/	n.	weariness, tiredness 疲劳，劳累
sustained	/səˈsteɪnd/	adj.	continuing for a long time 持续的
obstinate	/ˈɒbstɪnɪt/	adj.	refusing to change one's opinion 固执的，倔强的 **obstinacy** n. unwillingness to obey 倔强
evaluation	/ɪˌvæljuˈeɪʃən/	n.	a judgment about how good, useful, or successful something is 评估，评价
hamper	/ˈhæmpə/	vt.	to make it difficult for someone to do something 阻碍，妨碍
novice	/ˈnɒvɪs/	n.	someone who has no experience in a skill, subject, or activity 新手，初学者
obedience	/əˈbiːdɪəns/	n.	action of obeying 服从，顺从
underlie	/ˌʌndəˈlaɪ/	vt.	to be the basis or the cause of something 构成……的基础（原因）

Unit 4 Universities

apprenticeship	/əˈprentɪsʃɪp/	n.	a fixed period of time for someone who works for an employer in order to learn a particular skill or job 学徒期,学徒身份
drudgery	/ˈdrʌdʒərɪ/	n.	hard boring work 繁重、乏味的工作
a blind rule of thumb			a rough practical method of assessing or measuring something, usually based on past experience rather than on exact measurement, thus not completely reliable in every case or in every detail 基于实际经验的)粗略的计算

Notes:

1. **the tropics** the hottest part of the world, which is around the equator.
2. **temperate zone** (of climate or climate region) region with a mild temperature without extremes of heat of cold.

Reading Comprehension

I. **Fill in the blanks to complete the summary of the text.**

The universities are schools of education, and _____. The atmosphere of excitement in a university, arising from imaginative consideration, transforms knowledge. Youth is imaginative, and if _____
_____
_____. However, the tragedy of the world is that fools act on imagination without knowledge; pedants act on knowledge without imagination. The universities have trained the intellectual pioneers of our civilization—_____
_____. The way which a university should function in the preparation for an intellectual career is by _____
_____
_____.

II. **Answer the following questions.**

1. What is the chief function of a university in the author's eyes?
2. How does imagination work to illuminate facts?
3. Do you agree that "Fools act on imagination without knowledge; pedants act on knowledge

without imagination"? Why or why not? Is there a similar saying in Chinese?
4. What does the business school exemplify?
5. What are required of today's business organizations? List some of them.
6. What does the sentence "A university is imaginative or it is nothing—at least nothing useful (Para. 10)" mean?

III. Paraphrase the following sentences within the context of the reading passage.

1. (Para. 2) It is no longer a burden on the memory: it is energizing as the poet of our dreams, and as the architect of our purposes.
2. (Para. 5) We need not flinch from the assertion that the main function of such a school is to produce men with a greater zest for business.
3. (Para. 6) It requires an imaginative vision of the binding forces of any human organization, a sympathetic vision of the limits of human nature and of the conditions which evoke loyalty of service.
4. (Para. 6) It requires that discipline of character which can say "yes" and "no" to other men, not by reason of blind obstinacy, but with firmness derived from a conscious evaluation of relevant alternatives.
5. (Para. 8) In any larger organization the younger men, who are novices, must be set to jobs which consist in carrying out fixed duties in obedience to orders.
6. (Para. 9) Hence, instead of a drudgery issuing in a blind rule of thumb, the properly trained man has some hope of obtaining an imagination disciplined by detailed facts and by necessary habits.

IV. Based on the text, decide whether the following statements are true or false. For false statements, write the facts in parentheses.

1. Neither the opportunities for research nor the knowledge conveyed to the students is the primary reason for the existence of universities.
   (   )
2. If a university fails to impart knowledge imaginatively, then there is no need for its existence.
   (   )
3. The task of a university is to link together knowledge and experience.
   (   )
4. The universities have trained intellectual pioneers of our civilization.
   (   )
5. The proper function of a university is the practical acquisition of knowledge.
   (   )

Unit 4 Universities

Vocabulary Exercises

I. Fill in the blank in each sentence with a word or phrase taken from the box below. Make sure the appropriate form of the word is used.

| rule of thumb | hamper | feeble | evoke | interlocking |
| illuminate | weld | impart | elicit | derive from |

1. She was too _____ to leave the hospital on her own.
2. To _____ positive leisure attitudes to the general public is essential for motivating them to use their leisure in creative and satisfying ways.
3. As a general _____, children should not spend more than one hour on their homework.
4. He tried to run, but was _____ by his heavy suitcase.
5. The lawyer successfully _____ the truth from a witness.
6. They believed in a united national economy—one _____ system of labor, trade and investment.
7. My job is now to _____ the players into a single team.
8. His report _____ the difficult issues at the heart of science policy.
9. The photographs _____ sweet memories of our childhood in a small French town.
10. The Roman name of Paris, *Lutetia*, is said to _____ the Latin word for mud (*lutum*).

II. Fill in the blanks with the appropriate forms of the given words.

1. It is important to find the _____ (underlie) causes of her depression.
2. Your father is the most _____ (obstinacy) man I've ever met.
3. Running with _____ (fatigue) legs, most athletes failed to perform at a level that matches their ability in the Ironman marathon
4. The primary cause of _____ (variation) in global temperature is the cycles of the sun and Earth's orbit about the sun.
5. Researchers have suggested that _____ (assertion) buffers or moderates reactions to stressful events.

III. Replace the italicized words or phrases with simple, everyday words.

1. We need not flinch from the assertion that *drudgery*... (   )
2. ...but also with the power to *construe* them in terms of the particular circumstances of a concrete business. (   )
3. ...to produce men with a greater *zest* for business. (   )
4. ...hampers all the higher types of human *endeavor*. (   )
5. In any larger organization the younger men, ... must *be set to jobs* which consist in carrying out fixed duties ...

IV. Choose a word or phrase that best completes each of the following sentences.
1. In ancient times, it was very common for people to _____ meat _____ salt.
   A. protect...with   B. preserve...in   C. keep...through   D. store...by
2. The one-child policy has helped not only slow down population growth, but also reduce the extent of problems _____ overpopulation.
   A. arising in   B. arisen in   C. arising from   D. arisen from
3. It is our _____ policy that we will achieve unity through peaceful means.
   A. consistent   B. continuous   C. considerate   D. continual
4. She is acting _____ the advice of her lawyers.
   A. up   B. as   C. out   D. on
5. Senator Smith is very _____ towards environmental issues.
   A. sympathetic   B. indifferent   C. optimistic   D. confused
6. The _____ provided by the adoptive parents helped the orphan grow into a happy and successful adult.
   A. obedience   B. nurture   C. escort   D. diagnosis
7. _____ his earnings as a baseball coach, he also owns and runs a chain of sports shops.
   A. Other than   B. Except for   C. In addition   D. Apart from
8. Kathy _____ a lot of Spanish by playing with the native boys and girls.
   A. made up   B. took up   C. picked up   D. turned up

Translation Exercises

I. Translate each of the following sentences into English, using the word or phrase given in the brackets.
1. 具备传授知识的能力并能赢得学生的尊重是教师的基本素质。(impart; command respect)

2. 在西方,仍然有很多人认为奥林匹克运动不能掺杂政治因素。(be invested with)

3. 我们制定的政策和措施不能与国家和人民的实际需要脱节。(divorce... from...)

4. 这位体操运动员精彩的表演博得了观众阵阵的掌声。(elicit)

5. 他把未经训练的一群新兵组织成有战斗力的部队,这让敌人感到害怕。(weld)

6. 为了打击恐怖势力,俄罗斯不会停止在那一带的军事行动。(not flinch from)

Unit 4　Universities

II. Translate the following paragraph into English.

　　进入耶鲁大学的校园,看到莘莘学子青春洋溢的脸庞,呼吸着书香浓郁的空气,我不由回想起40年前在北京清华大学度过的美好时光。学生时代,对人的一生都会产生重要影响。当年老师们对我的教诲,同学们给我的启发,我至今仍受用不尽。耶鲁大学以悠久的发展历史、独特的办学风格、卓著的学术成就闻名于世。如果时光能够倒流几十年,我真希望成为你们中的一员。耶鲁大学校训强调追求光明和真理,这符合人类进步的法则,也符合每个有志青年的心愿。

III. Translate the following paragraph into Chinese.

　　Youth is imaginative, and if the imagination be strengthened by discipline this energy of imagination can in great measure be preserved through life. The tragedy of the world is that those who are imaginative have but slight experience, and those who are experienced have feeble imaginations. Fools act on imagination without knowledge; pedants act on knowledge without imagination. The task of a university is to weld together imagination and experience.

Language Appreciation

I. Read the text carefully, then pick up the sentences that you think is well-written. Pay close attention to the italicized words or phrases of the following sentences. The following sentences are some for your references. Try to appreciate the way in which the author expresses his/her ideas. Learn how to use them in your own writing.

1. It is no longer a burden on the memory: it is energizing as *the poet of our dreams*, and as *the architect of our purposes*.
2. Imagination is not to be *divorced* from the facts: it is a way of illuminating the facts.
3. Fools act on imagination without knowledge; pedants act on knowledge without imagination.
4. The task of a university is to *weld* together imagination and experience.
5. We need not *flinch from* the assertion that the main function of such a school is to produce men with a greater zest for business.

II. Read aloud and recite paragraphs 4 and 6.

III. Stylistics Study

Antithesis and Symmetry—The Beauty of Balanced Structure

Examples: 1) *The power of French literature is in its prose writers, the power of English literature is in its poets.*

—From Matthew Arnold, *Essays in Criticism*

2) It was the best of times, it was the worst of times; it was the age of wisdom, it was the age of foolishness; it was the epoch of belief, it was the epoch of incredulity; it was the season of Light, it was the season of Darkness; it was the spring of hope, it was the winter of despair; we had everything before us, we had nothing before us; we were all going directly to Heaven, we were all going the other way.

—From Charles Dickens, *A Tale of Two Cities*

3) Ask not what your country can do for you—ask what you can do for your country.

—From John F. Kennedy

4) Where there's marriage without love, there will be love without marriage.

—From Benjamin Franklin

Questions: 1) Describe the syntactic characteristics for the above sentences.

2) What does the writer intend to stress, similarity or contrast? What effects are achieved through the use of antithesis or symmetry?

3) In what kinds of styles of writing are antithesis and symmetry frequently used? How often do we use them in everyday language?

4) In what situation did President Kennedy use symmetry in Example 3? What was his intended purpose?

Text II

"Illuminating One's Bright Virtue": Higher Education in a Changing World

Pre-reading Questions

1. What is your interpretation of the title "Illuminating One's Bright Virtue"?
2. What changes can you envision in higher education? (*i.e.* the teaching / learning style, the functions of a university, the disciplines, the research, etc.)

1   Thank you, President Xu, distinguished faculty, students, and friends. It is an honor to receive such a generous welcome on my first visit to Peking University. China has nourished the world's most ancient traditions of learning,

and I am privileged to be invited here in the year you celebrate this great university's 110th anniversary. For 80 of those years, from the time of the founding of the Harvard-Yenching Institute in 1928, Harvard has cherished its connections with Beida, and we now see these ties growing even closer—as undergraduate students meet and discuss subjects from Confucius, to macroeconomics, to karaoke, as graduate students and faculty launch programs and projects in business, law, government, science, education, and the humanities. Today we celebrate those historic connections and reaffirm our shared commitment to the pursuit of learning and truth.

2   We do so in a time of great change. At Harvard and at Peking University alike, we have seen dramatic transformations in higher education even within our own lifetimes. In China, the pace and scale of change are breathtaking. The number of students attending Chinese universities has increased sixfold in the past decade. China will produce more graduates this year than any other nation in the world. In the United States we have seen a similar expansion, though over a longer period of time.

3   An important part of this expansion has been the growing access to higher education for minorities, women, immigrants, and those without substantial financial means. I was one of those who benefited from these changes. Neither my mother nor my grandmothers went to college. I attended a women's college, at a time when many leading American colleges were open only to men. Had I come to Harvard, I would not have been allowed inside its library for undergraduates, which in those days excluded women as a "distraction" from the serious scholarly pursuits of the young men. Even a generation ago, it would have been impossible to imagine that I would someday become president of Harvard or that I would have the privilege of standing on this platform before you. There are many of us at Harvard, students and faculty alike, just as there are many of you in this room, whose opportunities would have been unimaginable just a few years ago.

4   What does such sweeping change mean for places like Harvard and Beida? Part of the expansion in higher education in both our countries arises from the growing recognition that knowledge is the key driver of economic growth and of prosperity for all. But more than that, we recognize that knowledge and learning are as essential to human beings as food—especially as we confront the rapid pace of social, political, and technological change—and as we struggle to

understand what it means to be human amid such disorienting shifts in our societies and our lives. Both Beida and Harvard have grown from long traditions of dedication to knowledge. We share with you the challenge of learning to use those traditions in new times.

5   In the past few weeks, preparing for my trip here, I have spoken with a great many people—Chinese students at Harvard, Harvard students who have studied in China, faculty members who have made China the focus of their intellectual lives. And I have learned a bit about how you in China have faced this challenge of the old and the new, beginning with Confucius, who observed in his Analects, that "One who reanimates the old so as to understand the new may become a teacher." I would like to speak with you today about some of the ways my university has done this—how we pursue truth, become teachers, reanimate the old within the new—and about what such efforts might mean for universities as standard bearers in a time of profound change.

6   Harvard has a long association with the word "truth." It first appeared as our motto just a few years after Harvard's founding. The word we use for it is not even in our own language, but in Latin—a language that represents even longer traditions and histories. The word is *"veritas"*—*"zhenli"* perhaps in Chinese. Our forebears inscribed *"Veritas"* on the original design for the Harvard shield in 1643, with the letters written on three open books. In that era, *"veritas"* invoked divine truth, which in Puritan New England of the 17th century meant the revealed wisdom of a Christian God. The bottom book on the shield was face down, to symbolize the limits of human knowledge. But through the centuries, the image on the shield changed. Christian words appeared then disappeared. The bottom book turned upward. But always there is the word *"veritas."* Truth remains, but we see that old truth changes, turns over into the new. Today we seek a different sort of *"veritas"* than our forebears did —one based in reason rather than in faith. But as in the ancient Chinese notion of *"dao,"* we understand truth to be more than mere knowledge. It is not a possession, but an aspiration—a way to understanding. It is something never acquired but always to be pursued. Any answer simply shapes the next question. We must seek it in a spirit of challenge and restlessness and doubt—whether we are exploring the science of the brain or the history of a nation, the ethical dimensions of a law, the design of a health care system or of a sustainable city, the origins of the universe or the very nature of the human condition as

expressed in literature or philosophy or art.

7   I have learned that one of the basic texts of Chinese civilization describes education this way: "The way of Great Learning lies in illuminating one's bright virtue." This is at the heart of a great university. It is even captured in the Chinese word for "university."

8   But how do we find this illumination? How do we pursue truth from day to day? One of the fundamental commitments of the American research university as it has evolved over the decades is that the discovery of truth and the imparting of truth must be connected. The process of scholarly research and the teaching of students have been fundamentally intertwined. Students at Harvard are instructed by faculty working at the frontiers of their fields, and we seek to engage students themselves directly in the research process. We have begun to restructure our introductory science classes so that students working in laboratories will not just repeat experiments with known outcomes but will learn techniques and principles by exploring unsolved problems together with their professors. In every field from sciences to social sciences and humanities we encourage students to undertake original research, and nearly half of our undergraduates write theses during their final year of college pursuing original questions, seeking new truths within their chosen areas of study.

9   If research is the pursuit of truth, teaching is the instrument of its propagation. Our ideas about teaching have continuously evolved throughout Harvard's history. In its early days, teaching centered on rote learning through recitation. But as we have come to see truth as pursuit rather than possession, our teaching has come to focus more on questioning, interchange, challenge—on equipping our students with the skills and attitudes they need for a lifetime of learning—and we have structured more of our classes as debates and discussions.

10 Our Law and Business schools have proud traditions of classrooms centered on fast moving interchange between students and professors. In our undergraduate college we have recently revised the curriculum to create more such opportunities, especially through smaller classes that encourage close faculty-student interaction. For these students, we are introducing a new

curriculum designed to help them become thoughtful citizens of the 21st century. In this program of study we reaffirm our commitment to the liberal arts, to the belief that undergraduate education should not consist of training for a profession or immersion in one specialized area of inquiry. Instead we ask our students to undertake a broad range of study, including fields very distant from those in which they may eventually become expert and distant from careers they may later pursue. We ask them to stretch beyond the familiar and the comfortable.

11   In the words of the report on our curricular reform, we aim to "unsettle students' presumptions, to reveal what is going on beneath and behind appearances, to disorient" our students and then "help them to find ways to reorient themselves." Or, perhaps one could say, to "illuminate their bright virtue." Truth emerges from debate, from disagreement, from questions and doubt. "We provoke students to think and argue," one professor says, "not only with us and each other but with themselves." The restless mind, the challenging mind is the expanding and creative mind, the mind prepared for the changes that will confront us all in the years to come.

12   Just as we are seeking truth in new ways, so we are finding it in new places. The disciplinary fields into which knowledge has been traditionally structured are shifting and merging. We find ourselves increasingly crossing intellectual boundaries. The sciences are transforming one another. Life and physical sciences combine as we explore emerging fields like bioengineering or computational biology. And science reaches out beyond its own domain to the social sciences and humanities to find its proper place in the world.

13   It is not just the sciences that are embarked on new paths in search of truth. The humanities and social sciences engage across disciplines as well. The impact of the history of imperialism on literature has yielded an area of rich inquiry known as "post colonial studies." The intersections of law and economics produce new approaches to understanding the nature of both legal systems and government policies. The literary imagination of Shakespeare in "The Merchant of Venice" helps us grasp the impact of capital punishment in a Law School course on moral and legal reasoning.

14   The search for truth in the 21st century demands that we cross not just disciplinary borders, but national ones, as my presence here attests. As our global connections increase, we find that truths must be conceived internationally. Our sociologists' understanding of the family, our architects' notions of design,

must be global in reach; our Business School writes the case studies that provide the core of its curriculum about firms and organizations in China and India and other countries as well as the United States; our law students are now required to study international law during their very first year at Harvard.

15   A hundred years ago, in Beida's early years, Harvard faculty and students would have been very different people than they are today, and they would have taught, studied, and pursued learning in very different ways. But they would even then have understood themselves to be seeking the truths of knowledge, the illumination of their bright virtue. Our presence here today is one result of that pursuit, of the questions they asked, of the challenges they mounted to the assumptions of an earlier era, of the changes their discoveries brought to the world.

16   As products and as beneficiaries of these traditions, we hold special obligations. But we owe these debts not merely to the past but to the future. It is our responsibility that the principles of openness, the habits of curiosity, the dedication to a community of learning be sustained and nourished for the next century to come. And it is ours to ensure that the new meanings of the word truth—*veritas*—that I have described today both inspire us and define our progress.

By Harvard President Drew Faust at Peking University

(1,931 words)

Reading Comprehension

I.   **Answer the following questions with the information you read from the passage.**
   1. What is the reason for expansion in higher education?
   2. What is the most important pursuit for a university? Why is it so important at Harvard?
   3. What are the students encouraged to do at Harvard University?
   4. How can we find truth in the context of a university?
   5. What are the new trends for the development of truth?

II. **Topics for discussion and reflection.**
   1. "We find ourselves increasingly crossing intellectual boundaries." Explain what this means with examples.

2. Do you think the expansion in higher education is good? Present your ideas in class based on the topic—*Pros and Cons of Expansion in Higher Education*.

Exercises for Integrated Skills

I. Dictation

   Listen to the following passage. The passage will be read to you four times. During the first reading, which will be read at normal speed, listen and try to understand the meaning. For the second and third readings, the passage will be read sentence by sentence, or phrase by phrase, with intervals of 15 to 20 seconds. The last reading will be done at normal speed again and during this time check your work. You will then be given 2 minutes to check through your work a second time.

II. Cloze

| funnel | employ | vital | amateur | innovate |
| curriculum | account | marvelous | logistics | assure |

   Teaching is at the heart of what we do at a research university. The students of Harvard College are not only part of a much larger place, as I urged upon you in September, they are at its ___1___ center. Unlike a century ago when Josiah Royce could tout "the divine skill of the born teacher's instincts" and leave it at that, the faculty has recently spent a lot of time and effort to ___2___ that outstanding teaching is a fundamental part of the undergraduate experience. In the past four years they have designed a new ___3___, called for ___4___ and more highly rewarded teaching, and designed a classroom action plan that encourages undergraduate women and minorities to enter the sciences.

   Most remarkably, the Internet is changing the ___5___ of learning, enhancing classroom teaching in unexpected and ___6___ ways—not replacing the essential exchange between teacher and student, but giving it new forms and rich variety. Students themselves, who grew up online, are pulling us forward. One of our best ideas in years is a technology fellows program that ___7___ students to help professors teach with the Web. I hope some

Unit 4   Universities

of you have already found your way there.

Beyond being ___8___ for good teaching, the University is accountable to guide these undergraduates to experience a different person from the one who came to us. This cannot wait. Where else can it happen? Graduate school is a ___9___ for narrowing down ___10___ into experts. Jobs demand consistency. College, by contrast, cultivates a culture of unruliness, a zone of deconstruction and openness and new creation. As W.B. Yeats put it, "education is not filling a bucket, but lighting a fire."

Oral Activities

1: Discussion
  a) What attracts you most about university?
  b) Comment on your college life. What do you think can make one's college life more meaningful?
  c) Compare the differences in teaching and learning styles between high school and university.

2: Short Play

Each June, Chinese students applying for overseas study queue up in front of foreign embassies to wait and see if their visas have been approved. In 2005, the number of juveniles who applied for overseas study accounted for 70 to 80 percent of the total number of people going abroad. In Guangdong Province, the youngest overseas student was just five years old.

Work in groups to stage a short play based on the following situation. A high school student has failed to be accepted by a famous university in China. His parents want him to go to Britain in order that he can have a better job when he comes back.

Writing Practice

Composition Writing

From your discussions in the oral activities, write a composition of about 200 words about the advantages and disadvantages of studying overseas.

Unit 5 In a Lifetime

Warm-up Questions

1. Describe a goal that you once had but changed because of some unforeseen event. Did you regret changing your goal? Do you think you could have achieved your goal anyway?
2. Discuss a life-changing event. What kind of impact did it have on you?

Text I

It's Not About the Bike: My Journey Back to Life

Pre-reading Questions

1. Who is Lance Armstrong and what are some things he's known for?
2. Some people say, "Where there's a will, there's a way." Do you agree or disagree with this statement and belief? Why or why not?

1   I want to die at a hundred years old with an American flag on my back and the star of Texas on my helmet, after screaming down an Alpine descent on a bicycle at 75 miles per hour. I want to cross one last finish line as my stud wife and my ten children applaud, and then I want to lie down in a field of those famous French sunflowers and gracefully expire, the perfect contradiction to my once-anticipated poignant early demise.

2   A slow death is not for me. I don't do anything slow, not even breathe. I do everything at a fast cadence: eat fast, sleep fast. It makes me crazy when my wife, Kristin, drives our car, because she brakes at all the yellow caution lights,

while I squirm impatiently in the passenger seat.

3   I've spent my life racing my bike, from the back roads of Austin, Texas to the Champs-Élysées, and I always figured if I died an untimely death, it would be because some rancher in his Dodge 4x4 ran me headfirst into a ditch. Believe me, it could happen. Cyclists fight an ongoing war with guys in big trucks, and so many vehicles have hit me, so many times, in so many countries, I've lost count. I've learned how to take out my own stitches: all you need is a pair of fingernail clippers and a strong stomach.

4   If you saw my body underneath my racing jersey, you'd know what I'm talking about. I've got marbled scars on both arms and discolored marks up and down my legs, which I keep clean-shaven. Maybe that's why trucks are always trying to run me over; they see my sissy-boy calves and decide not to brake. But cyclists have to shave, because when the gravel gets into your skin, it's easier to clean and bandage if you have no hair.

5   One minute you're pedaling along a highway, and the next minute, boom, you're face-down in the dirt. A blast of hot air hits you, you taste the acrid, oily exhaust in the roof of your mouth, and all you can do is wave a fist at the disappearing taillights.

6   Cancer was like that. It was like being run off the road by a truck, and I've got the scars to prove it.

7   When I was 25, I got testicular cancer and nearly died. I was given less than a 40 percent chance of surviving, and frankly, some of my doctors were just being kind when they gave me those odds. Death is not exactly cocktail-party conversation, I know, and neither is cancer, or brain surgery, or matters below the waist. But I'm not here to make polite conversation. I want to tell the truth. I'm sure you'd like to hear about how Lance Armstrong became a great American and an inspiration to us all, how he won the Tour de France, the 2,290-mile road race that's considered the single most grueling sporting event on the face of the earth. You want to hear about faith and mystery, and my miraculous comeback, and how I joined towering figures in the record book. You want to hear about my lyrical climb through the Alps and my heroic conquering of the Pyrenees, and how it felt. But the Tour was the least of the story.

8   Some of it is not easy to tell or comfortable to hear. I'm asking you now, at

the outset, to put aside your ideas about heroes and miracles, because I'm not storybook material. This is not Disneyland, or Hollywood. I'll give you an example: I've read that I flew up the hills and mountains of France. But you don't fly up a hill. You struggle slowly and painfully up a hill, and maybe, if you work very hard, you get to the top ahead of everybody else.

9   My illness was humbling and starkly revealing, and it forced me to survey my life with an unforgiving eye. There are some shameful episodes in it: instances of meanness, unfinished tasks, weakness, and regrets. I had to ask myself, "If I live, who is it that I intend to be?" I found that I had a lot of growing to do as a man.

10   I won't kid you. There are two Lance Armstrongs, pre-cancer, and post. Everybody's favorite question is "How did cancer change you?" The real question is how didn't it change me? I left my house on October 2, 1996, as one person and came home another. I was a world-class athlete with a mansion on a riverbank, keys to a Porsche, and a self-made fortune in the bank. I was one of the top riders in the world and my career was moving along a perfect arc of success. I returned a different person, literally. In a way, the old me did die, and I was given a second life. Even my body is different, because during the chemotherapy I lost all the muscle I had ever built up, and when I recovered, it didn't come back in the same way.

11   The truth is that cancer was the best thing that ever happened to me. I don't know why I got the illness, but it did wonders for me, and I wouldn't want to walk away from it. Why would I want to change, even for a day, the most important and shaping event in my life? People die. That truth is so disheartening that at times I can't bear to articulate it. Why should we go on, you might ask? Why don't we all just stop and lie down where we are? But there is another truth, too. People live. It's an equal and opposing truth. People live, and in the most remarkable ways. When I was sick, I saw more beauty and triumph and truth in a single day than I ever did in a bike race—but they were human moments, not miraculous ones. I met a guy in a fraying sweatsuit who turned out to be a brilliant surgeon. I became friends with a harassed and overscheduled

nurse, who gave me such care that it could only be the result of the deepest sympathetic affinity.

12   Of course I should have known that something was wrong with me. But athletes, especially cyclists, are in the business of denial. You deny all the aches and pains because you have to in order to finish the race. It's a sport of self-abuse. You're on your bike for the whole day, six to seven hours, in all kinds of weather and conditions, over cobblestones and gravel, in mud and wind and rain, and even hail, and you do not give in to pain.

13   Everything hurts. Your back hurts, your feet hurt, your hands hurt, your neck hurts, your legs hurt, and of course, your butt hurts. So no, I didn't pay attention to the fact that I didn't feel well in 1996. I was riding strong, as well as I ever had, actually, and there was no reason to stop.

14   Cycling is a sport that rewards mature champions. It takes physical endurance built up over years, and a head for strategy that comes only with experience. By 1996 I felt I was finally coming into my prime. I was about to break into the top five in the international rankings for the first time in my career.

15   But cycling fans noted something odd: usually, when I won a race, I pumped my fists like pistons as I crossed the finish line. But one day, I was too exhausted to celebrate on the bike. My eyes were bloodshot and my face was flushed. I should have been confident and energized by my spring performances. Instead, I was just tired. My nipples were sore. If I had known better, I would have realized it was a sign of illness. Suck it up, I said to myself, you can't afford to be tired. Ahead of me I still had the two most important races of the season: the Tour de France and the Olympic Games in Atlanta, and they were everything I had been training and racing for. I dropped out of the Tour de France after just five days. I rode through a rainstorm, and developed a sore throat and bronchitis. I was coughing and had lower-back pain, and I was simply unable to get back on the bike. "I couldn't breathe," I told the press. Looking back, they were ominous words.

16   We each cope differently with the specter of our deaths. Some people deny it. Some pray. Some numb themselves with tequila. I was tempted to do a little of each of those things. But I think we are supposed to try to face it straightforwardly, armed with nothing but courage. The definition of courage is:

the quality of spirit that enables one to encounter danger with firmness and without fear.

By Lance Armstrong (abridged)
(1,485 words)

Words and Expressions

expire	/ɪksˈpaɪə/	vi.	to die 死亡,逝世
poignant	/ˈpɒmjənt/	adj.	making one feel sad or full of pity 令人伤心(辛酸)的,令人充满同情(惋惜)的
demise	/dɪˈmaɪz/	n.	death 死亡
cadence	/ˈkeɪdəns/	n.	a regular repeated pattern of sounds or movements 韵律
squirm	/skwɜːm/	vi.	to twist your body from side to side because you are uncomfortable or nervous, or to get free from something which is holding you (尤因不舒服或紧张而)扭动身体
untimely	/ʌnˈtaɪmlɪ/	adj.	happening too soon or sooner than you expected 过早死亡(结束)
rancher	/ˈrɑːntʃə/	n.	someone who owns or works on a ranch 牧场(农场)主
headfirst	/ˌhedˈfɜːst/	adv.	moving forward with the rest of your body following your head 头朝前地
stitch	/stɪtʃ/	n.	a piece of special thread which has been used to sew the edges of a wound together (缝合伤口的)缝线
clippers	/ˈklɪpəz/	n.	a special tool with two blades, used for cutting small pieces from something 剪子,大剪刀
jersey	/ˈdʒɜːzɪ/	n.	a shirt worn as part of a sports uniform 运动衫
discolor	/dɪsˈkʌlə/	vi.	to change colour, or to make something change colour, so that it looks unattractive (使)变色,(使)退色
sissy	/ˈsɪsɪ/	n.	a boy that other boys dislike because he prefers doing things that girls enjoy 女孩子气的男孩儿

Unit 5 In a Lifetime

calf	/kɑːf/	n.	the back part of your leg between your knee and ankle 小腿肚
gravel	/ˈɡrævəl/	n.	small stones, used to make a surface for paths, roads, etc. 碎石，砾石
pedal	/ˈpedl/	vi.	to ride a bicycle 骑（自行车），踩动踏板
acrid	/ˈækrɪd/	adj.	describes a smell or taste that is strong and bitter and causes a burning feeling in the throat 刺激的，辛辣的
testicle	/ˈtestɪkəl/	n.	one of the two round organs that produce sperm in a male, that are enclosed in a bag of skin behind and below the penis 睾丸
miraculous	/mɪˈrækjʊləs/	adj.	very good, completely unexpected, and often very lucky 非凡的，神奇的，不可思议的
comeback	/ˈkʌmbæk/	n.	a situation in a sports competition in which a person or team begins playing better after playing badly（在体育比赛中）反超，反败为胜
towering	/ˈtaʊərɪŋ/	adj.	much better than other people of the same kind 出类拔萃的，出众的
lyrical	/ˈlɪrɪkəl/	adj.	beautifully expressed in words, poetry, or music 像诗歌（音乐）般抒情的
chemotherapy	/ˌkiːməʊˈθerəpɪ/	n.	the use of drugs to control and try to cure cancer（治疗癌症的）化学疗法，化疗
disheartening	/dɪsˈhɑːtənɪŋ/	adj.	making one lose hope and determination 令人灰心（气馁）的
sweatsuit	/ˈswetsuːt/	n.	a set of loose warm clothes, worn especially for sport or relaxation 运动服，厚套装
harassed	/ˈhærəst/	adj.	anxious and tired because you have too many problems or things to do 疲惫焦虑的
denial	/dɪˈnaɪəl/	n.	a condition in which you refuse to admit or believe that something bad exists or has happened 拒绝承认，拒绝相信
cobblestone	/ˈkɒbəlstəʊn/	n.	a small round stone set in the ground, especially in the past, to make a hard surface for a road 鹅卵石，圆石
endurance	/ɪnˈdjʊərəns/	n.	the ability to continue doing something difficult or painful over a long period of time（忍）耐力

prime	/praɪm/	n.	the time in your life when you are strongest and most active 盛年，壮年时期，风华正茂
piston	/ˈpɪstən/	n.	a part of an engine consisting of a short solid piece of metal inside a tube, which moves up and down to make the other parts of the engine move 活塞
bloodshot	/ˈblʌdʃɒt/	adj.	(of an eye) reddened as a result of locally congested blood vessels（眼睛）充血的，有血丝的
flushed	/flʌʃt/	adj.	red in the face 脸红的
energize	/ˈenədʒaɪz/	vt.	to make someone feel more determined and energetic 使充满活力，使增强信心
drop out			to no longer do an activity or belong to a group 中途退出
bronchitis	/brɒŋˈkaɪtɪs/	n.	an illness which affects your bronchial tubes and makes you cough 支气管炎
ominous	/ˈɒmɪnəs/	adj.	making you feel that something bad is going to happen 不吉的，不祥的
specter	/ˈspektə/	n.	something that people are afraid of because it may affect them badly 引起恐惧的某物
tequila	/təˈkiːlə/	n.	a strong alcoholic drink made in Mexico from agave plant 特奎拉酒（一种用墨西哥产植物龙舌兰制成的烈酒）

Notes:

1. **Texas** is the second-largest U.S. state in both area and population, and the largest state in the contiguous United States.
2. **Champs-Élysées** is a prestigious avenue in Paris, France. With its cinemas, cafés, luxury specialty shops and clipped horse-chestnut trees, the Avenue des Champs-Élysées is one of the most famous streets in the world.
3. **Dodge** is a United States-based brand of automobiles, minivans, sport utility vehicles, and, until 2009, pickup trucks, manufactured and marketed by Chrysler Group LLC in more than 60 different countries and territories worldwide.
4. **Tour de France** is an annual bicycle race that covers approximately 3,500 kilometres throughout France and bordering countries. The race lasts three weeks and attracts cyclists

from around the world.

5. **Alps**   are one of the great mountain range systems of Europe, stretching from Austria and the Slovenia in the east; through Italy, Switzerland, Liechtenstein and Germany; to France in the west.
6. **the Pyrenees**   are a range of mountains in southwest Europe that form a natural border between France and Spain.
7. **Porsche**   is a German automotive manufacturer of luxury high performance automobiles.

Reading Comprehension

I. **Summarize Lance Armstrong's reflections on his illness.**

_____

_____

_____

_____

_____

II. **Answer the following questions.**

1. Why do cyclists have to shave their legs?
2. What was the best thing that ever happened to Lance Armstrong? Why?
3. How do you interpret the sentence "But athletes, especially cyclists, are in the business of denial (Para.12)"?
4. Before he was diagnosed with cancer, how would Lance Armstrong feel after a race?
5. What do people do to cope with deaths? How did Lance Armstrong deal with it?

III. **Paraphrase the following sentences within the context of the reading passage.**

1. (Para.1) ...and then I want to lie down in a field of those famous French sunflowers and gracefully expire, the perfect contradiction to my once-anticipated poignant early demise.
2. (Para. 5) A blast of hot air hits you, you taste the acrid, oily exhaust in the roof of your mouth, and all you can do is wave a fist at the disappearing taillights.
3. (Para.8) I'm asking you now, at the outset, to put aside your ideas about heroes and miracles, because I'm not storybook material.
4. (Para.9) My illness was humbling and starkly revealing, and it forced me to survey my life with an unforgiving eye.

5. (Para.11) I became friends with a harassed and overscheduled nurse, who gave me such care that it could only be the result of the deepest sympathetic affinity.

IV. **Based on the text, decide whether the following statements are true or false. For false statements, write the facts in parentheses.**

1. Lance Armstrong is very fast in almost everything, and he feels uncomfortable when his wife brakes at a yellow light.
   (   )
2. Lance Armstrong was hit countless times by trucks and other vehicles.
   (   )
3. Some of Lance's doctors were trying to be encouraging when they told him he had a 40 percent chance of survival.
   (   )
4. During chemotherapy, Lance lost all his muscle, but it came back in the same way when he recovered.
   (   )
5. By the year 1996, Lance thought that he was in an excellent condition.
   (   )

Vocabulary Exercises

I. **Fill in the blank in each sentence with a word or phrase from the box below. Make sure the appropriate form of the word is used.**

| cadence | miraculous | build up | ominous | ongoing | expire |
| fray | bloodshot | energize | towering | acrid | drop out |

1. The office was filled with white _____ smoke which made breathing difficult.
2. The U.S. President's speech is intended to _____ the nation's youths to seek academic success, for their own sake and for their country's.
3. There is a certain _____ to the roles of each of the musicians and the importance of ebbs and flows throughout the song.
4. There are a variety of reasons in developing _____ eyes ranging from eyestrain and fatigue to colds and allergies.
5. The dresses he designed were in white cotton jersey, often with _____ garlands of lace or tulle around the side, or with a yoke of seed pearls.
6. It is possible to _____ confidence in ourselves if we take the right attitude to our

Unit 5　In a Lifetime

abilities.
7. One common stereotype of witches is the ever popular broomstick, along with the pointy black hat and _____ black cat.
8. As many as half of the bright students in graduate schools—many of whom have never tasted failure-will _____ before they can claim their prize.
9. Even though Cuba has one of the lowest AIDS prevalence rates in the Caribbean region, there are still _____ education efforts to reduce the number of new infections.
10. The old man _____ as he was being carried from the train by ambulance men.
11. He was remembered as a(n) _____ personality known for his commitment to the cause of human emancipation.
12. She has made a(n) _____ recovery from her injuries and is now on her way to fulfilling her dreams of becoming a writer.

II. Fill in the blanks with the appropriate forms of the given words.
1. Young children easily grow _____ (disheartening) if they don't see quick results.
2. Most world religions and wisdom traditions include teachings on the nature of _____ (unforgiving).
3. The whole team is still _____ (flushed) with success after their weekend victory.
4. Many women employees claimed that they had been victims of workplace _____ (harassed).
5. Skin _____ (discolor) results from several factors. Some are natural, such as birthmarks. Others are related to factors such as sun exposure, allergy and immune reaction.

III. Replace the italicized words or phrases with simple, everyday words.
1. ...the perfect contradiction to my once-anticipated *poignant* early *demise*. (　　)
2. ...while I *squirm* impatiently in the passenger seat. (　　)
3. We each cope differently with *the specter of* our deaths. (　　)
4. ...the single most *grueling* sporting event on the face of the earth. (　　)
5. I've got *marbled* scars on both arms... (　　)

IV. Choose the word or phrase that best completes each of the following sentences.
1. The two cars and the bikes between them have been _____ by the train.
   A. run over　　B. run into　　C. run through　　D. run down
2. Don't be _____ by products claiming to help you lose weight in a week.
   A. taken after　　B. taken aback　　C. taken in　　D. taken out
3. Two students were sent to hospital immediately after the school bus crash yesterday, but

the doctors don't _____ that they will live much longer.
   A. articulate   B. manifest   C. anticipate   D. monitor
4. _____ and family ties thus play a critical role in facilitating trust and relations within the organizations of Chinese family firms.
   A. Affinity   B. Proximity   C. Kinship   D. Affiliation
5. That was the first time he spoke in public; no wonder he was _____ with nerves.
   A. overcome   B. numbed   C. frozen   D. inhibited

Translation Exercises

I. **Translate each of the following sentences into English, using the word or phrase given in the brackets.**

1. 那位风华正茂的足球运动员在世界杯中为他的球队踢入了制胜的一球。(prime)

2. 上半场惨败之后，这个球队奇迹般地在下半场中反败为胜。(miraculous; comeback)

3. 他的英年早逝至少有部分原因是由于过度劳累和缺乏锻炼。(untimely death)

4. 飞机经过的时候，我们感觉一阵强风从头顶呼啸而过。(blast of)

5. 资历较高的人在职业生涯一开始就能找到报酬丰厚的工作。(at the outset of)

II. **Translate the following paragraph into English.**

   假如我又回到了童年，我要事事乐观。生活犹如一面镜子：你朝它笑，它也朝你笑；如果你双眉紧锁，向它投以怀疑的目光，它也将还以你同样的目光。凡事都有危险，但镇定沉着往往能克服最严重的危险。对一切祸福做好准备，那么就没有什么灾难可以害怕的了。

III. **Translate the following paragraph into Chinese.**

   We each cope differently with the specter of our deaths. Some people deny it. Some pray. Some numb themselves with tequila. I was tempted to do a little of each of those things. But I think we are supposed to try to face it straightforwardly, armed with nothing but courage. The definition of courage is: the quality of spirit that enables one to encounter danger with firmness and without fear.

Unit 5 In a Lifetime

Language Appreciation

I. **Read the text carefully, then pick out the sentences that you think are well-written. Pay close attention to the italicized words or phrases of the following sentences. Try to appreciate the way in which the author expresses his/her ideas. Learn how to use them in your own writing.**

1. I want to die at a hundred years old *with an American flag on my back and the star of Texas on my helmet, after screaming down an Alpine descent on a bicycle at 75 miles per hour.*
2. I've got *marbled scars* on both arms and *discolored marks* up and down my legs, which I keep clean-shaven.

II. Read aloud and recite paragraphs 11 and 12.

III. Stylistics Study

Rhetorical Question—Is It a Real Question?

Example:

   I ask gentlemen, sir, what means this martial array, if its purpose be not to force us to submission? Can gentlemen assign any other possible motives for it? Has Great Britain any enemy, in this quarter of the world, to call for all this accumulation of navies and armies? No, sir, she has none. ...Have we anything new to offer on the subject? Nothing. ...Shall we resort to entreaty and humble supplication? What terms shall we find which have not been already exhausted? Let us not, I beseech you, sir, deceive ourselves longer.
—From Patrick Henry, 1775

Questions:

1) Read the short paragraph aloud. Which questions are asked for a purpose other than to obtain the information the question asks?
2) What is the function of those questions? What kind of effects does the author achieve through this technique? Is it an effective way to achieve this effect? Why or why not?
3) In what kinds of occasions are rhetorical questions frequently used?

Text II

The Old Man and the Sea

> *Pre-reading Questions*
>
> 1. In your opinion, is fishing considered cruelty to animals? How is fishing similar or different from hunting?
> 2. Re-tell a story, real or fictional, about man's relationship with nature.

1   The old man was thin and gaunt with deep wrinkles in the back of his neck. The brown blotches of the benevolent skin cancer the sun brings from its reflection on the tropic sea were on his cheeks. The blotches ran well down the sides of his face and his hands had the deep-creased scars from handling heavy fish on the cords. But none of these scars were fresh. They were as old as erosions in a fishless desert. Everything about him was old except his eyes and they were the same color as the sea and were cheerful and undefeated.

...

2   The shark was not an accident. He had come up from deep down in the water as the dark cloud of blood had settled and dispersed in the mile deep sea. He had come up so fast and absolutely without caution that he broke the surface of the blue water and was in the sun. Then he fell back into the sea and picked up the scent and started swimming on the course the skiff and the fish had taken.

3   Sometimes he lost the scent. But he would pick it up again, or have just a trace of it, and he swam fast and hard on the course. He was a very big Make shark built to swim as fast as the fastest fish in the sea and everything about him was beautiful except his jaws. His back was as blue as a sword fish's and his belly was silver and his hide was smooth and handsome. He was built as a sword fish except for his huge jaws which were tight shut now as he swam fast, just under the surface with his high dorsal fin knifing through the water without wavering. Inside the closed double lip of his jaws all of his eight rows of teeth were slanted inwards. They were not the ordinary pyramid-shaped teeth of most sharks. They were shaped like a man's fingers when they are crisped like claws. They were nearly as long as the fingers of the old man and they had razor-sharp cutting edges on both sides. This was a fish built to feed on all the fishes in the

sea, that were so fast and strong and well armed that they had no other enemy. Now he speeded up as he smelled the fresher scent and his blue dorsal fin cut the water.

4   When the old man saw him coming he knew that this was a shark that had no fear at all and would do exactly what he wished. He prepared the harpoon and made the rope fast while he watched the shark come on. The rope was short as it lacked what he had cut away to lash the fish.

5   The old man's head was clear and good now and he was full of resolution but he had little hope. It was too good to last, he thought. He took one look at the great fish as he watched the shark close in. It might as well have been a dream, he thought. I cannot keep him from hitting me but maybe I can get him. Dentuso, he thought. Bad luck to your mother.

6   The shark closed fast astern and when he hit the fish the old man saw his mouth open and his strange eyes and the clicking chop of the teeth as he drove forward in the meat just above the tail. The shark's head was out of water and his back was coming out and the old man could hear the noise of skin and flesh ripping on the big fish when he rammed the harpoon down onto the shark's head at a spot where the line between his eyes intersected with the line that ran straight back from his nose. There were no such lines. There was only the heavy sharp blue head and the big eyes and the clicking, thrusting all-swallowing jaws. But that was the location of the brain and the old man hit it. He hit it with his blood mushed hands driving a good harpoon with all his strength. He hit it without hope but with resolution and complete malignancy.

7   The shark swung over and the old man saw his eye was not alive and then he swung over once again, wrapping himself in two loops of the rope. The old man knew that he was dead but the shark would not accept it. Then, on his back, with his tail lashing and his jaws clicking, the shark plowed over the water as a speedboat does. The water was white where his tail beat it and three-quarters of his body was clear above the water when the rope came taut, shivered, and then snapped. The shark lay quietly for a little while on the surface and the old man

watched him. Then he went down very slowly.

8   "He took about forty pounds," the old man said aloud. He took my harpoon too and all the rope, he thought, and now my fish bleeds again and there will be others.

9   He did not like to look at the fish anymore since he had been mutilated. When the fish had been hit it was as though he himself were hit.

10   But I killed the shark that hit my fish, he thought. And he was the biggest dentuso that I have ever seen. And God knows that I have seen big ones.

11   It was too good to last, he thought. I wish it had been a dream now and that I had never hooked the fish and was alone in bed on the newspapers.

12   "But man is not made for defeat," he said. "A man can be destroyed but not defeated." I am sorry that I killed the fish though, he thought. Now the bad time is coming and I do not even have the harpoon. The dentuso is cruel and able and strong and intelligent. But I was more intelligent than he was. Perhaps not, he thought. Perhaps I was only better armed.

...

13   That afternoon there was a party of tourists at the Terrace and looking down in the water among the empty beer cans and dead barracudas a woman saw a great long white spine with a huge tail at the end that lifted and swung with the tide while the east wind blew a heavy steady sea outside the entrance to the harbour.

14   "What's that?" she asked a waiter and pointed to the long backbone of the great fish that was now just garbage waiting to go out with the tide.

15   "Tiburon," the waiter said. "Eshark." He was meaning to explain what had happened.

16   "I didn't know sharks had such handsome, beautifully formed tails."

17   "I didn't either," her male companion said.

18   Up the road, in his shack, the old man was sleeping again. He was still sleeping on his face and the boy was sitting by him watching him. The old man was dreaming about the lions.

By Ernest Hemingway (abridged)
(1,169 word)

Unit 5　In a Lifetime

Reading Comprehension

I. Answer the following questions with the information you read from the passage.
   1. What does the old man look like?
   2. How could the shark follow the course of the skiff and the fish?
   3. What did the old man do when he saw the shark coming? And what did he think?
   4. How did the old man kill the shark?
   5. Why didn't the old man like to look at his fish after he killed the shark?

II. Topics for discussion and reflection.
   1. Many believe that human beings are the highest level creatures on the planet. Other cultures believe that nature ultimately overrides all. What is your opinion on this? What are some instances of humans disrupting nature and what kind of effect has it had on our planet?
   2. Humans have long since had companionship relationships with animals. Why do you think this is so? Give examples.

Exercises for Integrated Skills

I. **Dictation**

   Listen to the following passage. The passage will be read to you four times. During the first reading, which will be read at normal speed, listen and try to understand the meaning. For the second and third readings, the passage will be read sentence by sentence, or phrase by phrase, with intervals of 15 to 20 seconds. The last reading will be done at normal speed again and during this time check your work. You will then be given 2 minutes to check through your work a second time.

   _____
   _____
   _____
   _____

II. **Cloze**

   I am standing in line at the _____1_____ with my mom waiting to have my prescription

_____2_____. What brought me here was _____3_____ my mother's old car. What led me here has _____4_____ the course of my lifetime. A _____5_____ of blackened days each exactly like the one before it has led me to this place.

This morning after waking up for about the fourth time, I finally forced myself _____6_____ bed. Here I am fifteen years old, a time of life _____7_____ most kids race to greet the dawn, and _____8_____ I try my best to sleep the time away.

Slowly I move toward my mirrored bureau feeling _____9_____ I'm walking through Jell-O. Each step is a deliberate effort, _____10_____ my body is young and healthy. I often wish that life came with a conveyor belt that I could just step on and ride to get where I need to go.

1. A. medicine   B. pharmacy   C. hospital   D. drugs
2. A. bought   B. dispersed   C. filled   D. prepared
3. A. more than   B. just   C. not more than   D. less than
4. A. crossed   B. spanned   C. included   D. covered
5. A. group   B. swarm   C. series   D. gang
6. A. out of   B. off   C. from   D. outside
7. A. which   B. of which   C. that   D. when
8. A. then   B. however   C. yet   D. but
9. A. though   B. as though   C. like   D. as
10. A. because   B. while   C. although   D. and

Oral Activities

1. Describe three places that you would like to visit in your lifetime. Include when, why, and with whom you would like to go, why they would be a trip of a lifetime, and what you plan on doing there.
2. Some say that making a difference (contribution) is what gives life meaning. What kind of contribution do you want to make?

Writing Practice

Composition Writing

Everyone has goals he/she wants to accomplish in life. Whether they be big or small, all are important for that person. What is the most important goal you want to achieve in your lifetime? Write a composition of about 200 words on the topic: In a Lifetime.

Unit 6 Nutrition

Warm-up Activities

1. Write down everything you ate today and compare it with your classmates. Use the food pyramid to see whether your diet includes all four food groups in its proper proportions.
2. Describe your idea of a healthy body image, be as specific as possible (i.e. weight, etc.)

Text I

Nutrition for Exercise and Health

Pre-reading Questions

1. What is considered a well-balanced diet? Give examples and reasons to support your answer.
2. Do you think your current diet provides sufficient nutrition to support an active lifestyle with daily exercise? How would you improve your diet?

1   Research on the role of nutrition in exercise and sport has increased dramatically over the last 15 years. Today there is no doubt that nutrition plays a vital role in exercise performance and training. Carbohydrates are important for endurance exercise performance and during times of high-intensity training. Fluid intake plays important roles in both short-term and endurance exercise. There is no question that competitive athletes can benefit from adequate energy, nutrient, and fluid intakes. Good nutrition can also help competitive or recreational athletes recover from strenuous physical activity: refueling and rehydrating the body, while providing nutrients to build and repair muscles, enable individuals to engage in the next bout of physical activity without

adverse effects. This is especially important for athletes during sport tournaments, or for any individuals who engage in strenuous physical activity on a daily or more than daily basis. For example, a triathlete may do an hour swim in the morning and a 3-hour cycle workout in the afternoon. Between these workouts, the athlete must replenish the body's glycogen stores and consume adequate fluid to ensure optimal exercise performance.

2   Well-fueled and well-hydrated athletes reduce their risk of injury during exercise—risk that increases as individuals become fatigued and lose their ability to concentrate, and as they deplete the substrates that fuel exercise. Proper nutrition can help speed the healing process for injured athletes; recovery from muscle or bone injuries or from surgery requires extra energy and nutrients, including protein, vitamins, and minerals.

3   Nutrition also plays an important role in weight control and body composition. Few individuals today are happy with their weight, body fat levels, or body shape. Helping active individuals develop realistic approaches to weight maintenance (or weight loss /gain) can significantly improve health and reduce stress levels. For many active individuals, weight control is of primary concern. If concerns about weight and body image become overwhelming, an individual is at increased risk of disordered eating or even of developing a clinical eating disorder.

4   As interest in sport nutrition increases, the number of products promising improved exercise performance, gains in muscle strength, quick weight loss, and changes in body composition increases exponentially—which makes it difficult to sort fact from fiction. You cannot pick up a popular fitness, nutrition, or health magazine without being bombarded with advertisements for various nutrient supplements, ergogenic aids, and sport foods. If you combine these advertisements with the myriad of advertisements for weight loss or weight gain, it is not surprising that the public is confused and distrustful. Since nutrition and exercise research is still in its infancy, there are many unanswered questions.

5   Over the last 70 years, nutrition research has identified a number of

specific nutrients in foods that are essential to good health. Various organizations and governments have used this information to make dietary recommendations to ensure the health of their citizens. These dietary recommendations can also be used as general guidelines in designing diets for active individuals.

6   The concept of essential nutrients evolved from observations that certain diseases occurred in populations that consumed poor diets, and that including certain foods in the diet could correct or prevent the diseases. Nutrients that could be deleted from the diet with no adverse health effects were classified as dispensable or non-essential nutrients. Food constituents that prevent diseases or health problems were classified as indispensable or essential nutrients. These concepts are sometimes confusing because a nutrient can be *physiologically* essential for the body, but classified as nonessential for the diet since the body can synthesize it. Many nutritionists therefore prefer the terms indispensable (essential) or dispensable (nonessential). Although all nutrients are important for growth and good health, they need not all come from the diet.

7   Classification of a nutrient as essential or indispensable clearly requires careful and extensive scientific examination. By the 1950s, 35 nutrients were identified as essential. All of the nutrients listed in the Recommended Dietary Allowances (RDAs) and the Dietary Reference Intakes (DRIs) are currently accepted as essential for humans. However, as the science of human nutrition has developed, classifying nutrients as either essential or nonessential has not always worked.

8   New research showed that the body could synthesize some "essential" nutrients from precursors, that interactions between nutrients could alter requirements, and that some disease states or genetic defects altered essential nutrients needs. A third category, conditional essentiality, has therefore been suggested. For example, a premature infant may require certain nutrients not required in a full-term infant. In order for the premature infant to grow and thrive, these nutrients must be added to the diet, even if they are not classified as essential nutrients for full-term infants.

9   In the last 20 years, the science of nutrition has taken a new direction. Nutritionists no longer focus only on preventing deficiency diseases—they now recognize many nutrients which, although not classified as essential nutrients, are important for good health and disease prevention. This has prompted researchers to suggest a fourth nutrient category called "desirable or beneficial

for health." Nutrients that might fit into this category are fiber, various phytochemicals, betacarotene, and fluoride. While many of these nutrients are now recommended for good health, they are not classified as essential nutrients. As the science of nutrition progresses, we may see this fourth category of nutrients evolve with specific inclusion criteria, which would then stimulate the rigorous research required for their inclusion.

By Melinda Manore (abridged)

(867 words)

Words and Expressions

carbohydrate	/ˌkɑːbəʊˈhaɪdreɪt/	n.	a substance that is in foods such as sugar, bread, potatoes etc., which provides your body with heat and energy and which consists of oxygen, hydrogen, and carbon 碳水化合物
intensity	/ɪnˈtensɪtɪ/	n.	the quality of being felt very strongly or having a strong effect 强烈,剧烈,紧张,极度
intake	/ˈɪnteɪk/	n.	the amount of food, drink etc. that you take into your body 纳入量
nutrient	/ˈnjuːtrɪənt/	n.	a chemical or food that provides what is needed for plants or animals to live and grow 营养物,养分,营养品
strenuous	/ˈstrenjuəs/	adj.	needing a lot of effort or strength 繁重的,艰苦的
tournament	/ˈtʊənəmənt/	n.	a competition in which players compete against each other in a series of games until there is one winner 锦标赛
workout	/ˈwɜːkaʊt/	n.	a period of physical exercise, especially as training for a sport 训练,赛前训练(时间)
replenish	/rɪˈplenɪʃ/	vt.	to put new supplies into something, or to fill something again 补充,再装满
glycogen	/ˈglaɪkəʊdʒən/	n.	a substance found in the liver and muscles which stores carbohydrate and is important in controlling suger levels in the blood 糖原
hydrate	/ˈhaɪdreɪt/	vt.	to supply someone or something with water to keep them healthy and in good condition

Unit 6　Nutrition

			为……补水，给……供水
fatigued	/fəˈtiːgd/	adj.	extremely tired 疲惫的，筋疲力尽的
deplete	/dɪˈpliːt/	vt.	to reduce the amount of something that is present or available 削减，损耗
substrate	/ˈsʌbstreɪt/	n.	a substance which an enzyme (= chemical made by living cells) acts on to produce a chemical reaction〈生〉酶作用物
protein	/ˈprəʊtiːn/	n.	one of several natural substances that exist in foods such as meat, eggs, and beans, which your body needs in order to grow and remain strong and healthy 蛋白质
overwhelming	/ˌəʊvəˈwelmɪŋ/	adj.	having such a great effect on you that you feel confused and do not know how to react 无法抗拒的，不可遏制的
exponential	/ˌekspəˈnenʃəl/	adj.	using a sign that shows how many times a number is to be multiplied by itself 指数的 **exponentially** adv. 以指数方式
infancy	/ˈɪnfənsɪ/	n.	the time when something is just starting to be developed 在某事物的初期（早期）
dietary	/ˈdaɪətərɪ/	adj.	related to the food someone eats 与饮食有关的
constituent	/kənˈstɪtjʊənt/	n.	one of the substances or components that combine to form something 成分，构成部分，要素
indispensable	/ˌɪndɪˈspensəbəl/	adj.	someone or something that is indispensable is so important or useful that it is impossible to manage without them 不可或缺的，必需的
synthesize	/ˈsɪnθɪsaɪz/	vt.	to make something by combining different components or substances 合成
classification	/ˌklæsɪfɪˈkeɪʃən/	n.	the process of putting something into the group or class it belongs to 归类，分类
precursor	/prɪˈkɜːsə/	n.	a compound that participates in the chemical reaction that produces another compound 前体
defect	/dɪˈfekt/	n.	a fault or a lack of something that results in something or someone in not being perfect 缺陷，瑕疵

premature	/ˌpreməˈtʃʊə/	adj.	happening or done too soon, especially before the natural or suitable time 早产的, 未成熟的
thrive	/θraɪv/	vi.	to become very successful or very strong and healthy 茁壮成长, 兴旺, 欣欣向荣
deficiency	/dɪˈfɪʃənsɪ/	n.	a lack of something that is necessary 缺乏, 不足
phytochemicals	/ˌfaɪtəʊˈkemɪkəlz/	n.	chemical compounds that occur naturally in plants 植物化学物质
fluoride	/ˈflʊəraɪd/	n.	a chemical which is believed to help protect teeth against decay （有助于防止龋齿的）氟化物
inclusion	/ɪnˈkluːʒən/	n.	the act of including someone or something in a larger group or set, or the fact of being included in one 包含, 包括
rigorous	/ˈrɪgərəs/	adj.	careful, thorough, and exact 严密的, 缜密的, 精确的

Notes:

1. **Ergogenic aids** are any external influences that can be determined to enhance performance.
2. **Recommended Dietary Allowances** are guidelines on what quantities of the various nutrients should be eaten by human males and females at various ages. They were established by the United States National Academy of Sciences.
3. **Dietary Reference Intakes** is a system of nutrition recommendations from the Institute of Medicine (IOM) of the U.S. National Academy of Sciences.
4. **Betacarotene** is a strongly-coloured red-orange pigment abundant in plants and fruits. It is a precursor of vitamin A.

Reading Comprehension

I. Explain the following terms according to the text.
   1. Indispensable nutrients: _____
   _____

Unit 6   Nutrition

2. **Dispensable nutrients:** _____
   _____

3. **Conditional essentiality:** _____
   _____

4. **Beneficial nutrients for health:** _____
   _____

II. **Answer the following questions.**
   1. What benefits does good nutrition have for athletes?
   2. How can well-fueled and well-hydrated athletes reduce their risk of injury?
   3. How does nutrition help people in weight control and body composition?
   4. Why has classifying nutrients as either essential or nonessential not always worked?
   5. What does a premature infant need?

III. **Paraphrase the following sentences within the context of the reading passage.**
   1. (Para.1) Between these workouts, the athlete must replenish the body's glycogen stores and consume adequate fluid to ensure optimal exercise performance.
   2. (Para.3) If concerns about weight and body image become overwhelming, an individual is at increased risk of disordered eating or even of developing a clinical eating disorder.
   3. (Para.4) You cannot pick up a popular fitness, nutrition, or health magazine without being bombarded with advertisements for various nutrient supplements, ergogenic aids, and sport foods.
   4. (Para.8) New research showed that the body could synthesize some "essential" nutrients from precursors, that interactions between nutrients could alter requirements, and that some disease states or genetic defects altered essential nutrients needs.

IV. **Based on the text, decide whether the following statements are true or false. For false statements, write the facts in parentheses.**
   1. Today there is still doubt as to whether nutrition plays a vital role in exercise performance and training.
      (   )
   2. Proper nutrition can help speed up recovery of muscle or bone injuries.
      (   )
   3. Even though nutrition science has entered a very advanced stage, there are still many unanswered questions in the field.
      (   )

4. All the nutrients listed in the RDAs and the DRIs are regarded as essential for humans.
   ( )
5. All nutrients are important for growth and good health, and they are only found in a proper diet.
   ( )

Vocabulary Exercises

I. Fill in the blank in each sentence with a word or phrase taken from the box below. Make sure the appropriate form of the word is used.

| strenuous | replenish | intake | evolve | refuel |
| premature | thrive | rigorous | at the risk of | |

1. Will they go ahead with their project, even _____ offending their professor?
2. Yoga while traveling is a healthful way for women to _____ the mind, body and spirit.
3. Preemies, known as _____ infants, have many special needs that make their care different from that of full-term infants.
4. More than 50 clinical studies have demonstrated that reductions in sodium _____ beneficially reduce blood pressure in adult age groups.
5. Old people are advised to engage in less _____ exercises since they can often do more harm than good.
6. Over more than four decades, the Super Bowl has _____ into a separate universe, as if pro football did not really exist before.
7. As the English saying goes, "If you want to live and _____, let the spider run alive."
8. Anthropology is a science where anthropologists use a _____ set of methods and techniques to document observations that can be checked by others.
9. The plane was _____ in Paris and declared ready for service again.

II. Fill in the blanks with the appropriate forms of the given words.

1. _____ (exponentially) growth occurs when some quantity regularly increases by a fixed percentage.
2. Peking Opera is a _____ (synthesize) of different arts and has an elegant form of expression, which can help develop students' aesthetic ability.
3. Young people should be encouraged to communicate with their peers and develop their interpersonal skills, which are _____ (nonessential) in the maintenance of healthy mental condition.

Unit 6   Nutrition

4. Nowadays, mobile phones have become an _____ (indispensable) part of our lives.
5. Seeing her daughter graduate from graduate school, he was _____ (overwhelming) with a flash of unspeakable love and pride.

III. Replace the italicized words or phrases with simple, everyday words.
   1. ...enable individuals to *engage* in the next bout of physical activity without adverse effects. (   )
   2. ...consume adequate fluid to ensure *optimal* exercise performance. (   )
   3. ...weight control is of *primary concern*. (   )
   4. If you combine these advertisements with the *myriad of* advertisements for weight loss or weight gain... (   )
   5. ...which would then *stimulate* the rigorous research required for their inclusion. (   )

IV. Choose a word or phrase that best completes each of the following sentences.
   1. You should discuss your idea with your classmates because when you explain it to someone else, the process helps you to sort _____ your problems.
      A. from   B. out   C. through   D. into
   2. According to the investigation, one of the problems for the new immigrants is they may find it hard to _____ the mainstream.
      A. fit into   B. fit out   C. fit onto   D. fit for
   3. If you exercise regularly, your blood _____ will be improved, and you will feel more energetic.
      A. fatigue   B. tranquility C. pressure   D. circulation
   4. The gym is closed on Monday for routine _____ work. The facilities are kept in good condition by the regular checking and repairing.
      A. disturbance   B. sustainable C. maintenance   D. alliance
   5. As a government spokesman, you shouldn't have said like that, for such tendentious statements are likely to _____ strong opposition nationwide.
      A. promote   B. provoke   C. propel   D. prompt

Translation Exercises

I. Translate each of the following sentences into English, using the word or phrase given in the brackets.
   1. 我非常渴望每天都能得到关于切尔西(Chelsea)的最新消息,球队或好或坏的成绩对我一整天的情绪都有积极或消极的影响。(on a daily basis)

2. 由于过度捕杀,这个地区的大马哈鱼的数量已大大减少。(deplete)

3. 新闻发布会上,记者们连珠炮似的提问使这个年轻导演感到措手不及。(bombard)

4. 尽管在过去的几年里取得了一些进展,基因工程领域仍处于起步阶段。(in infancy)

5. 作为一名研究人员,你必须了解如何以自己独特的视角来综合文献中的观点并提出新的见解。(synthesize)

II. Translate the following paragraph into English.

营养的"面孔"几乎天天都有变化。科学家和伪科学家每天都向公众发布时尚饮食和有关食品和补品的最新研究。全世界的营养学家一致认为适当的营养是取得最佳运动成绩不可或缺的。当今社会快餐文化盛行,人们在路上边走边吃,很难做到选择适当的饮食。然而,运动员们必须如执行训练计划一般来保证营养膳食。

III. Translate the following paragraph into Chinese.

As interest in sport nutrition increases, the number of products promising improved exercise performance, gains in muscle strength, quick weight loss, and changes in body composition increases exponentially—which makes it difficult to sort fact from fiction. You cannot pick up a popular fitness, nutrition, or health magazine without being bombarded with advertisements for various nutrient supplements, ergogenic aids, and sport foods. If you combine these advertisements with the myriad of advertisements for weight loss or weight gain, it is not surprising that the public is confused and distrustful. Since nutrition and exercise research is still in its infancy, there are many unanswered questions.

Language Appreciation

I. Read the text carefully, then pick out the sentences that you think are well-written. Pay close attention to the italicized words or phrases of the following sentences. Try to appreciate the way in which the author expresses his/her ideas. Learn how to use them in your own writing.

1. *There is no question* that competitive athletes can benefit from adequate energy, nutrient, and fluid intakes.

2. Since nutrition and exercise research is still *in its infancy*, there are many unanswered questions.

II. **Read aloud and recite paragraphs 2 and 3.**

III. **Stylistics Study**

Ellipsis—Subtraction in Stylistics

Ellipsis is often used in literature for extra emotive force. With less important elements relieved, the author can stress what he considers to be more significant.

1. Ellipsis can be easily found in advertising, headlines, idioms and slogans.

Examples: 1) *Equal rights for women!*

2) *City's New Plan on Affordable Housing: Build Less, Preserve More*

3) *No pain, no gain.*

4) *High quality with low price.*

Questions: 1) In the above sentences, which one is an advertisement, headline, idiom, and slogan respectively?

2) What kind of effect does ellipsis have on the reader? Why do advertisements, headlines, idioms and slogans use this technique?

2. Ellipsis is often found in an exclamatory style for an outburst of strong emotions. Its tempo and rhythm are an apt vehicle to carry the turbulent flow of feelings.

Example:

"Good gracious! Lord bless me! Only think! Dear me! Mr. Darcy! Who would have thought it! And is it really true? Oh my sweetest Lizzy! How rich and how great you will be! What pin-money, what jewels, what carriages you will have! Jane's is nothing to it—nothing at all. I am so pleased —so happy. Such a charming man! —So handsome! So tall! —Oh, my dear Lizzy! Pray apologise for my having disliked him so much before. I hope he will overlook it. Dear, dear Lizzy. A house in town! Every thing that is charming! Three daughters married! Ten thousand a year! Oh, Lord! What will become of me. I shall go distracted."

— From Jane Austen, *Pride and Prejudice*

Text II

Combat Stress with Good Nutrition

Pre-reading Questions

1. What happens to your body when it is under stress? What do you do to combat stress?
2. How are stress and nutrition related in terms of one's health?

1   I can hear you now... "Diet? I thought stress relief was all about long, hot soaks in an aromatic bath or lying in a hammock, being soothed by the sounds of nature. I don't even want to think about diets. I've been on so many different diets I can't count them all! Diets never do any good..."

2   But, we're not talking about dieting for weight-loss.

3   People who are faced with a serious health condition like heart disease, high blood pressure or diabetes have certain dietary guidelines to follow in order to help their system cope with the illness. Excessive stress is another condition that can be managed with proper nutrition and, as with other health conditions, proper nutrition is also preventative medicine.

4   Stress should not be taken lightly, or thought of as something you "just have to learn to live with." It can lead to serious health problems, so it's important to be aware of how your diet can affect your stress levels for better or worse.

5   First, let's talk about substances you should avoid if you are dealing with a lot of stress in your life.

Caffeine

6   Caffeine is a stimulant. Drinking coffee only increases feelings of stress. If you are drinking many cups of coffee a day, then you may find that you can reduce a lot of stress by switching to good decaffeinated coffee for a portion of your daily intake.

Alcohol

7   In small amounts, alcohol may help you relax. In larger amounts, it may increase stress as it disrupts sleep. In large amounts over a long term alcohol

will damage your body and will also exacerbate the symptoms of any depression you may be experiencing.

Nicotine

8   In the short term, nicotine can cause relaxation but its toxic effects eventually raise the heart rate and stress the body. If you smoke, try taking your pulse before and after a cigarette, and notice the difference. The long term negative effects of smoking on your body aren't worth the temporary, short-term relief you feel after smoking a cigarette.

Sugar

9   Sugar-rich foods can raise energy in the short term. The problem with this is that your body copes with high levels of sugar by secreting insulin, which reduces the amount of sugar in your blood stream. Insulin can persist and continue acting after it has normalized levels of blood sugar. This can cause an energy dip or what I refer to as a "sugar coma." You may feel good after that candy bar but, you will eventually crash and feel worse than you did before you ate it.

10   The above substances actually rob your body of its stores of nutrients. They also stimulate your heart rate, affect mood, behaviors and brain chemistry, and can lead to dependence. These are all things that will only compound the health issues associated with stress.

11   There are some specific nutritional elements that are especially helpful in dealing with stress. When stress occurs in our lives, proper nutrition reinforces our resistance against the effects of stress.

Complex carbohydrates

12   A good diet fights against stress. Complex carbohydrates cause the brain to release serotonin, a naturally occurring chemical that has a calming effect on the body and mind. So, when you feel really stressed, try a piece of whole grain bread or maybe some oatmeal, knowing that your brain will soon provide nature's own tranquilizer. Complex carbohydrates are found in whole grains (bread, pasta, cereal, etc.), vegetables (broccoli, leafy greens, etc.), potatoes, corn, and also in bananas (although bananas are the only fruit that has this effect).

Magnesium

13   Magnesium is an essential mineral that the body uses to fight stress, relax muscles and promote restful sleep. Not only is magnesium reduced by stress, but

also by the consumption of alcohol, caffeine, sugar and fatty foods. You can boost your magnesium intake by eating plenty of leafy vegetables, nuts, seeds and whole grains. Be sure to make these a part of your daily diet.

Vitamin B6

14   The B vitamins are calming nutrients and B6 helps deliver magnesium into the cells. Again, fruits, vegetables and whole grains are your best sources of B vitamins. If you want to supplement your diet, look for a B-complex supplement that includes all of the B vitamins, thiamin, riboflavin, niacin, B6, folic acid, B12 and biotin. The B vitamins are most effective when combined in the proper balance.

Vitamin C

15   Because vitamin C is not stored in the body, we need a steady supply of this nutrient in order to reap its immune benefits. Unfortunately, stress (and many common substances like nicotine, caffeine and birth control pills) depletes the level of vitamin C in the bloodstream, leaving us vulnerable to all types of illnesses. For this reason, it is vital to include plenty of vitamin C in the diet especially when under excessive stress. Eat plenty of citrus fruits and consider a vitamin C supplement.

Calcium

16   The benefits derived from calcium are widely recognized, especially with the recent heightened awareness of osteoporosis. Not as commonly known is the relaxing effect that calcium, in combination with magnesium, has on the muscles. This is an obvious plus when under stress. As stress is known to deplete calcium levels, calcium in the diet should be increased especially in stressful times. You may want to add a combined calcium/magnesium supplement to your daily intake.

Amino Acids

17   Amino acids support brain function, especially that of neurotransmitters, which can dramatically influence mood and behaviors. Because of this, amino acids can help relieve symptoms of stress. Foods that contain amino acids include eggs, meat, fish, and beans.

18   Good nutrition is the foundation for good health. It is especially important

Unit 6   Nutrition

during times of stress. When pressures in our life increase, maintaining good nutrition can help us through those stressful times.

By Heather Haapoja (abridged)

(976 word)

Reading Comprehension

I.   Answer the following questions with the information you read from the passage.
1. What will be the result if someone drinks alcohol in large amounts over a long term?
2. How does the body cope with high levels of sugar?
3. What is the function of complex carbohydrates?
4. How can people increase their magnesium intake?
5. What is the benefit of vitamin C? How can one keep plenty of vitamin C in the body?

II. Topics for discussion and reflection
1. People often use alcohol, cigarettes or various other addictions to cope with stress. Why do you think people choose such alternatives?
2. What are some positive ways of dealing with stress?

Exercises for Integrated Skills

I.   Dictation

Listen to the following passage. The passage will be read to you four times. During the first reading, which will be read at normal speed, listen and try to understand the meaning. For the second and third readings, the passage will be read sentence by sentence, or phrase by phrase, with intervals of 15 to 20 seconds. The last reading will be done at normal speed again and during this time check your work. You will then be given 2 minutes to check through your work a second time.

_____

_____

_____

_____

II. Cloze

Vitamins are ___1___ which are essential for health but which the body ___2___ make for itself either in sufficient quantity or at all. Vitamin D is an exceptional case. Some vitamins are needed ___3___ only minute amounts, ___4___ others are required in relatively large amounts, such as vitamin C.

During the early work on vitamins, their nature was unknown. ___5___ was clearly established, though, was that highly purified fat, carbohydrate, protein, minerals and water could not keep animals in good health ___6___ some unrefined (natural) food was added to the diet. For example, as ___7___ as one teaspoonful of milk per day was enough to enable young animals to ___8___ on the experimental refined diet. It has been known for centuries that an unvaried diet containing only a few different food ___9___ was likely to be unsatisfactory, the best-known circumstance being the ___10___ of scurvy, often fatal, among sailors on long journeys. This calamitous disease could be prevented or cured by quite small amounts of citrus fruit juice.

1. A. components   B. substances   C. ingredients   D. participles
2. A. needn't   B. shouldn't   C. cannot   D. mustn't
3. A. in   B. by   C. for   D. to
4. A. but   B. while   C. still   D. however
5. A. That   B. It   C. One   D. What
6. A. if   B. unless   C. in spite of   D. despite
7. A. small   B. less   C. little   D. much
8. A. enjoy   B. thrive   C. depend   D. succeed
9. A. items   B. substances   C. elements   D. compositions
10. A. appearance   B. incidence   C. occurrence   D. emergence

Oral Activities

1. Discuss the importance of health and nutrition in our daily lives.
2. Group discussion: How far can academic performance improve health and nutrition?

Writing Practice

Composition Writing

There is a popular English saying: "You are what you eat." How far do you agree with (or disagree) this saying? Write a composition of about 200 words to express your thoughts.

Unit 7 Success and Failure

Warm-up Activities

1. Discuss your thoughts on the old adage, "Cheaters never prosper." What do you consider to be cheating? Why?
2. How do you deal with success and failure in your life?

Text I

The Art of Turning Failure into Success

Pre-reading Questions

1. What are some measures of success and failure?
2. Are you invigorated or defeated by failure? Why?

1   Vicky—beautiful, talented, very bright, voted "Most Likely to Succeed" in college—got a promising job with a large company after graduation. Then, after two years without promotions, she was fired. She suffered a complete nervous breakdown. "It was panic," she told me later. "Everything had always gone so well for me that I had no experience in coping with rejection. I felt I was a failure."

2   Vicky's reaction is an extreme example of a common phenomenon. Our society places so much emphasis on "making it" that we come to believe that winning is not the only thing and any failure is bad. What we don't always recognize is that what looks like failure may, in the long run, prove beneficial. When Vicky was able to think coolly about why she was fired, for example, she realized that she was simply not suited for a job dealing with people all the

time. In her new position as a copy editor, she works independently, is happy and once again "successful."

3   Success and failure are relative terms. Is the honest man laid off in hard times less of a success than the swindler who's making money? Is the devoted college teacher a failure if he never makes full professor? Is the full professor a failure if his son abandons higher education in favor of organic farming? Political success, business success, social success, professional success, personal success—all have different values depending on who's judging. You may think your neighbor a failure because he works at a low-prestige factory. But to his family, his many bowling trophies are a mark of success. On the other hand, the woman you see as a dazzling success—because of her beautiful home, lovely children and fascinating husband—may feel like a failure because she's never had a career of her own.

4   People are generally prone to what language expert S. I. Hayakawa calls "the two-valued orientation." We talk about seeing both sides of a question as if every question had only two sides. We assume that everyone is either a success or a failure when, in fact, infinite degrees of both are possible. As Hayakawa points out, there's a world of difference between "I have failed three times" and "I am a failure." Indeed, the words failure and success cannot be reasonably applied to a complex, living, changing human being. They can only describe the situation at a particular time and place.

5   Obviously no one can be a whiz at everything. In fact, success in one area often precludes success in another. Some kinds of professional success interfere with personal life. An eminent politician once told me that his career had practically destroyed his marriage. "I have no time for my family," he explained. "I travel a lot. And even when I'm home, I hardly see my wife and kids. I've got power, money, prestige—but as a husband and father, I'm a flop."

6   Certain kinds of success can indeed be destructive. The danger of too early success is particularly acute. I recall, from my childhood, a girl whose skill on ice skates marked her as "Olympic material." While the rest of us were playing, bicycling, reading and just idling, this girl skated—every day after

Unit 7 Success and Failure

school and all weekend. Her picture often appeared in the papers, and the rest of us envied her glamorous life. Years later, however, she spoke bitterly of those early triumphs. "I never prepared myself for anything but the ice," she said. "I peaked at 17—and it's been downhill ever since."

7   Success that comes too easily is also damaging: the child who wins a prize for a carelessly-written essay, the adult who distinguishes himself at a first job by lucky accident, faces probable disappointment when real challenges arise.

8   Success is bad when it prevents growth—when, like an actor "typed" by one successful role, an individual is forced to go on doing the same thing because he does it so well. Success is also bad when it's achieved at the cost of the total quality of an experience. Successful students sometimes become so obsessed with grades that they never enjoy their school years. They never branch out into tempting new areas, because they don't want to risk their grade-point average.

9   Why are so many people so afraid of failure? I suppose it's because, though we hear a lot about how to succeed, no one tells us how to fail so that failure becomes a growing experience. We forget that failure is part of the human condition and that "every person has the right to fail."

10   Most parents work hard at either preventing failure or shielding their children from the knowledge that they have failed. In the first instance, they rush to rescue a child from the consequences of his or her misjudgement, negligence or inadequacy for the task in hand. Another technique for preventing failure is the constant pushing that makes a child feel that nothing he does is quite good enough. This approach may produce dramatically opposite results. The child may run more desperately after elusive triumphs—or even opt out of the race entirely.

11   On those frequent occasions when parents can't save a child from failure, the temptation is to keep the youngster from facing up to the fact that he or she has failed. One way is to lower standards. A mother describes her child's hastily-made table as "perfect!" even though it wobbles on uneven legs. Another way is to shift blame. If John fails math, his teacher is unfair or stupid.

12   The trouble with failure-prevention devices is that they leave a child unequipped for life in the real world. The young need to learn that no one can

be best at everything, no one can win all the time—and that it's possible to enjoy a game even when you don't win. A child who's not invited to a birthday party, who doesn't make the honor roll or the baseball team feels terrible, of course. But parents should not offer a quick consolation prize or say, "It doesn't matter," because it does. The youngster should be allowed to experience disappointment—and then be helped to master it. Parental rescue operations encourage omnipotence fantasies and delay the recognition of limits that is part of growing up. The person who is regularly rescued will keep plunging into deep waters—and become increasingly hostile towards his rescuers. And withholding from children the knowledge that they've done badly is simply irresponsible.

13 Failure is never pleasurable. It hurts adults and children alike. But it can make a positive contribution to your life once you learn to use it. Step one is to ask, "Why did I fail?" Resist the natural impulse to blame someone else. Ask yourself what you did wrong, how you can improve. If someone else can help, don't be shy about inquiring. When I was a teenager and failed to get a job I'd counted on, I telephoned the interviewer to ask why. "Because you came ten minutes late," I was told. "We can't afford employees who waste other people's time." The explanation was reassuring (I hadn't been rejected as a person) and helpful, too. I don't think I've been late for anything since.

14 Success, which encourages repetition of old behavior, is not nearly as good a teacher as failure. You can learn from a disastrous party how to give a good one, from an ill-chosen first house what to look for in a second. Even a failure that seems definitive can prompt fresh thinking, a change of direction. A friend of mine, after 12 years of studying ballet, auditioned for a professional company and was turned down by the ballet master, who said, "You haven't the body for it." In such cases, the way to use failure is to take stock courageously, asking, "What have I left? What else can I do?" My friend put away her toe shoes and moved into dance therapy, a field where she's both competent and useful.

15 Oddly enough, failure often brings with it a peculiar kind of freedom. It's like the first dent in a new car. Whether the accident is your fault or not, you feel terrible at first, then you relax. At last, your can enjoy driving. Who cares about the second dent or the third? Similarly, even a major life failure can be

followed by a sense of "It's happened. I wish it hadn't, but it's over now—and I survived." Failure frees one to take risks because there's less to lose. Often there's resurgence of energy, an awareness of new possibilities.

16   Faced, absorbed and accepted, failure contributes to personal growth. The man who once raged against the unemployed finally understands, when his own plant closes, that a man can be out of work through no fault of his own. Setbacks often lead to improved personal relationships, too. The officially "successful" person remains closed off and self-protective, but failure allows one to reveal simple human vulnerability.

17   Though we may envy the assurance that comes with success, most of us are attracted by courage in defeat. There is what might be called the noble failure—the special heroism of aiming high, doing your best and then, when that proves not enough, moving bravely on. As Ralph Waldo Emerson said: "A man's success is made up of failures, because he experiments and ventures every day, and the more falls he gets, moves faster on ... I have heard that in horsemanship—a man will never be a good rider until he is thrown; then he will not be haunted any longer by the terror that he shall tumble, and will ride whither he is bound."

By Fredelle Maynard
(1,615 words)

Words and Expressions

breakdown	/ˈbreɪkdaʊn/	n.	a serious medical condition in which someone becomes mentally ill and is unable to work or deal with ordinary situations in life 崩溃
reject	/rɪˈdʒekt/	vt.	to refuse to give someone any love or attention 冷落 **rejection** n. 冷落，嫌弃
lay off			to stop employing someone because there is no work for them to do 解雇（雇员）
swindle	/ˈswɪndl/	vt.	to get money from someone by deceiving them 诈骗，欺诈，骗取（钱财）**swindler** n. 骗子
organic	/ɔːˈɡænɪk/	adj.	relating to farming or gardening methods of

			growing food without using artificial chemicals, or produced or grown by these methods 施用有机肥料的，不使用化肥（农药）生产的
bowling	/ˈbəʊlɪŋ/	n.	an indoor game in which you roll a large heavy ball along a wooden track in order to knock down a group of pins 保龄球运动
trophy	/ˈtrəʊfi/	n.	a large object such as a silver cup or plate that someone receives as a prize for winning a competition 奖杯，奖品，奖牌
dazzling	/ˈdæzəlɪŋ/	adj.	very impressive and attractive 给人印象深刻的，特别吸引人的
orientation	/ˌɔːriːenˈteɪʃən/	n.	the particular preferences, tendencies, beliefs or opinions that a person has 态度，观点，信仰
whiz	/wɪz/	n.	(BrE. whizz, infl) someone who is very fast, intelligent, or skilled in a particular activity 能手，专家
preclude	/prɪˈkluːd/	vt.	to prevent something or make something impossible 阻止，防止，使不可能
flop	/flɒp/	n.	a film, play, product, etc. that is not successful 失败
glamorous	/ˈɡlæmərəs/	adj.	attractive, exciting, and related to wealth and success 富有而成功的，有魅力的，刺激的
bitterly	/ˈbɪtəli/	adv.	in a way that produces or shows feelings of great sadness or anger 痛苦地，愤恨地
damaging	/ˈdæmɪdʒɪŋ/	adj.	affecting someone or something in a bad way 对（某人或某物）有不利影响的
distinguish oneself			to do something so well that people notice and remember 表现突出
be obsessed with			thinking or worrying about something or someone all the time 困扰，使心神不宁
branch out			to do something new in addition to what you usually do 开辟新的领域，扩大范围
shield	/ʃiːld/	vt.	to protect someone or something from being harmed or damaged 保护，保卫

Unit 7 Success and Failure

misjudge	/ˌmɪsˈdʒʌdʒ/	vt.	to form a wrong or unfair opinion about a person or a situation 错误地判断 **misjudgement** n. 错误的判断
negligence	/ˈneglɪdʒəns/	n.	failure to take enough care over something that one is responsible for 疏忽大意，玩忽职守
inadequacy	/ɪnˈædɪkwəsɪ/	n.	the fact of not being good enough in quality, ability, size, etc. for a particular purpose 欠缺，不足
elusive	/ɪˈluːsɪv/	adj.	being difficult to achieve 难实现的，困难的
opt out of			to decide not to be part of a group or system 决定不加入（不参与）
wobble	/ˈwɒbəl/	n.	a movement from side to side which shows poor balance 摇晃，抖动
uneven	/ʌnˈiːvən/	adj.	not equal or equally balanced 不平衡的，不平等的
honor roll			a list of the best students in a school or college 优等生名单，光荣榜
consolation	/ˌkɒnsəˈleɪʃən/	n.	something that makes one feel better when he is sad or disappointed 安慰
omnipotent	/ɒmˈnɪpətənt/	adj.	able to do everything 全能的，无所不能的 **omnipotence** n. 全能
fantasy	/ˈfæntəsɪ/	n.	an idea or belief that is based only on imagination, not on real facts 想象，幻想
withhold	/wɪðˈhəʊld/	vt.	to refuse to give someone something 拒给，扣留
inquire	/ɪnˈkwaɪə/	vi.&vt.	to ask someone for information 询问，打听
count on			to expect something 期望，料想
definitive	/dɪˈfɪnɪtɪv/	adj.	not able to be changed or improved 最终的，不可更改的，不容怀疑的
prompt	/prɒmpt/		to make someone decide to do something 促使，使下决心
ballet	/ˈbæleɪ/	n.	a type of dance, often with costumes and scenery, combined with music, that tells a story 芭蕾舞（艺术）
audition	/ɔːˈdɪʃən/	vi.	to be judged by a trial performance or try-out 进行试演（试唱），评判试演（试唱）

113

take stock			to think carefully about the things that have happened in a situation in order to decide what to do next（对形势）做出估计（判断）
courageous	/kəˈreɪdʒəs/	adj.	brave 勇敢的，有胆量的 **courageously** adv. 勇敢地
oddly	/ˈɒdlɪ/	adv.	in a strange or unusual way 奇怪地，古怪地，异常地
dent	/dent/	n.	a hollow area in the surface of something, usually made by something hitting it 凹陷,凹痕
resurgence	/rɪˈsɜːdʒəns/	n.	the reappearance and growth of something that was common in the past 复苏,再起
setback	/ˈsetbæk/	n.	a problem that delays or prevents progress, or makes things worse than they were 挫折,阻碍前进的事物
assurance	/əˈʃʊərəns/	n.	a feeling of calm confidence about one's own abilities, or that he is right about something 自信,把握
horsemanship	/ˈhɔːsmənʃɪp/	n.	the skill involved in riding horses 骑术,马术
haunt	/hɔːnt/	vt.	to make someone worry, sad, or scared 烦扰,缠绕
tumble	/ˈtʌmbəl/	vi.	to fall down quickly and suddenly, especially with a rolling movement 滚下,跌倒,摔倒
whither	/ˈwɪðə/	adv.	a word used to ask if something will exist, or how it will develop, in the future 向何处去

Notes:

1. **S．I．Hayakawa (1906–1992)**　was a scholar, university president, and U.S. senator from California （1977–1983）. He is best known for his popular writings on semantics and for his career as president of San Francisco State College （now San Francisco State University）. His book, *Language in Action* (1941), was a popular treatment of semantic theories.

2. **Ralph Waldo Emerson (1803–1882)**　was an American essayist, philosopher, and poet, best remembered for leading the Transcendentalist movement of the mid 19th century.

Unit 7　Success and Failure

Reading Comprehension

I. **Classify the following people mentioned in the text into different groups and explain why they belong in those groups.**

    A. Vicky   B. an eminent politician

    C. the skating girl   D. my friend studying ballet for 12 years

    Success Group: _____   Failure Group: _____

II. **Answer the following questions.**

1. How do you interpret "Success and failure are relative terms"?
2. How did the eminent politician comment on his career and marriage?
3. Why are so many people afraid of failure according to the text?
4. What can parents do to keep the youngster from facing up to the fact that he or she has failed?
5. How can we make use of failure to make positive contributions to life?

III. **Paraphrase the following sentences within the context of the reading passage.**

1. (Para.8) They never branch out into tempting new areas, because they don't want to risk their grade-point average.
2. (Para.10) Most parents work hard at either preventing failure or shielding their children from the knowledge that they have failed.
3. (Para.10) The child may run more desperately after elusive triumphs—or even opt out of the race entirely.
4. (Para.12) Parental rescue operations encourage omnipotence fantasies and delay the recognition of limits that is part of growing up.
5. (Para.16) The officially "successful" person remains closed off and self-protective, but failure allows one to reveal simple human vulnerability.

IV. **Based on the text, decide whether the following statements are true or false. For false statements, write the facts in parentheses.**

1. Vicky felt panicky after she was fired, but she recovered later.
   (   )

2. A devoted college teacher is a failure if he never makes full professor.
   (   )

3. Too early success or too easy success can be destructive and damaging.
   (   )

4. Parents should offer an immediate consolation prize if their children fail.
    (   )
5. As a teenager, I failed to get a job I'd counted on for no reason at all.
    (   )

Vocabulary Exercises

I. Fill in the blank in each sentence with a word or phrase taken from the box below. Make sure the appropriate form of the word is used.

| elusive | prone | obsess | preclude | resurgence |
| prompt | whiz | count on | take stock | withhold |

1. Apparently, he was unaware that an unsatisfactory rating does not strictly _____ contractors from bidding on other projects.
2. Success that comes too easily makes people more _____ to failure when real challenges arise.
3. The revival of the language, particularly among young people, is part of a _____ of national identity sweeping through this small, proud nation.
4. The girl was so _____ with ice-skating that she never had time for normal childhood activities and experiences.
5. The army has made gains after sweeping operations against militants, but lasting success may prove _____.
6. In high school he was known as a _____ in physics and math who would patiently tutor his friends before tests.
7. The study was preliminary and uncontrolled, but convincing enough to _____ more methodical research.
8. Pauses in daily routines, after all, offer occasions to remove ourselves from the rush of what we do so we may _____ of who we are.
9. Even so, Obama may not be able to _____ one Republican senator who has worked with Democrats in the past.
10. It's not clear yet if publishers can _____ books from Amazon while giving them to other parties like Apple.

II. Fill in the blanks with the appropriate forms of the given words.
1. Some parents are upset about not sending their children to what they perceive to be a "_____ (prestige)" school.

Unit 7 Success and Failure

2. Candidates for this post should have training and _____ (practically) experience in basic electronics.
3. The girl _____ (distinguish) herself as a tennis player at a very early age, winning a junior tournament at Wimbledon before she was fifteen.
4. The word "Hollywood" represents all the dreams, despair, and _____ (glamorous) we associate with the movie business.
5. The _____ (reveal) of his scandalous past apparently put him under great stress.

III. Replace the italicized words or phrases with simple, everyday words.
1. ...what looks like failure may, *in the long run*, prove beneficial. (   )
2. People *are* generally *prone to* what language expert S. I. Hayakawa calls "the two-valued orientation." (   )
3. ...*make the honor roll* or the baseball team... (   )
4. Success, ..., is *not nearly* as good a teacher as failure. (   )
5. ...his career had *practically* destroyed his marriage. (   )
6. ...even though it's *wobbles* on uneven legs. (   )
7. Often there's *resurgence* of energy... (   )

IV. Choose a word or phrase that best completes each of the following sentences.
1. Youth means a temperamental predominance of courage over timidity, of the appetite for _____ over the love of ease.
   A. risk   B. venture   C. adventure   D. danger
2. Certain of the terms and conditions apply only _____ particular types of goods.
   A. in   B. to   C. for   D. on
3. You should face _____ the fact that your expectation of an ideal job is unrealistic under present circumstances.
   A. up to   B. up   C. with   D. off
4. Do you know Tim? He is _____ than his elder brother.
   A. much less sportsman   B. less of a sportsman
   C. less of sportsman   D. less a sportsman
5. A physical analysis of an airport can help close _____ areas where dangerous individuals may try to enter.
   A. up   B. in   C. out   D. off

Translation Exercises

I. Translate each of the following sentences into English, using the word or phrase given in the brackets.

1. 教育专家们认为失败与成功之间并无天壤之别。(a world of)

2. 庇护孩子,不让他们知道自己的失败对于孩子的成长是绝对无益的。(shield...from)

3. 她过于醉心于自己在舞蹈方面的成功,从未对现实世界中的挑战作好准备。(be obsessed with)

4. 琼斯太太在谈到她儿子的成功时,往往夸大其辞。(prone)

5. 我父亲起初收集邮票,现在又把收集范围扩大到了硬币。(branch out)

6. 那场大火造成的死亡和毁坏景象直到30年后还常常浮现在他脑海中。(haunt)

7. 最近我突然对弹奏乐器重燃热情,自己购买了钢琴并坚持练习。(resurgence)

II. Translate the following paragraph into English.

成功并无秘诀。成功是做你知道该去做的事,而不是做你知道不该做的事。成功不应局限于人格身心的某一方面,而与你身体、思维、心灵和精神的全面发展相关。成功是倾全力去执着追求你所热望的事业。成功并不以达到某个山峰为最终目标。它是一个不断盘旋上升的过程,它是永远进取。成功是以勇气来直面挫败而不被击败,它绝不会让当前的挫折妨碍你远大的目标。

III. Translate the following paragraph into Chinese.

Success is bad when it prevents growth—when, like an actor "typed" by one successful role, an individual is forced to go on doing the same thing because he does it so well. Success is also bad when it's achieved at the cost of the total quality of an experience. Successful students sometimes become so obsessed with grades that they never enjoy their school years. They never branch out into tempting new areas, because they don't want to risk their grade-point average.

Unit 7 Success and Failure

Language Appreciation

I. Read the text carefully, then pick out the sentences that you think are well-written. Pay close attention to the italicized words or phrases of the following sentences. Try to appreciate the way in which the author expresses his/her ideas. Learn how to use them in your own writing.

1. Success is also bad when it's achieved *at the cost of* the total quality of an experience.
2. Successful students sometimes become so *obsessed* with grades that they never enjoy their school years.
3. *Faced, absorbed and accepted,* failure contributes to personal growth.

II. Read aloud and recite paragraph 17.

III. Stylistics Study

Repetition—Addition in Stylistics

It is generally acknowledged that repetition should be avoided in writing as too much repetition can be tedious. But a deliberate repetition of the key words or phrases is a frequently used device for rhetorical build-up for emphasis and impression.

Examples: 1) *With this faith we will be able to work together, to pray together, to struggle together, to go to jail together, to stand up for freedom together, knowing that we will be free one day.*
—From Martin Luther King

2) *I love everything that's old: old friends, old times, old manners, old books, old wines; and, I believe, Dorothy, you'll own I have been pretty fond of an old wife.*
—From Oliver Goldsmith, *She Stoops to Conquer*

3) Work—work—work
Till the brain begins to swim,
Work—work—work
Till the eyes are heavy and dim!
Seam, and gusset, and band,
Band, and gusset, and seam,
Till over the buttons I fall asleep,
And sew them on in a dream!
—From Thomas Hood, *Song of the Shirt*

Questions: 1) How do repetition and parallelism differ from each other? Give examples.

2) Are the repetitions above unnecessary and tedious? Why or why not?

3) Find some more examples of repetition. Why do the authors use repetition in those contexts?

Text II

Born to Win

Pre-reading Questions

1. Do you think people are genetically determined to win or lose? In other words, are people "born" winners or losers?
2. Why do people care about winning or losing?

You cannot teach a man anything.
You can only help him discover it within himself.

—*Galileo*

"WINNERS AND LOSERS"

1   Each human being is born as something new, something that never existed before. He is born with what he needs to win at life. Each person in his own way can see, hear, touch, taste, and think for himself. Each has his unique potentials—his capabilities and limitations. Each can be a significant, thinking, aware, and creatively productive person in his own right—a winner.

2   The words "winner" and "loser" have many meanings. When we refer to a person as a winner, we do not mean one who beats the other guy by winning over him and making him lose. To us, a winner is one who responds authentically by being credible, trustworthy, responsive, and genuine, both as an individual and as a member of a society. A loser is one who fails to correspond authentically. Martin Buber expresses this idea as he retells an old story of a rabbi who on his death bed sees himself as a loser. The rabbi laments that, in the world to come, he will not be asked why he wasn't Moses, he will be asked why he wasn't himself.

Unit 7   Success and Failure

3   Few people are one hundred percent winners or one hundred percent losers. It's a matter of degree. However, once a person is on the road to being a winner, his chances are greater for becoming even more so.

"WINNERS"

4   Winners have different potentials. Achievement is not the most important thing. Authenticity is. The authentic person experiences the reality of himself by knowing himself, being himself, and becoming a credible, responsive person. He actualizes his own unprecedented uniqueness and appreciates the uniqueness of others.

5   A winner is not afraid to do his own thinking and to use his own knowledge. He can separate facts from opinion and doesn't pretend to have all the answers. He listens to others, evaluates what they say, but comes to his own conclusions. While he can admire and respect other people, he is not totally defined, bound, or awed by them.

6   A winner can be spontaneous. He does not have to respond in predetermined, rigid ways. He can change his plans when the situation calls for it. A winner has a zest for life. He enjoys work, play, food, other people, and the world of nature. Without guilt he enjoys his own accomplishments. Without envy he enjoys the accomplishments of others.

7   Although a winner can freely enjoy himself, he can also postpone enjoyment. He can discipline himself in the present to enhance his enjoyment in the future. He is not afraid to go after what he wants but does so in appropriate ways.   He does not get his security by controlling others.

8   A winner cares about the world and its peoples. He is not isolated from the general problems of society. He is concerned, compassionate and committed to improving the quality of life. Even in the face of national and international adversity, he does not see himself as totally powerless. He does what he can to make the world a better place.

"LOSERS"

9   Although people are born to win, they are also born helpless and totally dependent on their environment. Winners successfully make the transition from total helplessness to independence, and then to interdependence. Losers do not.

Somewhere along the line they begin to avoid becoming self-responsible.

10   As we have noted, few people are total winners or losers. Most of them are winners in some areas of their lives and losers in others. Their winning or losing is influenced by what happens to them in childhood.

11   A lack of response to dependency needs, poor nutrition, brutality, unhappy relationships, disease, continuing disappointments, inadequate physical care, and traumatic events are among the many experiences that contribute to making people losers. Such experiences interrupt, deter, or prevent the normal progress toward autonomy and self-actualization. To cope with negative experiences a child learns to manipulate himself and others. These manipulative techniques are hard to give up later in life and often become set patterns. A winner works to shed them. A loser hangs on to them.

12   A loser represses his capacity to express spontaneously and appropriately his full range of possible behavior. He may be unaware of other options for his life if the path he chooses goes nowhere. He is afraid to try new things. He maintains his own status quo. He is a repeater. He repeats not only his own mistakes, he often repeats those of his family and culture.

13   A loser has difficulty giving and receiving affection. He does not enter into intimate, honest and direct relationships with others. Instead, he tries to manipulate them into living up to his expectations and channels his energies into living up to their expectations.

14   When a person wants to discover and change his "losing streak," when he wants to become more like the winner he was born to be, he can use gestalt-type experiments and transactional analysis to make change happen. These are two new exciting, psychological approaches to human problems. The first was given new life by Dr. Frederick Perls; the second was developed by Dr. Eric Berne.

15   Perls was born in Germany in 1893 and left the country when Hitler came into power. Berne was born in Montreal in 1910. Both men were trained as Freudian psychoanalysts; both broke away from the use of orthodox psychoanalysis; both found their greatest popularity and acceptance in the United States.

16   Gestalt therapy is not new. However, its current popularity has grown rapidly since it was given new impetus and direction by Dr. Frederick Perls. Gestalt is a German word for which there is no exact English equivalent; it means,

roughly, the forming of an organized, meaningful whole.

17 Perls perceives many personalities as lacking wholeness, as being fragmented. He claims people are often aware of only parts of themselves rather than of the whole self. For example, a woman may not know or want to admit that sometimes she acts like her mother; a man may not know or admit that sometimes he wants to cry like a baby.

18 The aim of gestalt therapy is to help one to become whole—to help the person become aware of, admit to, reclaim, and integrate his fragmented parts. Integration helps a person make the transition from dependency to self-sufficiency, from authoritarian outer support to authentic inner support.

By Muriel James and Dorothy Jongeward
(1,076 words)

Reading Comprehension

I. Answer the following questions with the information you read from the passage.
   1. What did the rabbi lament on his death bed?
   2. What are the potentials of winners?
   3. What contributes to making people losers?
   4. Who is Dr. Eric Berne?
   5. What is *gestalt* therapy? And what is the aim of *gestalt* therapy?

II. Topics for reflection and discussion.
   1. What role does personality play in winning or losing?
   2. Some people say that one can never win alone, but one always loses by oneself. Do you agree or disagree with this statement? Why or why not?

Exercises for Integrated Skills

I. **Dictation**

   Listen to the following passage. The passage will be read a total of four times. During the first reading, which will be read at normal speed, listen and try to understand the meaning. For the second and third readings, the passage will be read sentence by sentence, or phrase by phrase, with intervals of 15 to 20 seconds. The last reading will be done at normal speed again and during this time check your work. You will then be given 2 minutes to check through your work a second time.

II. Cloze

Whereas superior ___1___ athletic talent allows youths to be good all-around athletes, ___2___ they get older and involved in higher levels of competition, the unique requirements of particular sports make ___3___ difficult for them to be stars in more than one sport. At the ___4___ level, if an athlete is ___5___ in one sport, he or she is ___6___ to be even near that same level in another. At the high school level, an 82-mile-an-hour fastball will blow hitters away, but even in the low ___7___ leagues it will get you a quick shower. In pro football, cornerbacks ___8___ be able to run forty yards in 4.4 or 4.5 seconds. That is not just fast; that is blazing fast. Tennis players must be extremely quick and possess remarkable hand-and-eye ___9___. Basketball players must have great agility and, usually, height way above the norm. John Stockton, an all-star guard in the NBA for years, is an unremarkable-looking person, that is, ___10___ you check out his hands—they are enormous. His huge hands give him a great advantage when handling the basketball.

1. A. usual	B. general	C. certain	D. particular
2. A. as	B. when	C. along with	D. with
3. A. /	B. that	C. it	D. this
4. A. superior	B. excellent	C. super	D. elite
5. A. proficient	B. sufficient	C. efficient	D. persistent
6. A. probable	B. unlikely	C. possible	D. doubtable
7. A. small	B. minor	C. menial	D. humble
8. A. need	B. may	C. have to	D. would
9. A. coordination	B. cooperation	C. connection	D. collaboration
10. A. if	B. until	C. when	D. even if

Unit 7 Success and Failure

Oral Activities

1. How would you define success? In your opinion, who are some of the biggest winners or most successful people in the world? Why?
2. Some people believe that failure is not problematic, but rather is a learning opportunity. Discuss your thoughts on this statement and whether you agree or disagree and reasons for your position.

Writing Practice

Composition Writing

Artist Corita Kent once said that flowers grow out of dark moments; the same goes with life. Recall a time in your past when you experienced "failure" and write a composition of about 200 words, stating how that failure inspired success. You may also write about the life experiences of others around you.

Unit 8 Aesthetics

Warm-up Activities

1. In your opinion, what characteristics make something aesthetically pleasing? Why?
2. Give some examples of how the aesthetics of appearances have changed throughout time and how they can vary from culture to culture.

Text I

The Beauty Industry

Pre-reading Questions

1. Why do people care so much about their appearance? Some people go through surgery to alter their appearance. Would you? Why or why not?
2. The notions of beauty have changed throughout history. What do you consider to be "beautiful" in a person?

1   The one American industry unaffected by the general depression of trade is the beauty industry. American women continue to spend on their faces and bodies as much as they spent before the coming of the slump—about three million pounds a week. These facts and figures are "official," and can be accepted as being substantially true. Reading them, I was only surprised by the comparative smallness of the sums expended. From the prodigious number of advertisements of aids to beauty contained in the American magazines, I had imagined that the personal appearance business must stand high up among the champions of American industry—the equal, or only just less than the equal, of

Unit 8   Aesthetics

bootlegging and racketeering, movies and automobiles. Still, one hundred and fifty-six million pounds a year is a tidy sum. Rather more than twice the revenue of India, if I remember rightly.

2   I do not know what the European figures are. Much smaller undoubtedly. Europe is poor, and a face can cost as much in upkeep as a Rolls-Royce. The most that the majority of European women can do is just to wash and hope for the best. Perhaps the soap will produce its loudly advertised effects; perhaps it will transform them into the likeness of those ravishing creatures who smile so rosily and creamily, so peachily and pearlily, from every hoarding. Perhaps, on the other hand, it may not. In any case, the most costly experiments in beautification are still as much beyond most European means as are high-powered motor-cars and electric refrigerators. Even in Europe, however, much more is now spent on beauty than was ever spent in the past. Not quite so much more as in America, that is all. But, everywhere, the increase has been undoubtedly enormous.

3   The fact is significant. To what is it due? In part, I supposed, to a general increase in prosperity. The rich have always cultivated their personal appearance. The diffusion of wealth—such as it is—now permits those of the poor who are less badly off than their fathers to do the same.

4   But this is, clearly, not the whole story. The modern cult of beauty is not exclusively a function (in the mathematical sense) of wealth. If it were, then the personal appearance industries would have been as hardly hit by the trade depression as any other business. But, as we have seen, they have not suffered. Women are retrenching on other things than their faces. The cult of beauty must therefore be symptomatic of changes than have taken place outside the economic sphere. Of what changes? Of the changes, I suggest, in the status of women; of the changes in our attitude towards "the merely physical."

5   Women, it is obvious, are freer than in the past. Freer not only to perform the generally unenviable social functions hitherto reserved to the male, but also freer to exercise the more pleasing, feminine privilege of being attractive. They have the right, if not to be less virtuous than their grandmothers, at any rate to

look less virtuous. The British Matron, not long since a creature of austere and even terrifying aspect, now does her best to achieve and perennially preserve the appearance of what her predecessor would have described as a Lost Woman. She often succeeds. But we are not shocked—at any rate, not morally shocked. Aesthetically shocked—yes; we may sometimes be that. But morally, no. We concede that the Matron is morally justified in being preoccupied with her personal appearance. This concession depends on another of a more general nature—a concession to the Body, with a large B, to the Manichaean principle of evil. For we have now come to admit that body has its rights. And not only rights—duties, actually duties. It has, for example, a duty to do the best it can for itself in the way of strength and beauty. Christian-ascetic ideas no longer trouble us. We demand justice for the body as well as for the soul. Hence, among other things, the fortunes made by face cream manufacturers and beauty-specialists, by the vendors of rubber reducing belts and massage machines, by the patentees of hair lotions and the authors of books on the culture of the abdomen.

6   What are the practical results of this modern cult of beauty? The exercises and the massage, the health motors and the skin foods—to what have they led? Are women more beautiful than they were? Do they get something for the enormous expenditure of energy, time, and money demanded of them by the beauty-cult? These are questions which it is difficult to answer. For the facts seem to contradict themselves. The campaign for more physical beauty seems to be both a tremendous success and a lamentable failure. It depends how you look at the results.

7   It is a success in so far as more women retain their youthful appearance to a greater age than in the past. "Old ladies" are already becoming rare. In a few years, we may well believe, they will be extinct. White hair and wrinkles, a bent back and hollow cheeks will come to be regarded as medievally old-fashioned. The crone of the future will be golden, curly and cherry-lipped, neat-ankled and slender. The Portrait of the Artist's Mother will come to be almost indistinguishable, at future picture shows, from the Portrait of the Artist's Daughter. This desirable consummation will be due in part to skin foods and injections of paraffin-wax, facial surgery, mud baths, and paint, in part to improved health, due in its turn to a more rational mode of life. Ugliness

is one of the symptoms of disease, beauty of health. In so far as the campaign for more beauty is also a campaign for more health, it is admirable and, up to a point, genuinely successful. Beauty that is merely the artificial shadow of these symptoms of health is intrinsically of poorer quality than the genuine article. Still, it is a sufficiently good imitation to be sometimes mistakable for the real thing. The apparatus for mimicking the symptoms of health is now within the reach of every moderately prosperous person; the knowledge of the way in which real health can be achieved is growing, and will in time, no doubt, be universally acted upon. When that happy moment comes, will every woman be beautiful—as beautiful, at any rate, as the natural shape of her features, with or without surgical and chemical aid, permits?

8   The answer is emphatically: No. For real beauty is as much an affair of the inner as of the outer self. The beauty of a porcelain jar is a matter of shape, of colour, of surface texture. The jar may be empty or tenanted by spiders, full of honey or stinking slime—it makes no difference to its beauty or ugliness. But a woman is alive, and her beauty is therefore not skin deep. The surface of the human vessel is affected by the nature of its spiritual contents. I have seen women who, by the standards of a connoisseur of porcelain, were ravishingly lovely. Their shape, their colour, their surface texture were perfect. And yet they were not beautiful. For the lovely vase was either empty or filled with some corruption. Spiritual emptiness or ugliness shows through. And conversely, there is an interior light that can transfigure forms that the pure aesthetician would regard as imperfect or downright ugly.

9   There are numerous forms of psychological ugliness. There is an ugliness of stupidity, for example, or unawareness (distressingly common among pretty women). An ugliness also of greed, of lasciviousness, of avarice. All the deadly sins, indeed, have their own peculiar negation of beauty. On the pretty faces of those especially who are trying to have a continuous "good time," one sees very often a kind of bored sullenness that ruins all their charm. I remember in particular two young American girls I once met in North Africa. From the porcelain specialist's point of view, they were beautiful. But the sullen boredom of which I have spoken was so deeply stamped into their fresh faces, their gait and gestures expressed so weary a listlessness, that it was unbearable to look at them. These exquisite creatures were positively repulsive.

10 Still commoner and no less repellent is the hardness which spoils so many pretty faces. Often, it is true, this air of hardness is due not to psychological causes, but to the contemporary habit of over-painting. In Paris, where this over-painting is most pronounced, many women have ceased to look human at all. Whitewashed and ruddled, they seem to be wearing masks. One must look closely to discover the soft and living face beneath. But often the face is not soft, often it turns out to be imperfectly alive. The hardness and deadness are from within. They are the outward and visible signs of some emotional or instinctive disharmony, accepted as a chronic condition of being. We do not need a Freudian to tell us that this disharmony is often of a sexual nature.

11 So long as such disharmonies continue to exist, so long as there is good reason for sullen boredom, so long as human beings allow themselves to be possessed and hagridden by monomaniacal vices, the cult of beauty is destined to be ineffectual. Successful in prolonging the appearance of youth, or realizing or simulating the symptoms of health, the campaign inspired by this cult remains fundamentally a failure. Its operations do not touch the deepest source of beauty—the experiencing soul. It is not by improving skin foods and point rollers, by cheapening health motors and electrical hair removers, that the human race will be made beautiful; it is not even by improving health. All men and women will be beautiful only when the social arrangements give to every one of them an opportunity to live completely and harmoniously, when there is no environmental incentive and no hereditary tendency towards monomaniacal vice. In other words, all men and women will never be beautiful. But there might easily be fewer ugly human beings in the world than there are at present. We must be content with moderate hopes.

By Aldous Huxley
(1,701 words)

Words and Expressions

prodigious	/prəˈdɪdʒəs/	adj.	very large or great in a surprising or impressive way 巨大的，庞大的
bootlegging	/ˈbuːtlegɪŋ/	n.	illegally making or selling products such as alcohol or recordings（酒、唱片等）的非法制

Unit 8　Aesthetics

造(销售)

racketeering	/ˌrækɪ'tɪərɪŋ/	n.	when someone earns money through crime and illegal activities 敲诈,勒索,诈骗
upkeep	/'ʌpkiːp/	n.	the process of keeping something in good condition 保养,维修
ravishing	/'rævɪʃɪŋ/	adj.	very beautiful 非常美丽的,十分标致的 **ravishingly** adv. 迷人地,醉人地
hoarding	/'hɔːdɪŋ/	n.	a large board fixed high on a wall outside on which large advertisements are shown 大幅广告牌
retrench	/rɪ'trentʃ/	vi.	to spend less money (开支)紧缩
cult	/kʌlt/	n.	a fashionable belief, idea, or attitude that influences people's lives 时尚观念(观点,态度)
sphere	/sfɪə/	n.	a particular area of activity, work, knowledge, etc. 领域,范围
unenviable	/ʌn'envɪəbəl/	adj.	difficult and unpleasant 尴尬的,令人不快的
hitherto	/ˌhɪðə'tuː/	adv.	up to this time 迄今,至今,到目前为止
virtuous	/'vɜːtjuəs/	adj.	behaving in a very honest and moral way 正直的,品德高尚的
matron	/'meɪtrən/	n.	an older married woman (较年长的)已婚妇女
austere	/ɔː'stɪə/	adj.	plain and simple and without any decoration 朴实的,古朴的
aesthetic	/iːs'θetɪk/	adj.	connected with beauty and the study of beauty 美学的,审美的 **aesthetically** adv. 审美地,美学地
concede	/kən'siːd/	vt.	to admit that something is true or correct, although you wish it were not true (勉强地)承认
preoccupied	/priː'ɒkjʊpaɪd/	adj.	thinking about something a lot, with the result that you do not pay attention to other things 全神贯注的,入神的
concession	/kən'seʃən/	n.	something you let someone have in order to end an argument 让步
Manichaean	/ˌmænɪ'kiːən/	adj.	one who believes in a combination of religions

			that includes Gnostic Christianity, Buddhism, Zoroastrianism, etc. with a basic doctrine of a conflict between light and dark, matter being regarded as dark and evil 摩尼教的
ascetic	/ə'setɪk/	*adj.*	living without any physical pleasures or comforts, especially for religious reasons (尤指宗教原因而)苦行的, 禁欲的
vendor	/'vendə/	*n.*	someone who sells things, especially on the street 街头小贩
patentee	/ˌpeɪtən'tiː/	*n.*	the party that possesses or has been granted a patent 专利权所有人
lotion	/'ləʊʃən/	*n.*	a liquid mixture that you put on your skin or hair to clean, soften, or protect it 护理液
abdomen	/'æbdəmən/	*n.*	the part of the body between the chest and legs which contains the stomach, bowels, etc. 腹(部)
lamentable	/'læməntəbəl/	*adj.*	very unsatisfactory or disappointing 令人惋惜的, 可叹的
crone	/krəʊn/	*n.*	an ugly or unpleasant old woman 丑老太婆, 卑劣的老女人
slender	/'slendə/	*adj.*	thin in an attractive or graceful way 苗条的, 修长的
consummation	/ˌkɒnsʌ'meɪʃən/	*n.*	the point at which something is complete or perfect 圆满, 完满, 完成
paraffin-wax		*n.*	a soft white substance used for making candles, made from petroleum or coal 石蜡
apparatus	/ˌæpə'reɪtəs/	*n.*	the set of tools and machines that are used for a particular scientific, medical, or technical purpose 设备, 用具, 仪器
mimic	/'mɪmɪk/	*vt.*	to behave or operate in exactly the same way as something or someone else 模仿, 酷似
act upon			to do something because of another person's advice or order, or because you have received information or had an idea

Unit 8　Aesthetics

			按照……行事
porcelain	/'pɔːslɪn/	n.	a hard shiny white substance that is used for making expensive plates, cups, etc. 瓷，瓷器
tenant	/'tenənt/	vt.	to hold, inhabit or occupy a place（作为租赁者）居住
stinking	/'stɪŋkɪŋ/	adj.	having a very strong unpleasant smell 臭的，有（恶）臭味的
slime	/slaɪm/	n.	an unpleasant thick slippery substance （难看的或难闻的）黏质物
conversely	/'kɒnvɜːslɪ/	adv.	used when one situation is the opposite of another 另一方面，相反地
transfigure	/træns'fɪgə/	vt.	to change the way someone or something looks, especially so that they become more beautiful 使改观，美化
aesthetician	/ˌiːsθɪ'tɪʃən/	n.	one versed in the theory of beauty and artistic expression 美学家
downright	/'daʊnraɪt/	adv.	used to emphasize that something is completely bad or untrue 十足地，彻底
lascivious	/lə'sɪvɪəs/	adj.	showing strong sexual desire, or making someone feel this way 好色的，淫荡的 **lasciviousness** n. 好色，淫荡
avarice	/'ævərɪs/	n.	a desire to have a lot of money that is considered to be too strong 贪婪，贪得无厌
deadly	/'dedlɪ/	adj.	complete or total 完全的
negate	/nɪ'geɪt/	vt.	to state that something does not exist or is not true 否认，否定 **negation** n. 否认，否定
sullen	/'sʌlən/	adj.	angry and silent, especially because you feel life has been unfair to you 闷闷不乐的 **sullenness** n. 闷闷不乐，阴沉
boredom	/'bɔːdəm/	n.	the feeling you have when you are bored, or the quality of being boring 厌倦，厌烦
gait	/geɪt/	n.	the way someone walks 步态，步伐
listless	/'lɪstləs/	adj.	feeling tired and not interested in things 倦怠的，无精打采的 **listlessness** n. 倦怠，无精打采
exquisite	/'ekskwɪzɪt/	adj.	extremely beautiful and very delicately made 精致的，精美的

repulsive	/rɪˈpʌlsɪv/	adj.	extremely unpleasant, in a way that almost makes you feel sick 令人厌恶的,使人反感的
repellent	/rɪˈpelənt/	adj.	very unpleasant 令人厌恶的,让人反感的
whitewash	/ˈwaɪtwɒʃ/	vt.	to cover something with whitewash 用石灰水粉刷(某物)
ruddle	/ˈrʌdl/	vt.	to dye or mark with or as if with red ocher 用红土做记号
hagride	/ˈhæɡraɪd/	vt.	to afflict with worry, dread, need, or the like 困扰,折磨
monomaniacal	/ˌmɒnəʊməˈnaɪəkəl/	adj.	obsessed with a single subject or idea 对一事狂热的,偏执的
ineffectual	/ˌɪnɪˈfektʃuəl/	adj.	not having the ability, confidence, or personal authority to get things done 无威望的,无能力的,无信心的

Notes:

1. **The author—Aldous Huxley** (1894–1963), British novelist, poet, essayist and one of the most prominent members of the famous Huxley family. His most important work *Brave New World* (1932), a science fiction, foretells the doom of mankind due to the development of modern science and technology.
2. **Rolls-Royce** is a very expensive and prestigious car made by a British company.
3. **The Portrait of the Artist's Mother** is an oil painting by Vincent Van Gogh.
4. **Facial surgery** is surgical procedures that alter the human face to bring its features closer in shape and size to those of an average female human.
5. **Freudian** is a person who accepts the basic tenets of the psychoanalytic theories of Sigmund Freud, especially a psychiatrist or psychologist who applies Freudian theories and methods in conducting psychotherapy.

Reading Comprehension

I. Fill in the blanks according to the main idea of the text.

The one American industry unaffected by the general depression of trade is _____.
The modern _____ of beauty is not exclusively a function (in the mathematical

Unit 8　Aesthetics

sense) of wealth. What are the practical results of this modern cult of beauty? Are women more beautiful than they were? The campaign for more physical beauty seems to be _____. The beauty of a porcelain jar is a matter of _____. However, spiritual emptiness or ugliness in humans shows through. There is an ugliness of _____ (distressingly common among pretty women). All the deadly sins, indeed, have their own _____ of beauty. _____ in prolonging the appearance of youth, or realizing or simulating the symptoms of health, the campaign inspired by this cult remains _____.

II. **Answer the following questions.**
   1. Why does the author say that the American beauty industry is an industry unaffected by the general depression of trade?
   2. What are the reasons for so many people spending so much money on beauty according to the text?
   3. Why does the author say "the campaign for more physical beauty seems to be both a tremendous success and a lamentable failure" (Para.6)?
   4. What are the possible forms of psychological ugliness?
   5. What are the author's comments on the two American girls he met in North Africa?

III. **Paraphrase the following sentences within the context of the reading passage.**
   1. (Para.3) The diffusion of wealth—such as it is—now permits those of the poor who are less badly off than their fathers to do the same.
   2. (Para.4) The cult of beauty must therefore be symptomatic of changes than have taken place outside the economic sphere.
   3. (Para.5) We concede that the Matron is morally justified in being preoccupied with her personal appearance.
   4. (Para.7) The apparatus for mimicking the symptoms of health is now within the reach of every moderately prosperous person; the knowledge of the way in which real health can be achieved is growing, and will in time, no doubt, be universally acted upon.
   5. (Para.9) But the sullen boredom of which I have spoken was so deeply stamped into their fresh faces, their gait and gestures expressed so weary a listlessness, that it was unbearable to look at them.

IV. **Based on the text, decide whether the following statements are true or false. For false statements, write the facts in parentheses.**
   1. In Europe, people don't spend as much money on beauty as Americans do.
      (   )

2. The beauty industry is a total success nowadays because more women retain their youthful appearance to a greater age.
(   )

3. For a jar, the beauty lies in its outer self: shape, color, surface texture, etc.
(   )

4. In Paris, many women have ceased to look human at all because they have become painters.
(   )

5. The deepest source of beauty is the experiencing soul.
(   )

Vocabulary Exercises

I. **Fill in the blank in each sentence with a word or phrase from the box below. Make sure the appropriate form of the word is used.**

| prodigious | emphatic | prosperity | exclusive | simulating |
| preoccupy | genuinely | peculiar | exquisite | compare |

1. Success in the marketplace can be achieved by countering this _____ disadvantage with high quality products and service, at the right price.

2. _____ discovers vice, adversity discovers virtue.

3. Yet, and very often, even a single _____ conventional gesture performed in a moment of stillness can be tremendously effective.

4. But he was back in a few moments, having discarded his broom and provided himself, from some mysterious source, with an _____ bouquet of flowers

5. Happy is he who has laid up in his youth, and held fast in all fortune, a _____ and passionate love for reading.

6. The best conclusion that one can draw is that the objectives model provides a useful tool for certain purposes, especially the basic levels of knowledge and skill acquisition, but that should not be used _____ without judgement.

7. A more inquiring mind might also have drawn a different conclusion from the most _____ episode in the book, which concerns the death in Liege in 1922 of a young man called Kleine.

8. The new exhibition of organic gardening, for example, would take visitors first through an electronic display which would _____ a magnified section of the sub-soil with its

Unit 8   Aesthetics

organisms and cycles.

9. Mixed with an old-fashioned respect for education, this means that tens of thousands of new jobs have to be generated each year to keep up with the _____ output of mothers and universities.

10. Alex had spilled some juice on the table top and was drawing his finger through the orange puddle with enjoyment; Sarah seemed completely _____ by the last mouthful of toast.

II. **Fill in the blanks with the appropriate forms of the given words.**

1. Most liberals have thought that we, unfortunately, needed the firm yoke of the law to ensure that the interests of weaker individuals and groups were not _____ (substantial) harmed by the irresponsible attitudes and actions of the more powerful.

2. It expressed resentment at the failure of the government to _____ (concession) majority rule.

3. There's often a _____ (contradict) as to whether programmes are addressed to their actual or potential audiences or to a hypothetical audience.

4. By his campaign for Fox, Lewis probably destroyed his own chances of promotion in the university, even though he was very obviously the most _____ (distinguish) member of the English faculty.

5. Any sensitive reading of a story demands a feeling for how far one is permitted to push the significance of its details, and an _____ (aware) of those questions that can properly be asked of it.

6. He makes up for the _____ (empty) of his own life by creating a dramatic emotional triangle for these puppets of his imagination.

7. Yet I do not doubt that Aristotle and St Paul have done more to frame the Prime Minister's mind and therefore the _____ (destined) of her government than any other thinkers who have been dead for less than 1,900 years.

8. The new legislation effectively ensures that badgers are as well protected by law as are species on the verge of _____ (extinct).

9. But the big rises in indebtedness came in industries where cash flow is more stable, such as public utilities, services and the _____ (manufacturer) of non-durables such as food and tobacco.

10. Founded by workers in 1886, the club enjoyed _____ (moderately) success in the next decade, playing in the all-red shirts originally donated by Nottingham Forest.

III. **Choose the word or phrase that best completes each of the following sentences.**

1. Economic studies of cleaning have shown that manual labour accounts for some 89 percent of energy costs which themselves account for _____ 96 per cent of the total

cleaning bill.
   A. as large as   B. as little as   C. as many as   D. as much as
2. In _____ literature would inevitably play a substantial part in any such course, the students reading it would learn the appropriate cultural codes rather than being expected to know them already.
   A. so far as   B. as far as   C. so much as   D. as much as
3. It encompasses a great diversity of questions around film as an instrument of dominant ideology, or, _____, as a tool for political resistance and subversion.
   A. furthermore   B. while   C. conversely   D. oppositely
4. Above all his move means leaving behind the double Olympic gold medallist _____ a number of other promising young British oarsmen.
   A. also   B. still   C. as well as   D. moreover
5. All that shows _____ reasonable doubt that eggs were not responsible for the increase in food poisoning
   A. beyond   B. surpass   C. for   D. out of

Translation Exercises

I. **Translate each of the following sentences into English, using the word or phrase given in the brackets.**

1. 他能在几分钟内记住数十个单词,我们都惊奇于他惊人的记忆力。(prodigious)

2. 这些设计师自1993年成立他们的工作室以来,一直专注于建筑设计和电子传媒。(preoccupied with)

3. 告诉成年的孩子遵照经验行事是行不通的,一方面因为他们不相信这些话,另一方面因为经历错误挫折是教育非常重要的一部分。(act upon)

4. 实践证明角色扮演是模拟实际生活情景的有效途径。(simulate)

5. 要把醉人的巴黎市全景尽览无遗,艾菲尔铁塔的瞭望台是最佳观赏点。(ravishing)

6. 他强调他对下属明察秋毫,无所不知。(emphatically)

Unit 8 Aesthetics

II. **Translate the following paragraph into English.**

人们对美持有不同观点，美的标准随时代和文化的不同而变化。传统和时尚如同社会本身是变化的，是与时代同步的。在19世纪的欧洲，男人们喜欢羊毛披肩，而在21世纪的今天，很难想象这样的穿着会有吸引力。现代社会，文化依然是决定我们审美观的重要因素。在一些国家，年轻女子为准备婚礼而减肥，而在其他文化中，身材略微丰满圆润才更迷人。

III. **Translate the following paragraph into Chinese.**

So long as such disharmonies continue to exist, so long as there is good reason for sullen boredom, so long as human beings allow themselves to be possessed and hagridden by monomaniacal vices, the cult of beauty is destined to be ineffectual…. All men and women will be beautiful only when the social arrangements give to every one of them an opportunity to live completely and harmoniously, when there is no environmental incentive and no hereditary tendency towards monomaniacal vice. In other words, all men and women will never be beautiful. But there might easily be fewer ugly human beings in the world than there are at present. We must be content with moderate hopes.

Language Appreciation

I. Read the text carefully, then pick out the sentences that you think are well-written. Pay close attention to the italicized words or phrases of the following sentences. Try to appreciate the way in which the author expresses his/her ideas. Learn how to use them in your own writing.

1. …perhaps it will transform them into the likeness of those ravishing creatures who smile *so rosily* and *creamily*, so *peachily* and *pearlily*, from every hoarding..
2. The crone of the future will be golden, curly and *cherry-lipped, neat-ankled* and slender.

II. Read aloud and recite paragraph 11.

III. Stylistics Study

Short Sentence—A Stylistic Miracle

Examples: 1) *They arrived, the carriage turned, the step was let down, and Mr. Elton, spruce, black and smiling, was with them instantly.*
—From Jane Austen, *Emma*

2) *The ball was over—and the breakfast was soon over too; the last kiss was given, and William was gone.*
—From Jane Austen, *Mansfield Park*

Generally speaking, a series of short coordinate sentences can produce a succession of fast-moving images to make their points with minimal use of language. Jane Austen is one of those great writers who often used short sentences to good effects.

Example: *...the figure of a man on horseback drew her eyes to the window. He stopt at their gate. It was a gentleman, it was Colonel Brandon himself. Now she should hear more; —and she trembled in expectation of it. But—it was not Colonel Brandon—neither his air —nor his height. Were it possible, she should say it must be Edward. She looked again. He had just dismounted; —she could not be mistaken; —it was Edward. She moved away and sat down. "He comes from Mr. Pratt's purposely to see us. I will be calm; I will be mistress of myself."*
—From Jane Austen, *Sense and Sensibility*

A succession of short sentences is also used for describing mental activities to mark a period of excitement or suspense.

Example: *I came, I saw, I conquered.*
   —Julius Caesar

A succession of short sentences is sometimes used for rhythm, in order to create a certain atmosphere for the reader to experience more vividly.

Text II

Sport and Physical Education As a Means of Aesthetic Education

Pre-reading Questions

1. When a superb athlete makes an amazing move (a great shot, a nice steal, a flawless stroke, etc.), do you consider that to be "beautiful?" Why or why not?
2. Choose an athlete that you admire. Describe some of his/her physical movements while engaging in his/her sport.

Unit 8 Aesthetics

1 Aesthetics, the study of the philosophy of beauty, is not commonly thought of as a factor in the sporting education. It can be surprising therefore to find that sport and physical education provide innumerable opportunities for increasing aesthetic awareness.

2 An aesthetic education can be attempted through the medium of the senses — visual, musical, verbal and physical. Gymnastics, at Olympic level, has become "artistic gymnastics" calling for musical feeling, imagination, and creative originality. Diving, skating, and other physical skills which demand a highly refined kinaesthetic sense, can also reach heights which are generally accepted as truly artistic. However, there are millions of ordinary people who do not watch the more sophisticated sports; neither do they attend the theatre, opera, symphony, or art gallery. They do watch football, the male element anyway, literally in their millions. Surveys, apparently show a large female, as well as male, tele-viewing audience for Rugby League. It is in this field of "mass sports", of which association football is the most popular, that the most gigantic possibilities for an aesthetic education lie.

3 A number of artists have pondered on the relationship of sport to art. As to an artist, a haystack is always a haystack yet each one is different, so in sport "each match pattern and design is unique". Deyneka, a Soviet painter, writes, "I love sport; I can spend hours watching runners, swimmers, skiers. It seems to me that sport, like everything beautiful, ennobles man." Laurent describes the affinity of feeling between the athlete and the artist. The athlete, "modelling his body by repeated drilling", shares the feelings of the artist, concerned as he is, "with the need to correct a faulty line, to attenuate a corpulence, despairing ever to acquire the line or the curve so ardently desired".

4 Coubertin, the founder of the modern Olympic Games, in his address to the Consultative Conference of Arts, Letters and Sports, in 1906, was passionately concerned that the fine arts and sports should not be alienated one from the other. "We are gathered," he said, "to celebrate a singular ceremony to reunite in the bonds of legitimate wedlock a long divorced couple—muscle and

mind." The programme of this Conference embraced architecture, dramatic art, choreography (processions, grouped movements, etc.), decorations, letters, music, painting, and sculpture. The immense love Coubertin had for sport is revealed in his "Ode to Sport".

"O Sport you are beauty! You, the architect of this house, the human body, which may become abject or sublime according to whether it is defiled by base passions or cherished with wholesome endeavour. There can be no beauty without poise and proportion and you are the incomparable master of both, for you create harmony, you fill movement with rhythm, you make strength gracious, and you lend power to supple things."

5   Within physical education there has been some heart-searching in recent years. Nasmark discusses how gymnastics can help to cultivate aesthetic taste. "He who holds himself straight, and moves well, controls his body and feels it as something which has been perfected. He experiences what may be regarded as an aesthetic feeling." Nasmark suggests that three fundamentals should always appear in gymnastics teaching—good order, good movement, and joy—and that these can contribute to an aesthetic education. Moreover a body which "looks good and moves well" is pleasing to others; the teacher encourages the search for movements which lack tension, which contain both "beauty and utility"...

6   Most sports have the straightforward, uncomplicated objective of scoring goals or points; any aesthetic element is incidental to the main aim. In some sports, such as gymnastics, diving, and skating, one major aim is aesthetic—to create a "good" or "artistic" movement. The gymnastic judge is given official guidance to look for "general beauty", "elegance", "rhythm and precision", "harmony" and "perfect artistic execution". His diving counterpart must look for "grace". In skating, marks are awarded for technical merit and for "artistic impression"; among the terms used in this latter section are: "harmonious composition of the whole"; "conformity with music"; and "carriage". On the trampoline a good performer must satisfy requirements such as "continuity and flow", "symmetrical placing of body segments", and "aesthetic manner", according to the "established standards of art". A partial survey of several movement "systems" shows that symmetry and asymmetry, rhythm, balance, harmony and

economy of effort, are among the most-mentioned qualities used in assessing what is a "good" movement.

7   It is not, however, only in doing or in teaching sports and other movement activities that an aesthetic experience can be secured. A majority of mankind apparently enjoy watching sport. Some pundits throw up their hands in horror bewailing the fact that "we are becoming a nation of onlookers". This is a strange reaction since few people dispute the value of the gallery, the museum, the professional theatre, in stimulating mass interest in the recognized arts. Similarly the stadium performances of the elite sports teams can be used to stimulate mass interest in sports—although perhaps in other sports more appropriate to the different ages and abilities of the spectator.

8   The good spectator is not a pawn in a passive culture; he is part of the active performance; by his efforts the player is uplifted. The French actor J. L. Barrault describes how the actor and the sportsman share several experiences; both get stage fright, both are prone to "swollen heads", both are weighed down by the presence of the audience when they are inexperienced and both then learn to use the presence of the audience to lift their own performances to previously unattained heights. Some researchers say that the sports spectator is not "recognized for his culture" yet "aesthetic emotion is one motive for watching sport". The match is embellished by ceremonials, by cheering and handshaking rituals, by flags, colours and distinctive dress. There can be an atmosphere of solemn magnificence and of colour and movement. The "sportive fight" must itself contain chivalry and other positive ethical elements. Those of us who follow sport know that the artistry and genius of a soccer player of the calibre of Eastham or Matthews can draw forth the appreciative "Oohs" and "Ahs" of tens and thousands of spectators; this is for them perhaps the only avenue in which they can experience, and sometimes create beauty.

9   Like fairplay and sportsmanship, a sense of aesthetic awareness must be deliberately awakened—it is not a natural concomitant of physical activities. For women, with the current emphasis on dance and dance-like movements the task is easier. For men, the first task is to show that aesthetic should not be a synonym of feminine. Whilst dance forms could of course further enrich the male's movement experience, much more could be done immediately to draw out the aesthetic elements from the dynamic sports which he currently

practises.

By D. W. J. Anthony (abridged)
(1,144 words)

Reading Comprehension

I. Answer the following questions with the information you read from the passage.

1. Which field do the most gigantic possibilities for an aesthetic education lie in?
2. How do you interpret De Coubertin's attitude towards fine arts and sports?
3. How does a judge evaluate a gymnastic performance according to the text? How about skating or diving?
4. What are the similarities between an actor and a sportsman according to J. L. Barrault?
5. Is it easy to awaken sportsmen's aesthetic awareness? Why or why not?

II. Topics for discussion and reflection.

1. Are chivalry and sportsmanship necessary characteristics in being an athlete? Why or why not?
2. Why do you think that so many ceremonies are associated with sports?

Exercises for Integrated Skills

I. Dictation

    Listen to the following passage. The passage will be read to you four times. During the first reading, which will be read at normal speed, listen and try to understand the meaning. For the second and third readings, the passage will be read sentence by sentence, or phrase by phrase, with intervals of 15 to 20 seconds. The last reading will be done at normal speed again and during this time check your work. You will then be given 2 minutes to check through your work a second time.

Unit 8 Aesthetics

II. Cloze

The human figure ___1___ any other object in nature exhibits an equally balanced ___2___ of fitness, strength, and beauty; consequently, there are three ___3___ classes of inquirers into the nature of this great work of creation—the anatomical, the physiological, and the aesthetical. But ___4___ its anatomy and physiology ___5___ considered amongst the most useful branches of scientific education, the nature of its aesthetical developments has remained a mystery. Although the ___6___ which govern beauty are in themselves perfect, ___7___ they operate throughout nature in the production of an infinite variety. It is this variety which has led some writers to doubt the ___8___ of a definite law of beauty, and to advance the doctrine ___9___ beauty is not a quality in the object itself, but a feeling of admiration ___10___ in the mind of the observer.

1. A. less than   B. not more than   C. more than   D. no more than
2. A. mix   B. combination   C. connection   D. link
3. A. distinct   B. diverse   C. distinguished   D. various
4. A. since   B. while   C. /   D. for
5. A. have long been   B. have long   C. was long   D. is long being
6. A. perspective   B. potential   C. principle   D. premise
7. A. yet   B. moreover   C. for   D. despite
8. A. emergence   B. occurrence   C. existence   D. appearance
9. A. which   B. that   C. for   D. of
10. A. originating   B. originated   C. having originated   D. being originated

Oral Activities

1. Manners, etiquette, and hygiene often come into play when evaluating someone's overall aesthetic appearance. Give some examples of how bad habits, impolite, rude behavior can negatively affect one's aesthetics.
2. You've been giving the task of writing a chapter in a parenting handbook. In groups of 3-4, list at least 10 lessons you think a parent should teach a child and choose one to elaborate on.

Writing Practice

Composition Writing

There is an increasing interest in watching various sports activities from an aesthetic point of view. Choose a specific sport or a work of art related to sport, (i.e. the famous Greek *Discus Thrower* sculpture). Write a composition of about 200 words, describing the beauty you have seen through it.

Unit 9 Humor

Warm-up Activities

1. What makes something funny?
2. What are some different kinds of humor found in books, movies, and everyday conversations?

Text I

On the Sense of Humor

Pre-reading Questions

1. How can you tell if a person has a good sense of humor?
2. Some say that you shouldn't take yourself too seriously and that being able to laugh at yourself is an important quality to have. Do you agree or disagree?

1   I doubt whether the importance of humor has been fully appreciated, or the possibility of its use in changing the quality and character of our entire cultural life—the place of humor in politics, humor in scholarship, and humor in life. Because its function is chemical, rather than physical, it alters the basic texture of our thought and experience. Its importance in national life we can take for granted. The inability to laugh cost the former Kaiser Wilhelm an empire, or as an American might say, cost the German people billions of dollars. Wilhelm Hohenzollern probably could laugh in his private life, but he always looked so terribly impressive with his upturned mustache in public, as if he was always angry with somebody. And then the quality of his laughter and

the things he laughed at—laughter at victory, at success, at getting on top of others—were just as important factors in determining his life fortune. Germany lost the war because Wilhelm Hohenzollern did not know when to laugh, or what to laugh at. His dreams were not restrained by laughter.

2   It seems to me the worst comment on dictatorships is that presidents of democracies can laugh, while dictators always look so serious—with a protruding jaw, a determined chin, and a pouched lower lip, as if they were doing something terribly important and the world could not be saved, except by them. Franklin D. Roosevelt often smiles in public—good for him, and good for the American people who like to see their president smile. But where are the smiles of the European dictators? Or don't their people want to see them smile? Or must they indeed look either frightened, or dignified, or angry, or in any case look frightfully serious in order to keep themselves in the saddle? ...

3   We are not indulging in idle fooling now, discussing the smiles of dictators; it is terribly serious when our rulers do not smile, because they have got all the guns. On the other hand, the tremendous importance of humor in politics can be realized only when we picture for ourselves a world of joking rulers. Send, for instance, five or six of the world's best humorists to an international conference, and give them the plenipotentiary powers of autocrats, and the world will be saved. As humor necessarily goes with good sense and the reasonable spirit, plus some exceptionally subtle powers of the mind in detecting inconsistencies and follies and bad logic, and as this is the highest form of human intelligence, we may be sure that each nation will thus be represented at the conference by its sanest and soundest mind. Let Shaw represent Ireland, Stephen Leacock represent Canada; G. K. Chesterton is dead, but P. G. Wodehouse or Aldous Huxley may represent England. Will Rogers is dead, otherwise he would make a fine diplomat representing the U.S.; we can have in his stead Robert Benchley or Heywood Broun. There will be others from Italy and France and Germany and Russia. Send these people to a conference on the eve of a great war, and see if they can start a European war, no

matter how hard they try. Can you imagine this bunch of international diplomats starting a war or even plotting for one? The sense of humor forbids it. All people are too serious and half-insane when they declare a war against another people. They are so sure that they are right and that God is on their side. The humorists, gifted with better horse-sense, don't think so. You will find George Bernard Shaw shouting that Ireland is wrong, and a Berlin cartoonist protesting that the mistake is all theirs, and Heywood Broun claiming the largest share of bungling for America, while Stephen Leacock in the chair makes a general apology for mankind, gently reminding us that in the matter of stupidity and sheer foolishness no nation can claim itself to be the superior of others. How in the name of humor are we going to start a war under these conditions?

4   For who have started wars for us? The ambitious, the able, the clever, the scheming, the cautious, the sagacious, the haughty, the over-patriotic, the people inspired with the desire to "serve" mankind, people who have a "career" to carve and an "impression" to make on the world, who expect and hope to look down the ages from the eyes of a bronze figure sitting on a bronze horse in some square. Curiously, the able, the clever, and the ambitious and haughty are at the same time the most cowardly and muddleheaded, lacking in the courage and depth and subtlety of the humorists. They are forever dealing with trivialities, while the humorists with their greater sweep of mind can envisage larger things. As it is, a diplomat who does not whisper in a low voice and look properly scared and intimidated and correct and cautious is no diplomat at all... But we don't even have to have a conference of international humorists to save the world. There is a sufficient stock of this desirable commodity called a sense of humor in all of us. When Europe seems to be on the brink of a catastrophic war, we may still send to the conferences our worst diplomats, the most "experienced" and self-assured, the most ambitious, the most whispering, most intimidated and correct and properly scared, even the most anxious to "serve" mankind. If it be required that, at the opening of every morning and afternoon session, ten minutes be devoted to the showing of a Mickey Mouse picture, at which all the diplomats are compelled to be present, any war can still be averted.

5   This I conceive to be the chemical function of humor: to change the character of our thought. I rather think that it goes to the very root of culture, and opens a way to the coming of the Reasonable Age in the future human world. For humanity I can visualize no greater ideal than that of the Reasonable Age. For that after all is the only important thing, the arrival of a race of men imbued with a greater reasonable spirit, with greater prevalence of good sense, simple thinking, a peaceable temper and a cultured outlook. The ideal world for mankind will not be a rational world, nor a perfect world in any sense, but a world in which imperfections are readily perceived and quarrels reasonably settled. For mankind, that is frankly the best we can hope for and the noblest dream that we can reasonably expect to come true. This seems to imply several things: a simplicity of thinking, a gaiety in philosophy and a subtle common sense, which will make this reasonable culture possible. Now it happens that subtle common sense, gaiety of philosophy and simplicity of thinking are characteristic of humor and must arise from it.

6   It is difficult to imagine this kind of a new world because our present world is so different. On the whole, our life is too complex, our scholarship too serious, our philosophy too somber, and our thoughts too involved. This seriousness and this involved complexity of our thought and scholarship make the present world such an unhappy one today.

7   Now it must be taken for granted that simplicity of life and thought is the highest and sanest ideal for civilization and culture, that when a civilization loses simplicity and the sophisticated do not return to unsophistication, civilization becomes increasingly full of troubles and degenerates. Man then becomes the slave of the ideas, thoughts, ambitions and social systems that are his own product. Mankind, overburdened with this load of ideas and ambitions and social systems, seems unable to rise above them. Luckily, however, there is a power of the human mind which can transcend all these ideas, thoughts and ambitions and treat them with a smile, and this power is the subtlety of the humorist. Humorists handle thoughts and ideas as golf or billiard champions handle their balls, or as cowboy champions handle their lariats. There is an ease, a sureness, a lightness of touch, that comes from mastery. After all, only he who handles his ideas lightly is master of his ideas, and only he who is master of his ideas is not enslaved by them. Seriousness, after all, is only a sign of effort, and effort is a sign of imperfect mastery. A serious writer is awkward

Unit 9   Humor

and ill at ease in the realm of ideas as a nouveau riche is awkward, ill at ease and self-conscious in society. He is serious because he has not come to feel at home with his ideas.

8   Now it is natural that the sense of humor nourishes this simplicity of thinking. Generally, a humorist keeps closer touch with facts, while a theorist dwells more on ideas, and it is only when one is dealing with ideas in themselves that his thoughts get incredibly complex. The humorist, on the other hand, indulges in flashes of common sense or wit, which show up the contradictions of our ideas with reality with lightning speed, thus greatly simplifying matters. Constant contact with reality gives the humorist a bounce, and also a lightness and subtlety. All forms of pose, sham, learned nonsense, academic stupidity and social humbug are politely but effectively shown the door. Man becomes wise because man becomes subtle and witty. All is simple. All is clear. It is for this reason that I believe a sane and reasonable spirit, characterized by simplicity of living and thinking, can be achieved only when there is a very much greater prevalence of humorous thinking.

By Lin Yutang (abridged)

(1,615 words)

Words and Expressions

upturned	/ˈʌpˈtɜːnd/	adj.	pointing or turning upwards 朝上翘的, 向上翻的
restrain	/rɪsˈtreɪn/	vt.	to control or limit something that is increasing too much 控制, 限制(趋于增长的东西)
dictatorship	/dɪkˈteɪtəʃɪp/	n.	government by a ruler who has complete power 独裁统治, 专政, 独裁政府
protrude	/prəˈtruːd/	vi.	to stick out from somewhere 突出, 伸出
determined	/dɪˈtɜːmɪnd/	adj.	showing determination, especially in a difficult situation 意志坚定的, 有决心的
dignify	/ˈdɪɡnɪfaɪ/	vt.	to make something or someone seem better or more important than they really are, especially by using a particular word to describe them 使有尊严, 抬高身价
frightfully	/ˈfraɪtfʊlɪ/	adv.	very 非常, 十分

in the saddle			in a position in which you have power or authority 在位,掌权
idle	/ˈaɪdl/	adj.	not serious, or not done with any definite intention 无价值的,无意义的
plenipotentiary	/ˌplenɪpəˈtenʃərɪ/	adj.	conferring or bestowing full power 全权大使的,全权代表的
autocrat	/ˈɔːtəukræt/	n.	a ruler who has complete power over a country 独裁者,专制者
exceptionally	/ɪkˈsepʃənlɪ/	adv.	extremely 极其
inconsistency	/ˌɪnkənˈsɪstənsɪ/	n.	when someone keeps changing their behaviour, reactions, etc. so that other people become confused 变化无常
folly	/ˈfɒlɪ/	n.	a very stupid thing to do, especially one that is likely to have serious results 蠢事,荒唐事
sane	/seɪn/	adj.	reasonable and using or showing sensible thinking 明智的,思路清晰的
do something in somebody's stead			to do something that someone else usually does or is going to do 代替某人做某事
insane	/ɪnˈseɪn/	adj.	completely stupid or crazy, often in a way that is dangerous 疯狂的,愚蠢的
horse sense		n.	sensible judgement gained from experience 常识
bungling	/ˈbʌŋɡəlɪŋ/	adj.	awkward, clumsy 笨拙的
sagacious	/səˈɡeɪʃəs/	adj.	able to understand and judge things very well 明智的,洞察事理的
haughty	/ˈhɔːtɪ/	adj.	behaving in a proud, unfriendly way 傲慢的,目中无人的,倨傲不逊的
muddleheaded	/ˌmʌdlˈhedɪd/	adj.	confused or not able to think clearly 头脑糊涂的
subtlety	/ˈsʌtltɪ/	n.	a thought, idea, or detail that is important but difficult to notice or understand 微妙的思想,(思想中的)细微之处
triviality	/ˌtrɪvɪˈælɪtɪ/	n.	something that is not important at all 琐事
envisage	/ɪnˈvɪzɪdʒ/	vt.	to think that something is likely to happen in the future 展望,设想
intimidated	/ɪnˈtɪmɪdeɪtɪd/	adj.	feeling worried and lacking confidence because of the situation you are in or the people you are with 胆怯的,畏缩的
commodity	/kəˈmɒdɪtɪ/	n.	a useful quality or thing 有用的特性

Unit 9 Humor

catastrophic	/ˌkætəˈstrɔfik/	adj.	extremely harmful, bringing physical or financial ruin 灾难的
self-assured	/ˌselfəˈʃuəd/	adj.	calm and confident about what you are doing 自信的
avert	/əˈvɜːt/	vt.	to prevent something unpleasant from happening 避免，防止
visualize	/ˈvɪzjuəlaɪz/	vt.	to form a picture of someone or something in one's mind 设想，想象
peaceable	/ˈpiːsəbəl/	adj.	being calm, without any violence or fighting 温和的，不爱争吵的，和睦的
gaiety	/ˈgeɪəti/	n.	a feeling of cheerfulness and fun 快乐，高兴
unsophisticated	/ˌʌnsəˈfɪstɪkeɪtɪd/	adj.	not having all the features of more modern ones 简单的，不复杂的 **unsophistication** n. 简单
billiards	/ˈbɪljədz/	n.	a game played on a cloth-covered table in which balls are hit with a cue (=a long stick) against each other and into pockets at the edge of the table 台球 **billiard** adj. 台球的
lariat	/ˈlærɪət/	n.	a rope with one end tied in a circle, used to catch cattle and horses, especially in the western U.S. 套索；系绳
enslave	/ɪnˈsleɪv/	vt.	to control 束缚，制约
nouveau riche		adj.	having only recently become rich and spending a lot of money, used to show disapproval 新贵，暴发户
self-conscious	/ˌselfˈkɒnʃəs/	adj.	worried and embarrassed about what you look like or what other people think of you 不自然的，害羞的
dwell on/upon something			to think or talk for too long about something, especially something unpleasant 老是想着，唠叨（令人不愉快的事情）
lightning	/ˈlaɪtnɪŋ/	adj.	extremely quick 闪电般的
sham	/ʃæm/	n.	someone or something that is not what they are claimed to be 伪善，欺骗，虚伪，假象
humbug	/ˈhʌmbʌg/	n.	something that is intended to trick or deceive people 诡计，花招
witty	/ˈwɪti/	adj.	using words in a clever and amusing way 说话风趣的，妙趣横生的

Notes:

1. **The author—Lin Yutang** (1895–1976) was a Chinese writer and inventor whose polished style in both Chinese and English made him one of the most influential writers of his generation. His compilations and translations of classic Chinese texts into English were bestsellers in the West. His important works include *My Country and My People* (1935), *The Importance of Living* (1937), *Moment in Peking* (1939), and *Chinese-English Dictionary of Modern Usage* (1973). He was nominated for the Nobel Prize in Literature several times in the 1970s.

2. **Kaiser Wilhelm** is a common reference to two German emperors: Wilhelm I (1797–1888), King of Prussia, became the first Kaiser (Emperor) of a united Germany; Wilhelm II (1859–1941), was Kaiser during World War I and abdicated the throne in 1918.

3. **Franklin D. Roosevelt** (1882–1945) was the 32nd President of the United States and a central figure in world events during the mid-20th century, leading the United States during a time of worldwide economic crisis and world war.

4. **George Bernard Shaw** (1856–1950) was an Irish playwright who wrote more than 60 plays. Nearly all his writings deal sternly with prevailing social problems, but have a vein of comedy to make their stark themes more palatable.

5. **Stephen Leacock** (1869–1944) was a Canadian writer and economist.

6. **G. K. Chesterton** (1874–1936) was one of the most influential English writers of the 20th century. His diverse output included philosophy, poetry, journalism, biography, fantasy, detective fiction, etc.

7. **P. G. Wodehouse** (1881–1975) was an English writer whose body of works include novels, collections of short stories, and musical theatre.

8. **Will Rogers** (1879–1935) was a Cherokee cowboy, comedian, humorist, social commentator, and actor. He was the father of U.S. Representative and WWII veteran Will Rogers, Jr.

9. **Robert Benchley** (1889–1945) was an American humorist best known for his work as a newspaper columnist and film actor.

10. **Heywood Broun** (1888–1939) was an American journalist who worked as a sportswriter, newspaper columnist, and editor in New York City. He founded the American Newspaper Guild, now known as The Newspaper Guild.

Unit 9   Humor

Reading Comprehension

I.   **Summarize the text in about 100 hundred words:**

_____
_____
_____
_____
_____
_____
_____
_____

II. **Answer the following questions.**
   1. Who was Wilhelm Hohenzollern? Why did Germany lose the war?
   2. What would happen if George Bernard Shaw representing Ireland, Stephen Leacock representing Canada, and Aldous Huxley representing England, were going to a conference on the eve of a great war?
   3. Who started wars for us according to the author?
   4. What makes the present world such an unhappy one today?
   5. How does a humorist differ from a theorist? Explain.

III. **Paraphrase the following sentences within the context of the reading passage.**
   1. (Para.4) They are forever dealing with trivialities, while the humorists with their greater sweep of mind can envisage larger things.
   2. (Para.4) If it be required that, at the opening of every morning and afternoon session, ten minutes be devoted to the showing of a Mickey Mouse picture, at which all the diplomats are compelled to be present, any war can still be averted.
   3. (Para.5) For that after all is the only important thing, the arrival of a race of men imbued with a greater reasonable spirit, with greater prevalence of good sense, simple thinking, a peaceable temper and a cultured outlook.
   4. (Para.8) A serious writer is awkward and ill at ease in the realm of ideas as a nouveau riche is awkward, ill at ease and self-conscious in society.
   5. (Para.9) The humorist, on the other hand, indulges in flashes of common sense or wit, which show up the contradictions of our ideas with reality with lightning speed, thus greatly simplifying matters.

IV. Based on the text, decide whether the following statements are true or false. For false statements, write the facts in parentheses.

1. The function of humor is chemical rather than physical, and it can change our thoughts and experience.
   (   )

2. From the author's viewpoint, the worst comment on dictatorship is that leaders of democracies can laugh, while dictators can't.
   (   )

3. Subtle common sense, gaiety of philosophy and simplicity of thinking are characteristic of humor, yet these characteristics don't necessarily come from humor.
   (   )

4. The humorists can't transcend the load of ideas, thoughts and ambitions, yet they can still treat them with a smile.
   (   )

5. We can take the importance of humor in national life for granted.
   (   )

Vocabulary Exercises

I. Fill in the blank in each sentence with a word or phrase from the box below. Make sure the appropriate form of the word is used.

| plot | inconsistency | transcend | envisage |
| frightfully | intimidate | dictatorship | degenerate |

1. It has also drawn support from several former high-ranking officials who were responsible for setting United States policy in Central America in the 1980s and '90s, when the region was struggling to break with the military_____ and guerrilla insurgencies that defined the cold war.

2. With each step, he was slowly distancing himself from the _____ stress of a traumatic experience.

3. A review of the hospital found _____ with reporting deaths and problems with patient safety, including surgeons performing procedures they were not authorized to do.

4. Rumors have swirled for weeks about government allegations that General Fonseka had _____ to overthrow the government or assassinate Mr. Rajapaksa with the help of army deserters loyal to him.

Unit 9 Humor

5. To curb the proliferation of nuclear weapons, the United States and Russia said during the weekend that they hoped to conclude a new agreement that would _____ deep cuts in land-based strategic missiles.
6. We pledge to each other, and to our fellow believers, that no power on earth, be it cultural or political, will _____ us into silence or acquiescence.
7. Street crime in the battered industrial center has _____ into something like chaos now that its youth gangs are fully armed and far more dangerous.
8. The beauty of her songs has _____ words and language.

II. **Fill in the blanks with the appropriate forms of the given words.**
   1. She seemed too _____ (restrain) to talk about anything other than the weather.
   2. Secretary of State Hillary Rodham Clinton and European leaders urged Nigeria's government on Thursday to adhere to its Constitution as the nation faced a "period of uncertainty" in the absence of its president, who is ill. That message came as a former military _____ (dictatorship) and a former civilian president joined the growing number of prominent Nigerians calling on President Umaru Yar'Adua to cede power to the nation's vice president.
   3. To courthouse officials, the unattended bag was potentially dangerous. When they put it through a scanning machine, they saw a laptop computer with wires _____ (protrude) from it, prompting them to declare a security alert that required the building's evacuation.
   4. I _____ (picture) myself cradling my miracle baby, talking to my imaginary husband.
   5. Devoted to art, music and theory, and more specifically to the _____ (subtlety) ways in which these disciplines intersect, the journal has so far been published twice, in limited editions.

III. **Replace the italicized words or phrases with simple, everyday words.**
   1. ..., and give them the plenipotentiary powers of *autocrats,* ... (   )
   2. ..., we may be sure that each nation will thus be represented at the conference by its *sanest* and soundest mind. (   )
   3. The ambitious, the able, the clever, the scheming, the cautious, the sagacious, the *haughty*, the over-patriotic, ... (   )
   4. ... , any war can still be *averted*. (   )
   5. ..., but a world in which *imperfections* are readily perceived and quarrels reasonably settled. (   )

IV. **Choose the word or phrase that best completes each of the following sentences.**
   1. For a group of affluent wine lovers, buying a French vineyard is similar to indulging _____ a yacht or a villa in the south of France.
      A. in   B. to   C. of   D. from

2. There is no doubt that we must be patient, avoid setting unrealistic deadlines and above all, keep in mind that peace, _____ difficult to achieve and imperfect, is better than perpetual conflict.
   A. whatever   B. no matter what   C. no matter how   D. how no matter
3. The cyclists in contention for the yellow jersey are the ones gifted _____ enough aerobic strength to motor through the mountain stages, but also have enough power to be fast in the time trials.
   A. with   B. at   C. on   D. over

Translation Exercises

I. Translate each of the following sentences into English, using the word or phrase given in the brackets.

1. 他设法抓住了悬崖上向外伸出的岩石。(protrude)

2. 他是不可能参加这个项目了,而要委任一个代替他的人也同样困难。(in one's stead)

3. 很难想象罗纳尔多会披上其他俱乐部的战袍。(envisage)

4. 过去的就让它过去吧,老是想着你过去的不幸毫无意义。(dwell on)

5. 有多少动物在以科学名义进行的残酷实验中丧生,谁也无法说清楚。(in the name of)

II. Translate the following paragraph into English.

幽默感被认为是人类最重要的特征,因为它和笑声结合在一起,而笑又是和幸福联系在一起。勇气、决心、创造力是我们和其他生命形式共享的特征,而幽默感是人类所独有的。如果幸福是我们生活的伟大目标,那么幽默感就是开启幸福的钥匙。

III. Translate the following paragraph into Chinese.

The ideal world for mankind will not be a rational world, nor a perfect world in any sense, but a world in which imperfections are readily perceived and quarrels reasonably settled. For mankind, that is frankly the best we can hope for and the noblest dream that we can reasonably expect to come true. This seems to imply several things: a simplicity of thinking, a gaiety in philosophy and a subtle common sense, which will make this reasonable culture possible. Now it happens that subtle common sense, gaiety of philosophy and simplicity of thinking are characteristic of humor and must arise from it.

Unit 9 Humor

Language Appreciation

I. Read the text carefully, then pick out the sentences that you think are well-written. Pay close attention to the italicized words or phrases of the following sentences. Try to appreciate the way in which the author expresses his/her ideas. Learn how to use them in your own writing.

1. *It seems to me* the worst comment on dictatorships is that presidents of democracies can laugh, while dictators always look so serious—with *a protruding jaw, a determined chin*, and *a pouched lower lip*, as if they were doing something terribly important and the world could not be saved, except by them..

2. Generally, a humorist keeps closer touch with facts, while a theorist *dwells* more on ideas, and it is only when one is dealing with ideas in themselves that his thoughts get incredibly complex.

II. Read aloud and recite paragraph 8.

III. Stylistics Study

Long Sentence

— A Formal and Complicated Way

Long sentences are often used in formal occasions to express complicated ideas in a more objective way, more specifically, like in academic papers, government documents, etc.

Example:

We the peoples of the United Nations determined to save succeeding generations from the scourge of war, which twice in our lifetime has brought untold sorrow to mankind, and to reaffirm faith in fundamental human rights, in the dignity and worth of the human person, in the equal rights of men and women and of nations large and small, and to establish conditions under which justice and respect for the obligations arising from treaties and other sources of international law can be maintained, and to promote social progress and better standards of life in larger freedom, and for these ends, to practice tolerance and live together in peace with one another as good neighbours, and to unite our strength to maintain international peace and security, and to ensure, by the acceptance of principles and the institution of methods, that armed force shall not be used, save in the common interest, and to employ international machinery for the promotion of the economic and social advancement of all peoples, have resolved to combine our efforts to accomplish these aims.

—From *Preamble to the U.N. Charter*

Long sentences are also used to describe people's complicated psychological changes since the syntactic character of long sentences is also marked by complexity.

Example:

> To take a dislike to a young man, only because he appeared to be of a different disposition from himself, was unworthy the real liberality of mind which she was always used to acknowledge in him; for with all the high opinion of himself, which she had often laid to his charge, she had never before for a moment supposed it could make him unjust to the merit of another.
>
> —From Jane Austen, *Emma*

Text II

The Ransom of Red Chief

Pre-reading Questions

1. What kind of writing is O. Henry best known for?
2. What is an "O. Henry" ending characterized as?

1 It looked like a good thing: but wait till I tell you. We were down South, in Alabama—Bill Driscoll and myself—when this kidnapping idea struck us. It was, as Bill afterward expressed it, "during a moment of temporary mental apparition"; but we didn't find that out till later.

2 We selected for our victim the only child of a prominent citizen named Ebenezer Dorset. The father was respectable and tight, a mortgage fancier and a stern, upright collection-plate passer and forecloser. The kid was a boy of ten, with bas-relief freckles, and hair the colour of the cover of the magazine you buy at the news-stand when you want to catch a train. Bill and me figured that Ebenezer would melt down for a ransom of two thousand dollars to a cent. But wait till I tell you.

3 About two miles from Summit was a little mountain, covered with a dense cedar brake. On the rear elevation of this mountain was a cave. There we stored provisions. One

evening after sundown, we drove in a buggy past old Dorset's house. The kid was in the street, throwing rocks at a kitten on the opposite fence.

"Hey, little boy!" says Bill, "would you like to have a bag of candy and a nice ride?"

The boy catches Bill neatly in the eye with a piece of brick.

"That will cost the old man an extra five hundred dollars," says Bill, climbing over the wheel.

That boy put up a fight like a welter-weight cinnamon bear; but, at last, we got him down in the bottom of the buggy and drove away. We took him up to the cave and I hitched the horse in the cedar brake. After dark I drove the buggy to the little village, three miles away, where we had hired it, and walked back to the mountain.

Bill was pasting court-plaster over the scratches and bruises on his features. There was a fire burning behind the big rock at the entrance of the cave, and the boy was watching a pot of boiling coffee, with two buzzard tail-feathers stuck in his red hair. He points a stick at me when I come up, and says:

"Ha! Cursed paleface, do you dare to enter the camp of Red Chief, the terror of the plains?"

"He's all right now," says Bill, rolling up his trousers and examining some bruises on his shins. "We're playing Indian. We're making Buffalo Bill's show look like magic-lantern views of Palestine in the town hall. I'm Old Hank, the Trapper, Red Chief's captive, and I'm to be scalped at daybreak. By Geronimo! That kid can kick hard."

Yes, sir, that boy seemed to be having the time of his life. The fun of camping out in a cave had made him forget that he was a captive himself. He immediately christened me Snake-eye, the Spy, and announced that, when his braves returned from the warpath, I was to be broiled at the stake at the rising of the sun.

"Red Chief," says I to the kid, "would you like to go home?"

"Aw, what for?" says he. "I don't have any fun at home. I hate to go to school. I like to camp out. You won't take me back home again, Snake-eye, will you?"

"Not right away," says I. "We'll stay here in the cave a while."

15 "All right!" says he. "That'll be fine. I never had such fun in all my life."

16 We went to bed about eleven o'clock. We spread down some wide blankets and quilts and put Red Chief between us. We weren't afraid he'd run away. He kept us awake for three hours, jumping up and reaching for his rifle and screeching: "Hist! pard," in mine and Bill's ears, as the fancied crackle of a twig or the rustle of a leaf revealed to his young imagination the stealthy approach of the outlaw band. At last, I fell into a troubled sleep, and dreamed that I had been kidnapped and chained to a tree by a ferocious pirate with red hair.

17 Just at daybreak, I was awakened by a series of awful screams from Bill. They weren't yells, or howls, or shouts, or whoops, or yawps, such as you'd expect from a manly set of vocal organs—they were simply indecent, terrifying, humiliating screams, such as women emit when they see ghosts or caterpillars. It's an awful thing to hear a strong, desperate, fat man scream incontinently in a cave at daybreak.

18 I jumped up to see what the matter was. Red Chief was sitting on Bill's chest, with one hand twined in Bill's hair. In the other he had the sharp case-knife we used for slicing bacon; and he was industriously and realistically trying to take Bill's scalp, according to the sentence that had been pronounced upon him the evening before.

19 I got the knife away from the kid and made him lie down again. But, from that moment, Bill's spirit was broken. He laid down on his side of the bed, but he never closed an eye again in sleep as long as that boy was with us. I dozed off for a while, but along toward sun-up I remembered that Red Chief had said I was to be burned at the stake at the rising of the sun. I wasn't nervous or afraid; but I sat up and lit my pipe and leaned against a rock.

...

20 I went up on the peak of the little mountain and ran my eye over the contiguous vicinity. Over toward Summit I expected to see the sturdy yeomanry of the village armed with scythes and pitchforks beating the countryside for the dastardly kidnappers. But what I saw was a peaceful landscape dotted with one man ploughing with a dun mule. Nobody was dragging the creek; no couriers dashed hither and yon, bringing tidings of no news to the distracted parents. There was a sylvan attitude of somnolent sleepiness pervading that section of

the external outward surface of Alabama that lay exposed to my view. "Perhaps," says I to myself, "it has not yet been discovered that the wolves have borne away the tender lambkin from the fold. Heaven help the wolves!" says I, and I went down the mountain to breakfast.

21   When I got to the cave I found Bill backed up against the side of it, breathing hard, and the boy threatening to smash him with a rock half as big as a coconut.

22   "He put a red-hot boiled potato down my back," explained Bill, "and then mashed it with his foot; and I boxed his ears. Have you got a gun about you, Sam?"

23   I took the rock away from the boy and kind of patched up the argument. "I'll fix you," says the kid to Bill. "No man ever yet struck the Red Chief but what he got paid for it. You better beware!"

24   After breakfast the kid takes a piece of leather with strings wrapped around it out of his pocket and goes outside the cave unwinding it.

25   "What's he up to now?" says Bill, anxiously. "You don't think he'll run away, do you, Sam?"

26   "No fear of it," says I. "He don't seem to be much of a home body. But we've got to fix up some plan about the ransom. There don't seem to be much excitement around Summit on account of his disappearance; but maybe they haven't realized yet that he's gone. His folks may think he's spending the night with Aunt Jane or one of the neighbours. Anyhow, he'll be missed to-day. To-night we must get a message to his father demanding the two thousand dollars for his return."

...

27   Bill and I got paper and pencil and worked on the letter while Red Chief, with a blanket wrapped around him, strutted up and down, guarding the mouth of the cave. Bill begged me tearfully to make the ransom fifteen hundred dollars instead of two thousand. "I ain't attempting," says he, "to decry the celebrated moral aspect of parental affection, but we're dealing with humans, and it ain't human for anybody to give up two thousand dollars for that forty-pound chunk of freckled wildcat. I'm willing to take a chance at fifteen hundred dollars. You can charge the difference up to me."

28   So, to relieve Bill, I acceded, and we collaborated a letter that ran this way:

Ebenezer Dorset, Esq.:

We have your boy concealed in a place far from Summit. It is useless for you or the most skilful detectives to attempt to find him. Absolutely, the only terms on which you can have him restored to you are these: We demand fifteen hundred dollars in large bills for his return; the money to be left at midnight to-night at the same spot and in the same box as your reply—as hereinafter described. If you agree to these terms, send your answer in writing by a solitary messenger to-night at half-past eight o'clock. After crossing Owl Creek, on the road to Poplar Cove, there are three large trees about a hundred yards apart, close to the fence of the wheat field on the right-hand side. At the bottom of the fence-post, opposite the third tree, will be found a small pasteboard box.

The messenger will place the answer in this box and return immediately to Summit.

If you attempt any treachery or fail to comply with our demand as stated, you will never see your boy again.

If you pay the money as demanded, he will be returned to you safe and well within three hours. These terms are final, and if you do not accede to them no further communication will be attempted.

TWO DESPERATE MEN.

29   I addressed this letter to Dorset, and put it in my pocket. As I was about to start, the kid comes up to me and says:

"Aw, Snake-eye, you said I could play the Black Scout while you was gone."

30   "Play it, of course," says I.

...

31   When I got back to the cave Bill and the boy were not to be found. I explored the vicinity of the cave, and risked a yodel or two, but there was no response.

32   So I lighted my pipe and sat down on a mossy bank to await developments.

33   In about half an hour I heard the bushes rustle, and Bill wabbled out into the little glade in front of the cave. Behind him was the kid, stepping softly like a scout, with a broad grin on his face. Bill stopped, took off his hat and wiped his face with a red handkerchief. The kid stopped about eight feet behind him.

34   "Sam," says Bill, "I suppose you'll think I'm a renegade, but I couldn't help it. I'm a grown person with masculine proclivities and habits of self-defense, but there is a time when all systems of egotism and predominance fail. The boy is gone. I have sent him home. All is off. There was martyrs in old times," goes on Bill, "that suffered death rather than give up the particular graft they enjoyed. None of 'em ever was subjugated to such supernatural tortures as I have been. I tried to be faithful to our articles of depredation; but there came a limit."

35   "But he's gone"—continues Bill —"gone home. I showed him the road to Summit and kicked him about eight feet nearer there at one kick. I'm sorry we lose the ransom; but it was either that or Bill Driscoll to the madhouse."

36   Bill is puffing and blowing, but there is a look of ineffable peace and growing content on his rose-pink features.

37   "Bill," says I, "there isn't any heart disease in your family, is there?

38   "No," says Bill, "nothing chronic except malaria and accidents. Why?"

39   "Then you might turn around," says I, "and have a look behind you."

40   Bill turns and sees the boy, and loses his complexion and sits down plump on the round and begins to pluck aimlessly at grass and little sticks. For an hour I was afraid for his mind. And then I told him that my scheme was to put the whole job through immediately and that we would get the ransom and be off with it by midnight if old Dorset fell in with our proposition. So Bill braced up enough to give the kid a weak sort of a smile and a promise to play the Russian in a Japanese war with him as soon as he felt a little better.

41   I had a scheme for collecting that ransom without danger of being caught by counterplots that ought to commend itself to professional kidnappers. The tree under which the answer was to be left—and the money later on—was close to the road fence with big, bare fields on all sides. If a gang of constables should be watching for any one to come for the note they could see him a long way off crossing the fields or in the road. But no, sirree! At half-past eight I was up in that tree as well hidden as a tree toad, waiting for the messenger to arrive.

42   Exactly on time, a half-grown boy rides up the road on a bicycle, locates the pasteboard box at the foot of the fence-post, slips a folded piece of paper into it and pedals away again back toward Summit.

43   I waited an hour and then concluded the thing was square. I slid down the tree, got the note, slipped along the fence till I struck the woods, and was back

at the cave in another half an hour. I opened the note, got near the lantern and read it to Bill. It was written with a pen in a crabbed hand, and the sum and substance of it was this:

Two Desperate Men.
Gentlemen:

  I received your letter to-day by post, in regard to the ransom you ask for the return of my son. I think you are a little high in your demands, and I hereby make you a counter-proposition, which I am inclined to believe you will accept. You bring Johnny home and pay me two hundred and fifty dollars in cash, and I agree to take him off your hands. You had better come at night, for the neighbours believe he is lost, and I couldn't be responsible for what they would do to anybody they saw bringing him back. Very respectfully,

EBENEZER DORSET.

44   "Great pirates of Penzance!" says I; "of all the impudent—"

45   But I glanced at Bill, and hesitated. He had the most appealing look in his eyes I ever saw on the face of a dumb or a talking brute.

46   We took him home that night. We got him to go by telling him that his father had bought a silver-mounted rifle and a pair of moccasins for him, and we were going to hunt bears the next day.

47   It was just twelve o'clock when we knocked at Ebenezer's front door. Just at the moment when I should have been abstracting the fifteen hundred dollars from the box under the tree, according to the original proposition, Bill was counting out two hundred and fifty dollars into Dorset's hand.

48   When the kid found out we were going to leave him at home he started up a howl like a calliope and fastened himself as tight as a leech to Bill's leg. His father peeled him away gradually, like a porous plaster.

49   "How long can you hold him?" asks Bill.

50   "I'm not as strong as I used to be," says old Dorset, "but I think I can promise you ten minutes."

52   "Enough," says Bill. "In ten minutes I shall cross the Central, Southern and Middle Western States, and be legging it trippingly for the Canadian border."

53   And, as dark as it was, and as fat as Bill was, and as good a runner as I am, he was a good mile and a half out of Summit before I could catch up with him.

By O. Henry (abridged)

(2,689 words)

Notes:

1. **The author—O. Henry** was the pseudonym of William Sydney Porter (1862–1910), a prolific American short-story writer, known for his surprise endings, who has been praised as "the poet with laurels in Manhattan" and "the father of modern short stories in America" by the critics. His works depicted the life of ordinary people in New York City and were honored as the "humorous encyclopedia of American life."

Reading Comprehension

I. Answer the following questions with the information you read from the passage.
   1. What did Bill and I plan to do?
   2. Who was Red Chief? What was he like?
   3. How was the first night like?
   4. What game(s) did the kid play with Bill?
   5. Did we get the ransom? Why?

II. Topics for discussion and reflection.
   1. How did the author use regionalism in the story?
   2. In order to get Red Chief to follow instructions, Sam uses a technique commonly known as "reverse psychology." What is reverse psychology? Did it work on Red Chief? Is it an effective way to take control of a situation?

Exercises for Integrated Skills

I. **Dictation**
   Listen to the following passage. The passage will be read to you four times. During the first reading, which will be read at normal speed, listen and try to understand the meaning. For the second and third readings, the passage will be read sentence by

sentence, or phrase by phrase, with intervals of 15 to 20 seconds. The last reading will be done at normal speed again and during this time check your work. You will then be given 2 minutes to check through your work a second time.

II. Cloze

___1___ possess a good sense of humor is regarded as thoroughly healthy and desirable by ___2___ all those who ___3___ concerned themselves with the subject of humor. The average man is also firmly ___4___ to the belief that having a(n) ___5___ for a keen sense of humor is something to be treasured and protected. Amongst ___6___ of college students Allport and Omwake found that only 6% and 14% ___7___ were prepared to admit to a lower-than-average sense of humor. In the ___8___ of Frank Moore Colby, "Men will confess to murder, false teeth or a wig. How many will own up to a lack of humor?" Man ___9___ always held humor and laughter on a pedestal of desirability. From a(n) ___10___ perspective, humor has often been characterized as degenerate, fit only for the ignorant and foolish.

1. A. To   B. /   C. That   D. For
2. A. exactly   B. actually   C. virtually   D. remarkably
3. A. have been   B. have   C. are   D. /
4. A. devoted   B. committed   C. clung   D. stick
5. A. reputation B. fame   C. honor   D. award
6. A. examples   B. some   C. samples   D. respondents
7. A. individually B. respectively C. alternatively D. correspondingly
8. A. light   B. perspective   C. angle   D. words
9. A. has not   B. has   C. /   D. is
10. A. historic   B. historical   C. ancient   D. history

Unit 9 Humor

Oral Activities

1. Stand-up comics often use insults, coarse language, and/or racial humor and stereotypes in their acts. Why is this considered funny?
2. When learning a second language, humor is often a difficult element to learn and appreciate fully. Discuss reasons for why this is the case and what has helped you better understand humor in other languages/cultures.

Writing Practice

Composition Writing

   Mark Twain, a well-known American novelist and humorist, once said, "Humor is the great thing, the saving thing. The minute it crops up, all our irritations and resentments slip away and a sunny spirit takes their place." Have you ever solved a problem with a touch of humor? Write a composition of about 200 words on the topic: **The Power of Humor**, stating how humor enables people to solve problems.

Unit 10 Medicine

Warm-up Activities

1. In pairs, brainstorm the ethical issues a doctor may face on a daily basis. How would you deal with some of the issues?
2. When you get sick, do you typically trust Western medicine or traditional Chinese medicine more? What do you base this on? Does your decision depend on what illness you have?

Text I

A Doctor's Vision of the Future of Medicine

Pre-reading Questions

1. How often do you and your family take part in preventative health care? Describe what measures are taken.
2. With the prevalence of medical information on the Internet, people will often look up treatment for some of their symptoms. How does this compare with seeing a doctor face to face?

1   It's June 2018. Sally picks up a handheld device and holds it to her finger. With a tiny pinprick, it draws off a fraction of a droplet of blood, makes 2,000 different measurements and sends the data wirelessly to a distant computer for analysis. A few minutes later, Sally gets the results via e-mail, and a copy goes to her physician. All of Sally's organs are fine, and her physician advises her to do another home medical checkup in six months.

2 This is what the not-so-distant future of medicine will look like. Over the next two decades, medicine will change from its current reactive mode, in which doctors wait for people to get sick, to a mode that is far more preventive and rational. I like to call it P4 medicine—predictive, personalized, preventive and participatory. What's driving this change are powerful new measurement technologies and the so-called systems approach to medicine. Whereas medical researchers in the past studied disease by analyzing the effects of one gene at a time, the systems approach will give them the ability to analyze all your genes at once. The average doctor's office visit today might involve blood work and a few measurements, such as blood pressure and temperature; in the near future physicians will collect billions of bytes of information about each individual—genes, blood proteins, cells and historical data. They will use this data to assess whether your cell's biological information-handling circuits have become perturbed by disease, whether from defective genes, exposure to bad things in the environment or both.

3 Several emerging technologies are making this holistic, molecular approach to disease possible. Nano-size devices will measure thousands of blood elements, and DNA sequencers will decode individual human genomes rapidly, accurately and inexpensively. New computers will sort through huge amounts of data gathered annually on each individual and boil down this information to clear results about health and disease.

4 Medicine will begin to get more predictive and personalized (the first two aspects of P4 medicine) over the next five to 10 years. First, doctors will be able to sequence the genome of each patient, which together with other data will yield useful predictions about his or her future health; it will be able to tell you, for example, that you have a 30 percent chance of developing ovarian cancer before age 30. Second, a biannual assessment of your blood will make it possible to get an update on the current state of your health for each of your 50 or so organ systems. These steps will place the focus of medicine on individual patients and on assessing the impact that genes and their interactions with the environment have in determining health or disease.

5 In preventive medicine (the third P), researchers will use systems medicine to develop drugs that help prevent disease. If, say, you have a 50 percent

chance of developing prostate cancer by the time you're 50, you may be able to start taking a drug when you're 30 that would substantially reduce that probability. In the next 10 to 20 years the focus of health care will shift from dealing with disease to maintaining wellness.

6   Participatory medicine acknowledges the unparalleled opportunities that patients will have to take control of their health care. To participate effectively, though, they will have to be educated as to the basic principles of P4 medicine. New companies that can analyze human genome variation, like 23andMe and Navigenics, are already planning to provide patients with genetic information that may be useful in modifying their behavior to avoid future health problems. In the future, patients will need not just genetic data but insight into how the environment is turning genes on and off to cause disease—just as smoking often causes lung cancer and exposure to sunlight can cause skin cancer.

7   P4 medicine will have a big impact on many industries, including pharmaceuticals, food and insurance, as well as health care. The interesting question is whether preexisting businesses and entrenched bureaucracies will be able to respond to these winds of change, or whether a host of new companies will emerge to replace them—focused precisely on these new opportunities.

8   Research will also have to change. Because most important diseases such as diabetes, cancer, heart disease, obesity and Alzheimer's are so complex, the traditional approaches to studying them have had only marginal results. Powerful new systems approaches, individual measurements and computational technologies will transform our ability to deal with complexity and fashion new drugs and approaches for therapy and prevention.

9   Medical education will also need to be transformed. Although today's medical students will be practicing P4 medicine within the next five to 20 years, their training is still focused on a classification of disease based on observation of relatively few measurements of health parameters. Tomorrow's physicians will need to be familiar with the complexity of the human biological system as never before, and they'll have to be handy with computer-based tools. Physicians will need to deal with patients who have an enormous amount of information at their disposal. And doctors will need to deal with maintaining wellness more than with disease.

10   The digitization of medicine—that is, our ability to extract and store disease-relevant information from DNA and molecules in the blood of each individual—together with the revolutionary changes in diagnosis, therapy and prevention will allow those of us in the developed world to export P4 medicine to the developing world and thus transform the quality of its health care. The new P4 medicine will eventually lead to a universal democratization of health care, bringing to billions the fundamental right of health, unimaginable even a few years ago.

By Leroy Hood
(941 words)

Words and Expressions

pinprick	/ˈpɪnprɪk/	n.	a very small hole in something, similar to one made by a pin (似针刺的)小孔
draw off			to remove some liquid from a larger supply 使流走,排掉
fraction	/ˈfrækʃən/	n.	a very small amount of something 少量,一点儿
droplet	/ˈdrɒplɪt/	n.	a very small drop of liquid (液体的)小滴
checkup	/ˈtʃekʌp/	n.	a general medical examination that a doctor or dentist gives you to make sure you are healthy 体格检查
personalize	/ˈpɜːsnəlaɪz/	vt.	to design or change something so that it is suitable for a particular person 使(某物)符合某人的特定要求
participatory	/pɑːˈtɪsɪpeɪtəri/	adj.	involving a particular person or group of people taking part in 众人参与的
byte	/baɪt/	n.	a unit for measuring computer information, equal to eight bits 字节
defective	/dɪˈfektɪv/	adj.	not made properly, or not working properly 有缺陷的,有问题的
molecule	/ˈmɒlɪkjuːl/	n.	the smallest unit into which any substance can be divided without losing its own chemical nature, usually consisting of two or more atoms 分子 **molecular** adj. 分子的

DNA sequencer			a scientific instrument used to automate the DNA sequencing process 脱氧核糖核酸(DNA)测序仪
decode	/diːˈkəʊd/	vt.	to translate a secret or complicated message, or a signal into a form that can be easily understood 解码
genome	/ˈdʒiːnəʊm/	n.	all the genes in one cell of a living organism 基因组,染色体组
boil down			to make a list or piece of writing shorter by not including anything that is not necessary 精简,压缩
yield	/jiːld/	vt.	to produce a result, answer, or piece of information 得出(结果、答案或信息)
ovary	/ˈəʊvərɪ/	n.	the part of a female that produces eggs 卵巢 **ovarian** adj. 卵巢的
biannual	/baɪˈænjuəl/	adj.	happening twice each year 一年两次的
prostate	/ˈprɒsteɪt/	n.	an organ in the body of male mammals that is near the bladder and that produces a liquid in which sperm are carried 前列腺
unparalleled	/ʌnˈpærəleld/	adj.	bigger, better, or worse than anything else 无比的,无双的
pharmaceutical	/ˌfɑːməˈsjuːtɪkəl/	adj.	relating to the production of drugs and medicines 制药的
bureaucracy	/bjʊˈrɒkrəsɪ/	n.	a complicated official system which is annoying or confusing because it has a lot of rules, processes, etc. 官僚制度,官僚主义
diabetes	/daɪəˈbiːtiːz/	n.	a serious disease in which there is too much sugar in the blood 糖尿病
parameter	/pəˈræmɪtə/	n.	a set of fixed limits that control the way that something should be done 参数,范围
handy with			good at using something, especially a tool 擅长使用
disposal	/dɪˈspəʊzəl/	n.	(at somebody's disposal) available for someone to use 供(人)使用
digitize	/ˈdɪdʒɪtaɪz/	vt.	to put information into a digital form 使数字化 **digitization** n. 数字化
extract	/ɪkˈstrækt/	vt.	to carefully remove a substance from something which contains it, using a machine, chemical process, etc. 采集,采掘,提炼

Unit 10 Medicine

> diagnosis   /ˌdaɪəɡˈnəʊsɪs/   n.   the process of discovering exactly what is wrong with someone or something, by examining them closely 诊断(结果)

Notes:

1. **Alzheimer's**   Alzheimer's disease is a brain disorder named after the German physician Alois Alzheimer, who first described it in 1906. It is characterized by the progressive loss of mental ability.

Reading Comprehension

I. **Summarize the following situations according to the text:**

1. Predictive and personalized aspect of future medicine:

2. Preventative medicine of the future:

3. Participatory medicine of the future:

II. **Answer the following questions.**

1. What will the not-so-distant future of medicine look like?
2. What does P4 medicine mean? What do you think of it?
3. How can P4 medicine influence other industries, such as food, insurance and health care?
4. Why will medical education need to be transformed?
5. What is the digitization of medicine?

III. **Paraphrase the following sentences within the context of the reading passage.**

1. (Para.2) They will use this data to assess whether your cell's biological information-handling circuits have become perturbed by disease, whether from detective genes, expose

to bad things in the environment or both.

2. (Para.3) New computers will sort through huge amounts of data gathered annually on each individual and boil down this information to clear results about health and disease.

3. (Para.6) Participatory medicine acknowledges the unparalleled opportunities that patients will have to take control of their health care.

4. (Para.7) The interesting question is whether preexisting business and entrenched bureaucracies will be able to these winds of change, or whether a host of new companies will emerge to replace them—focused precisely on these new opportunities.

5. (Para.9) Tomorrow's physicians will need to be familiar with the complexity of the human biological system as never before, and they'll have to be handy with computer-based tools.

IV. Based on the text, decide whether the following statements are true or false. For false statements, write the facts in parentheses.

1. Over the next 20 years, medicine will change from the current personalized mode to the reactive mode.
   (   )

2. DNA sequencers will decode individual human genomes rapidly, accurately and inexpensively.
   (   )

3. The focus of health care will change from dealing with disease to maintaining wellness in the near future.
   (   )

4. Today's medical students will be practicing P4 medicine in the future, therefore their training is quite different from the traditional medical students' training.
   (   )

5. The new P4 medicine will bring a more democratic medicine to people.
   (   )

Vocabulary Exercises

I. Fill in the blank in each sentence with a word or phrase from the box below. Make sure the appropriate form of the word is used.

| perturb | sequence | yield | unparallel |
| holistic | entrench | predictive | rational |

Unit 10   Medicine

1. The answer is to create a highly regulated insurance system with inefficiencies eliminated through _____ rules.
2. We're also able to do _____ analytics—predict what we think you might want based on what we already know about you.
3. She sat looking quiet and didn't seem _____ by the rumors around.
4. The hospital is among the first in the country to begin integrating a full program of _____ care into a more traditional medical system.
5. Using cells donated by a woman in her 50s who died of leukemia（白血病）, the scientists _____ all the DNA from her cancer cells and compared it to the DNA from her own normal, healthy skin cells.
6. The program, although still in its early stages, has already _____ some results.
7. His efforts were critical to the successes of all six American lunar landings. He was a leader in the space program for more than three decades, with scientific and programmatic experience that is _____.
8. The unequal treatment of men and women in the labour market is deeply _____ in our culture.

II. **Fill in the blanks with the appropriate forms of the given words.**
  1. It would be an enormous relief if the recent attacks on the science of global warming actually indicated that we do not face an unimaginable calamity requiring large-scale, _____ (prevention) measures to protect human civilization as we know it.
  2. Manufacturing businesses that embrace _____ (participate) management say it typically increases their productivity by 30 to 40 percent.
  3. When it comes to cars, the rapid growth of the auto industry here and of car ownership in the 1960s and '70s was accompanied by a spate of fatal accidents. A consumer movement soon emerged among owners of these _____ (deficiency) vehicles.
  4. Prolonged _____ (expose) to chemical pollutants causes cancer and other fatal diseases.
  5. In open virtual communities, which allow users access to the underlying computer code from which their universe is built, anyone who is sufficiently _____ (hand) with 3-D graphics programs is free to design amusement park rides, pirate galleons or anything else that can be dreamed up, and to incorporate them into the environment.
  6. In the announcement he underscored his government's desire to maintain control over France's cultural heritage in an era of _____ (digital).
  7. Whites were the most likely—at a rate of about 1 in 10—to have received a _____ (diagnose) of insomnia.

III. Choose the word or phrase that best completes each of the following sentences.

1. That open land would _____ floodwater from elsewhere in future storms.
   A. draw against   B. go against
   C. go off   D. draw off

2. This column is meant to help you, or a smoker close to you, sort _____ the options for quitting.
   A. with   B. at   C. through   D. in

3. For all the new marketing efforts, Starbucks's biggest mistakes and greatest challenges boil _____ to three words: location, location and location.
   A. off   B. down   C. on   D. up

4. Investors will get a handful of economic reports toward the end of the week that should provide some insight _____ the health of the economy.
   A. at   B. about   C. into   D. on

5. Within Europe, different countries have pursued a range of approaches _____ with Internet piracy.
   A. to deal   B. dealt   C. to be dealt   D. to dealing

Translation Exercises

I. Translate each of the following sentences into English, using the word or phrase given in the brackets.

1. 这个清单帮助我把混乱的思想理出了头绪。(sort through)

2. 老板要求他把繁琐的文件简化成一页报告。(boil down)

3. 当美洲殖民地民众拿起武器抗击大英帝国获得独立时,黑人奴隶制度早已根深蒂固。(entrench)

4. 跨国公司,全球市场营销,新兴通讯技术和文化融合的发展,使全球公共关系得到空前的发展。(unparalleled)

5. 信息系统可扩展健康保健的范围,提高卫生保健的质量,使个人生活更加舒适,并能使人们按自己的意愿增加休闲方式。(at one's disposal)

Unit 10　Medicine

II. Translate the following paragraph into English.

传统医学是维护健康以及预防、诊断、改善或治疗身心疾病方面所使用的知识、技能和实践总和。其他人群所采用的传统医学通常被称作替代或补充医学。在一些亚洲和非洲国家,80%的人口依赖传统医学提供初级卫生保健。在许多发达国家,70%—80%的人口使用某种形式的替代或补充医学(例如针灸)。草药治疗是最受欢迎的传统医学形式,在国际市场中非常赚钱:西欧国家2003—2004年年收入达50亿美元,中国2005年产品销售总额为140亿美元,巴西2007年的草药收入为1.6亿美元。

III. Translate the following paragraph into Chinese.

The digitization of medicine—that is, our ability to extract and store disease-relevant information from DNA and molecules in the blood of each individual—together with the revolutionary changes in diagnosis, therapy and prevention will allow those of us in the developed world to export P4 medicine to the developing world and thus transform the quality of its health care. The new P4 medicine will eventually lead to a universal democratization of health care, bringing to billions the fundamental right of health, unimaginable even a few years ago.

Language Appreciation

I. Read the text carefully, then pick out the sentences that you think are well-written. Pay close attention to the italicized words or phrases of the following sentences. Try to appreciate the way in which the author expresses his/her ideas. Learn how to use them in your own writing.

1. New computers will sort through huge amounts of data gathered annually on each individual and *boil down* this information to clear results about health and disease.
2. Powerful new systems approaches, individual measurements and computational technologies will transform our ability to deal with complexity and *fashion* new drugs and approaches for therapy and prevention.

II. Read aloud and recite paragraph 2.

III. Stylistics Study

Levels of Formality
— Stylistic Consciousness (1)

As a language learner, one should be aware that the language we use should be adjusted to the situation. Generally speaking, there are three main ranges of variation —written and

spoken English, formal and informal English, and polite and familiar language.

The English of speech and the English of writing are quite different in distinctive ways.

1. Written language tends to be explicit and balanced while the grammar of spoken sentences is simpler and less strictly constructed.

Examples: 1) —With a Greek-American family?
　　　　　　　—No. Hispanic.
　　　　　　　—From *Family Album U.S.A.*
　　　　　2) —Pleased to meet you.
　　　　　　　—[She shakes his hand.] Likewise, Mr. Riley.
　　　　　　　—Please, sit down. What can I do for you?
　　　　　　　—We'd like to discuss a mortgage.
　　　　　　　—For a house.
　　　　　　　—From *Family Album U.S.A.*

2. Spoken language tends to use more filler words or phrases such as "well," "you see," "it seems that," "I think," and "kind of," which carry little information but convey speaker's attitude.

Examples: —Yeah, I do. I need to get out more. Well, I mean there's a lot to do around the house, and I love being here with the family, you know, but I'm restless. Since I retired, I've got extra time on my hands.
　　　　　　—I understand, Grandpa.
　　　　　　—I think you do. Frankly, I'd like to use my brain a little more.
　　　　　　—From *Family Album U.S.A.*

3. "Language (Hesitation) fillers" like "er", "mm" and "um" are commonly used in spoken language.

Text II

Use of Stimulants in Doping

> **Pre-reading Questions**
>
> 1. Some athletes use nutritional supplements to help them increase muscle mass, get more energy faster, etc. What is your opinion of this?
> 2. Caffeine and nicotine are two of the most common addictive ingredients. What kinds of benefits can one receive from them? What are some adverse affects?

Unit 10   Medicine

1   The ergogenic aids that have raised the most concern among athletic-governing bodies are the pharmacological agents, or drugs. Doping, or the use of drugs by athletes in attempts to improve performance, has persisted for nearly a century, but it was not until after World War II that doping became rampant among athletes involved in international competition and professional sports. Doping eventually filtered down to college sports, and today appears to pervade sports at even the high school level.

2   Although doping in sports was a growing concern, drug use was not regulated until the death of a cyclist in the 1960 Olympic Games in Rome triggered the formation of the Medical Commission of the International Olympic Committee (IOC) and the initiation of anti-doping legislation for Olympic competition. The legislation developed by the IOC serves as a guideline for other athletic-governing bodies such as the International Amateur Cycling Federation, The Athletics Congress (TAC), and the National Collegiate Athletic Association (NCAA). The general definition of doping as developed by the IOC is as follows:

   Doping is the administration of or the use by a competing athlete of any substance foreign to the body or of any physiological substance taken in abnormal quantity or by an abnormal route of entry into the body, with the intention of increasing in an artificial and unfair manner his performance in competition. When necessity demands medical treatment with any substance which because of its nature, dosage, or application is able to boost the athlete's performance in competition in an artificial and unfair manner, this is to be regarded as doping.

3   The major purpose of this general rule was to discourage the use of drugs by athletes, and in this regard the IOC lists several pages of specific drugs banned in athletic competition. There is no need to list these specific drugs, however, the IOC does group these specific drugs into several distinct categories, such as stimulants, depressants, diuretics, and anabolic steroids.

4   Before we begin our discussion of some of the more obvious and commonly used drugs used to improve performance in sports, it is important to point out that all of the agents discussed, with some exceptions and limitations that shall be noted, are banned for use by most

athletic-governing bodies and are thus illegal for athletes to use.

5   In order to enforce anti-doping legislation, a highly technical and effective drug-testing system is available to most athletic-governing bodies. However, like many athletes, you may take drugs for a variety of medicinal purposes, such as a headache, a stuffed nose, a cold, or to heal an injury. Unfortunately, many over-the-counter medications that you may be able to purchase without a prescription for such conditions may contain drugs that are banned for athletic competition. If you will be competing in any athletic event involving drug testing, such as a TAC-sponsored race or NCAA contest, it would be advisable to check with the athletic-governing body about the legality of any medications you are taking.

6   Most of us consume stimulant drugs in one form or another almost daily. The most common stimulant available to us is, of course, *caffeine*, which is found in such beverages and foods as coffee, cocoa, tea, chocolate, and cola sodas. Caffeine is also found in aspirin, whereas many other over-the-counter preparations that we may take contain various stimulant drugs on the IOC doping list. For example, many nasal decongestants contain *ephedrine*, a stimulant that resulted in the loss of a gold medal when inadvertently used by an American swimmer in the 1972 Olympic Games.

7   A wide variety of stimulant drugs have been developed by medical researchers. Many of these drugs are designed to exert only very specific local effects. For example, *digitalis* is a cardiac stimulant designed to increase the contractile force of the heart, and thus is an important medication for some cardiac patients. On the other hand, many stimulant drugs exert widespread psychological and physiological effects throughout the body; it is this type of stimulant drug that has been of interest to athletes as a means of improving performance.

8   Historically, *amphetamines* have been the most widely used stimulant among athletes at all levels of competition. More recently, caffeine has become popular among many athletes, particularly endurance runners and cyclists. Although there may be some small differences in the psychological and physiological effects that various stimulants may exert in the body, there are many similarities regarding their possible effects on functions that are important during competition in sport.

9   Psychologically, such stimulants as amphetamines and caffeine may increase excitability, arousal, attention, concentration, motivation, and self-confidence, while concomitantly removing psychological inhibitions. In other words, psychological energy is increased. It is obvious that this psychological stimulation could be important to athletes in a variety of sports if it would add to the normal stimulation elicited by athletic competition itself. For example greater concentration in a tennis player might result in a faster reaction to a return. On the other hand, excessive excitability resulting in muscle tremor and unsteadiness may be deleterious to some athletic performances, such as archery and riflery.

10   Physiologically, stimulants have been used by athletes because they produce physiological responses in the body comparable to that of *epinephrine*, also called *adrenalin*, which is a natural hormone secreted by the adrenal gland. During exercise, your sympathetic nervous system activates the adrenal gland, which releases epinephrine into the blood for delivery to all tissues. Many stimulant drugs mimic this natural action of the sympathetic nervous system and thus are called sympathomimetic drugs. The resulting physiological responses that could be important for energy production during exercise include facilitation of contractile processes in the muscle, increased size of the bronchi delivering air to the lungs, increased amount of blood pumped by the heart, increased blood flow to the muscle, and increased availability of glucose and free fatty acids (FFA) in the blood to serve as energy sources. Many of these changes could be theorized to benefit the oxygen energy system and, thereby, aerobic endurance. One current popular theory suggests that the increased levels of blood FFA will increase the use of fat as an energy source in the muscle, thereby improving performance by sparing muscle glycogen for use during the latter stages of a prolonged endurance event.

11   In summary, stimulants are theorized to improve athletic performance, either through psychological or physiological mechanisms, and to increase energy production, but only if they can augment the natural psychological and physiological effects induced by the secretion of natural hormones in the body during athletic competition. On the other hand, as we shall see, there may be some potential adverse effects of these agents upon physical performance.

By Melvin H. Williams (abridged)

(1,105 words)

Reading Comprehension

I. Answer the following questions with the information you read from the passage.

1. What is the general definition of doping?
2. How do most people consume stimulant drugs in one form or another daily? Explain with examples.
3. Why did an American swimmer in the 1972 Olympic Games lose the gold medal?
4. What psychological effects do amphetamines and caffeine have on people?
5. What physiological effects do stimulants have on the human body?

II. Topics for discussion and reflection.

1. Should athletes be able to use drugs, or supplements, or other types of assistance in competitions?
2. How are nutritional supplements similar or different from drugs? Should they also be banned?
3. Would you ever risk your life to achieve a lifelong dream? Why or why not?

Exercises for Integrated Skills

I. Dictation

Listen to the following passage. The passage will be read to you four times. During the first reading, which will be read at normal speed, listen and try to understand the meaning. For the second and third readings, the passage will be read sentence by sentence, or phrase by phrase, with intervals of 15 to 20 seconds. The last reading will be done at normal speed again and during this time check your work. You will then be given 2 minutes to check through your work a second time.

_____
_____
_____
_____

II. Cloze

Sports medicine deals with injuries or illnesses ___1___ participation in sports and athletic activities. It ___2___ proper ___3___ of the human body and with the ___4___ and treatment of athletic injuries. This __5__ continues to __6__ for many reasons. Growing __7__ of people seek to improve or __8__ their fitness level by engaging in __9__ sports activities than ever before. __10__ the increase of sporting participants, there is an increase in types of high-risk sports. As a result, more people participate in more dangerous athletic activities.

1. A. resulting from   B. rising from   C. bringing about   D. leading from
2. A. concerning   B. concerned   C. is concerned with   D. is concerning
3. A. working   B. functioning   C. performing   D. playing
4. A. control   B. prevention   C. avoidance   D. aversion
5. A. area   B. scale   C. field   D. sphere
6. A. evolve   B. expand   C. spread   D. extend
7. A. number   B. amount   C. numbers   D. quantity
8. A. preserve   B. keep   C. maintain   D. stay
9. A. wider varieties of B. wider variety of C. a wider variety of D. various
10. A. Same to   B. Likely to   C. Even to   D. Parallel to

Oral Activities

Brainstorm and Debate

1. Animal research has often been used to test new drugs. Debate the pros and cons of animal testing.
2. Brainstorm the pros and cons of medical marijuana. Debate the issue of medical use and legalization of marijuana

Writing Practice

Composition Writing

In recent years, an alarming number of sports including football, track and field and cycling have been involved in doping scandals that taint the spirit of competitive sports. Today, the fight against doping is an uphill battle. What needs to be done to win this seemingly endless battle? Write a composition of about 200 words to express your thoughts.

Unit 11 Communication

Warm-up Activities

1. What are some key components of effective communication?
2. Discuss examples of non-verbal communication and what messages they send.

Text I

I Blog, Therefore I Am

Pre-reading Questions

1. What is a blog? Do you have one or do you follow somebody else's blog?
2. The word "blog" has entered the English language lexicon and can now be used as a noun, verb, and adjective—a blog, to blog, bloggy, and blogger. There are even "professional bloggers" now. Discuss your opinion of having blogging as a job.

1   On March 23, 2005, cartoonist Stephan Pastis published an installment of his *Pearls Before Swine* comic entitled "Rat's Book Signing" that seems especially relevant to the current debate over the impact of blogging on American media consumption habits.

2   In it, the humble Pig asks a passerby if he would be interested in buying his friend Rat's new book of comic strips.

3   "Comic strip? What's a comic strip?" asks the passerby.

4   Rat, ever the know-it-all, is ready with an answer: "It was a once thriving medium killed by decades of mediocrity, fueled by the insidious tradition of

older strips never going away, resulting in an apathetic generation of younger readers who no longer have reason to even open their newspaper."

5 The passerby looks confused: "Newspaper?" he asks.

6 Pastis thus took an ironic and well-timed poke at the current notion, popular in some blogging circles and even among a few establishment pundits, that the nation's established print and television media are going the way of the dinosaur as growing numbers of young people turn to blogs, podcasts, Google search, text messaging, niche TV programming, and other new and customized media.

7 Oh, to live in revolutionary times! It would all be so exciting if we hadn't heard it all before. For as anyone old enough to have a driver's license may recall, it was barely a decade ago that the evangelists of the early World Wide Web, online commerce, electronic publishing, and new interactive media claimed that "old media" was dead, the shopping mall was doomed, print-on-paper books would soon disappear—and that all the frantic efforts of traditional media and publishing companies to adapt to new media's insurgent threat would prove as useless as "rearranging the deck chairs on the Titanic."

8 Currently, citizen-created media is exploding. Blogs, video blogs, podcasts (or audio blogs), and customized on-demand television, radio, and online newspaper content are beginning to populate a richly diverse landscape of citizen-created media. As a sign of their belief in the potential for citizen-generated media, Mark Potts, a cofounder of Washingtonpost.com, and partner Susan DeFife recently launched Backfence.com, a network of local news sites relying entirely on reader-contributed content. Similar ventures are launching with regularity.

9 This is not the first time that citizens have created their own media, of course. During the Renaissance, for example, "commonplace books" helped educated citizens cope with the information overload of the then newly emerged printing era. In these self-published books, people wrote down their favorite sayings, poems, or speeches in order to help them organize and classify

information as well as remember key moral precepts. Much like blogs today, commonplace books reflected the personal experience and conscience of their authors. As Rachel Toor noted in an article for the *Chronicle of Higher Education*, "Reading the commonplace books of historical figures like George Washington, Thomas Jefferson, or any number of antebellum Southern ladies gives us an interior view of each person's self-image and the words that motivated him or her."

10 Citizens continued the practice of chronicling and making sense of their lives through self-created media throughout the nineteenth and twentieth centuries, observes the futurist Paul Saffo. "In the late 1900s," he explains, "people invented these little letterpress printing systems, and you could buy one cheaply and print up whatever you wanted. It was a big phenomenon, very exciting at the time. But it eventually disappeared."

11 In one sense, then, blogs are simply a continuation of a phenomenon that, at least in the form of oral storytelling, reaches back to antiquity. But in terms of its enormous scale, scope, and cultural impact, nothing in history compares to today's explosion of citizen-created media. Tens of millions of people around the world are now documenting their lives, exploring their religious and political beliefs, and engaging in public conversations on everything from poetry to classic cars to the latest advances in nanotechnology. And they do so not only through blogs, but also through virtually every digital communications tool they can get their hands on. They create and distribute their own movies, record and narrate their own audio and video podcasts, send text messages to their friends' handheld devices, and share photos via their camera phones.

12 Analyzing this explosion of amateur content, a fascinating new study entitled "The Pro-Am Revolution" by the British think tank Demos notes that "the twentieth century was shaped by the rise of professionals in most walks of life. As professionalism grew, often with hierarchical organizations and formal systems for accrediting knowledge, so amateurs came to be seen as second rate. Amateurism came to be a term of derision. Professionalism was a mark of seriousness and high standards." "But in the latest two decades," the Demos report continues, "a new breed of amateur has emerged: the Pro-Am, amateurs who work to professional standards. The Pro-Ams are knowledgeable, educated, committed and net-worked by new technology. The twentieth century

was shaped by large hierarchical organizations with professionals at the top. Pro-Ams are creating new, distributed organizational models that will be innovative, adaptive and low-cost." As a result, the study argues, "Knowledge, once held tightly in the hands of professionals and their institutions, will flow into networks of dedicated amateurs."

13   And therein lies a perfect description of the blogging phenomenon.

14   What accounts for this unprecedented new surge of citizen media? Certainly the fact that the tools for creating and publishing citizen-generated media are much more affordable and easier to use than ever before in history is part of the answer. Then, too, access to useful information—whether it be polling data used by political bloggers or photography tips and tricks for video-bloggers—is so much simpler and instantaneous than ever before. Finally, thanks to the Internet, the distribution of this amateur content to a worldwide yet targeted audience is now made possible by the costless click of the mouse.

15   But the fact that millions of people now have the means and opportunity to be publishers and broadcasters does not tell us *why* they wish to be. For that we need to look to the alienation, powerlessness, and crushing anonymity that seem to be such overpowering features of modern life.

16   As a response to these forces, then, blogs and other citizen-created media should properly be seen as the revolt of the voiceless against the heedless.

17   Blogs help break through the anonymity and isolation of modern life. They give people a voice and a forum with which to speak truth to power—or at least to reach out and touch someone. And although blogs certainly won't give rise to a million new citizen-Shakespeares, they do enable talented but heretofore unacknowledged people with something to say to find an audience—and thereby pluck from the indifference of daily life a bit of validation for themselves, their ideas, and their creative abilities.

18   In other words, blogging's ultimate product is empowerment. A weblog "creates a fluid and living form of self-representation, like an avatar in cyberspace that we wear like a skin," says the Web producer Tom Coates. "Through it we articulate ourselves."

19   Or, to put it another way, "I blog, therefore I am."

By David Kline
(1,180 words)

Words and Expressions

blog	/blɒg/	n.	a web page that is made up of information about a particular subject, in which the newest information is always at the top of the page 网络日志 **blogger** n. 博客 (即写网络日志的人)
installment	/ɪnˈstɔːlmənt/	n.	one of the parts of a story that appears as a series of parts, especially in a magazine, newspaper, etc. 一部分，一集（部）
entitle	/ɪnˈtaɪtl/	vt.	to give a title to a book, film, etc. 名为……
comic strip			a series of pictures drawn inside boxes that tell a story 连环漫画
know-it-all		n.	someone who behaves as if they know everything 自以为无所不知的人，自以为通晓一切事物的人
thriving	/ˈθraɪvɪŋ/	adj.	being very successful 兴旺发达的，欣欣向荣的
insidious	/ɪnˈsɪdɪəs/	adj.	spreading gradually without being noticed, and causing serious harm 暗中为害的，潜伏的
apathetic	/ˌæpəˈθetɪk/	adj.	not interested in something, and not willing to make any effort to change or improve things 无感情的，无兴趣的，冷漠的，无动于衷的
ironic	/aɪˈrɒnɪk/	adj.	using words that are the opposite of what you really mean, often in a joking way 讽刺的，挖苦的，嘲讽的
well-timed		adj.	said or done at the most suitable moment 时机合适的，及时的
poke	/pəʊk/	n.	a criticism of someone or something 批评（某人/某事）
pundit	/ˈpʌndɪt/	n.	someone who is often asked to give their opinion publicly of a situation or subject （某一方面的）权威，专家
customize	/ˈkʌstəmaɪz/	vt.	to change something to make it more suitable for you, or to make it look special or different from things of a similar type 定制，定做，按规格改

Unit 11 Communication

evangelist	/ɪˈvændʒəlɪst/	n.	someone who travels to different places and tries to persuade people to become Christians 巡回布道者
frantic	/ˈfræntɪk/	adj.	extremely hurried and using a lot of energy, but not very organized 紧张忙乱的, 匆忙的
insurgent	/ɪnˈsɜːdʒənt/	adj.	in opposition to a civil authority or government 叛乱的, 造反的
precept	/ˈpriːsept/	n.	a rule on which a way of thinking or behaving is based 准则, 戒律, 格言
chronicle	/ˈkrɒnɪkəl/	n.	a written record of a series of events, especially historical events, written in the order in which they happened 年代记, 编年史
		vt.	to describe events in the order in which they happened 记述, 记载(事), 载入编年史
futurist	/ˈfjuːtʃərɪst/	n.	someone who speculates about the future 未来主义者, 未来派艺术家
continuation	/kənˌtɪnjuˈeɪʃən/	n.	something that continues or follows something else that has happened before, without a stop or change 继续部分
antiquity	/ænˈtɪkwɪtɪ/	n.	ancient times 古代
nanotechnology	/ˌnænəʊtekˈnɒlədʒɪ/	n.	a science which involves developing and making extremely small but very powerful machines 纳米技术
think tank		n.	a group of people with experience or knowledge of a particular subject, who work to produce ideas and give advice 智囊团
hierarchical	/haɪəˈrɑːkɪkəl/	adj.	being divided into levels of importance 按等级划分的, 等级制度的
derision	/dɪˈrɪʒən/	n.	when you show that you think someone or something is stupid or silly 讥讽, 嘲笑, 嘲弄
adaptive	/əˈdæptɪv/	adj.	having a capacity for adaptation 有适应能力的, 适应的
therein lies sth.			used to say that something is caused by or comes from a particular situation 缘此, 此即
surge	/sɜːdʒ/	n.	a sudden increase in amount or number 急剧增加
instantaneous	/ˌɪnstənˈteɪnɪəs/	adj.	happening immediately 即刻的

alienation	/ˌeɪliəˈneɪʃən/	n.	the feeling of not being part of society or a group 疏离感
crushing	/ˈkrʌʃɪŋ/	adj.	very hard to deal with, and making you lose hope and confidence 使人受不了的,压倒的
overpowering	/ˌəʊvəˈpaʊərɪŋ/	adj.	very strong 很强的,强烈的
revolt	/rɪˈvəʊlt/	n.	a refusal to accept someone's authority or obey rules or laws 造反,起义,反叛
voiceless	/ˈvɔɪslɪs/	adj.	unable to get your opinions or concerns noticed by people in power 不受人重视的,无发言权的
heedless	/ˈhiːdlɪs/	adj.	not giving attention to a risk or possible difficulty 不注意的,不理会的
forum	/ˈfɔːrəm/	n.	a group of computer users who are interested in a particular subject and discuss it using email or the Internet 网络论坛
heretofore	/ˌhɪətʊˈfɔː/	adv.	before this time 此前,在此之前
unacknowledged	/ˌʌnəkˈnɒlɪdʒd/	adj.	ignored or not noticed 未受到注意(重视)的,未被接受的
thereby	/ðeəˈbaɪ/	adv.	with the result that something else happens 从而
pluck	/plʌk/	vt.	to take someone away from a place or situation that is dangerous or unpleasant in a quick and unexpected way 带某人/某物离开
validate	/ˈvælɪdeɪt/	vt.	to make someone feel that their ideas and feelings are respected and considered seriously 受人尊重,受到重视 **validation** n. 尊重
empower	/ɪmˈpaʊə/	vt.	to give someone more control over their own life or situation 使自主,给(某人)权利 **empowerment** n. 激励自主,授权,赋权
weblog	/ˈweblɒɡ/	n.	a website that is owned by a particular person or group of people rather than by an organization or company, and that has information about one or more subjects 网络日志
avatar	/ˈævətɑː/	n.	a person who represents an idea or quality 化身

Unit 11 Communication

Notes:

1. **Podcast** is a series of digital media files (either audio or video) that are released episodically and downloaded through web syndication.
2. **Google search** is a web search engine owned by Google Inc. and is the most-used search engine on the Web. It was originally developed by Larry Page and Sergey Brin in 1997.
3. **Text messaging** refers to the exchange of brief written messages between mobile phones over cellular networks.
4. **Niche TV programming** refers to a certain type of programming that is specific in content and attracts a narrow but highly interested audience.
5. **Washingtonpost** is Washington, D.C.'s largest and oldest newspaper, founded in 1877. Located in the nation's capital, the Post has a particular emphasis on national politics.
6. **Information overload** is a term popularized by Alvin Toffler that refers to the difficulty a person can have in understanding an issue or making decisions because of the presence of too much information.
7. **Thomas Jefferson** (1743–1826) was the third President of the United States (1801–1809), the principal author of the Declaration of Independence (1776), and one of the most influential Founding Fathers for his promotion of the ideals of republicanism in the United States.
8. **Antebellum** refers to Antebellum era, the history of the United States (1789–1849), i.e. before the US Civil War but after the American Revolution and the beginning of the US as sovereign nation.

Reading Comprehension

I. **Summarize the reasons** *why there is a surge of citizen media* *(such as blogging)* **in about 80 words.**

_____
_____
_____
_____
_____
_____

II. **Answer the following questions.**
   1. Who is Stephan Pastis?

2. What is a "comic strip" according to Rat?
3. What is the situation of blogging in comparison to the mainstream media?
4. Can you name some forms of citizen-created media?
5. What is the ultimate product of blogging? Explain.

III. Paraphrase the following sentences within the context of the reading passage.

1. (Para.6) Pastis thus took an ironic and well-timed poke at the current notion, popular in some blogging circles and even among a few establishment pundits, that the nation's established print and television media are going the way of the dinosaur ...
2. (Para.8) Similar ventures are launching with regularity.
3. (Para.12) As professionalism grew, often with hierarchical organizations and formal systems for accrediting knowledge, so amateurs came to be seen as second rate.
4. (Para.15) For that we need to look to the alienation, powerlessness, and crushing anonymity that seem to be such overpowering features of modern life.
5. (Para.17) ... and thereby pluck from the indifference of daily life a bit of validation for themselves, their ideas, and their creative abilities.

IV. Based on the text, decide whether the following statements are true or false. For false statements, write the facts in parentheses.

1. "Rat's Book Signing" is mainly relevant to the impact of blogging on American media consumption habits.
   (   )
2. Washingtonpost.com and Backfence.com are pioneers of citizen-generated media.
   (   )
3. In terms of scale, scope and cultural impact, today's explosion of citizen-created media is unprecedented.
   (   )
4. The tools for creating and publishing citizen-generated media are much cheaper, which partly contributes to the surge of citizen media.
   (   )
5. The conclusion of the *Pro-Am* study drawn by Demos is not applicable to the blogging phenomenon.
   (   )

Unit 11 Communication

Vocabulary Exercises

I. Fill in the blank in each sentence with a word or phrase from the box below. Make sure the appropriate form of the word is used.

| alienation | derision | unprecedented | pluck...from | apathetic |
| mediocrity | insidious | insurgent | hierarchical | accredit |

1. People who are unable to motivate themselves must be content with _____, no matter how impressive their other talents.
2. The audience greeted his speech with shouts of _____ .
3. Between 1938 and 1940, some 10,000 children from Germany, Austria and Poland were _____ the imminent threat of the Nazi inferno and brought to safety in Britain.
4. All approaches to the capital are now under the control of the _____ groups.
5. How can the young people of today be so _____ about the world and its problems?
6. Noise is a(n) _____ kind of pollution that particularly affects urban areas and invades our daily lives.
7. Families are viewed as a _____ structure in terms of cousinship, ancestry (as depicted in a family tree) and inheritance.
8. Racial discrimination, language barriers, and culture shock reinforce the sense of _____ and frustration among new immigrant students.
9. The global financial crisis of 2008 caused _____ levels of unemployment worldwide.
10. By 2009, there were 130 _____ medical schools in the United States and 1,000 teaching hospitals to train residents.

II. Fill in the blanks with the appropriate forms of the given words.

1. The Berlin International Film Festival is _____ (unacknowledged) to be a competitive film fest by the International Federation of Film Producers (FIAPF) since 1956.
2. Mongolia is one of the least densely _____ (populate) countries in the world.
3. Police said an _____ (anonymity) caller warned just after midnight yesterday that a bomb was about to go off.
4. They promised to unionize hundreds of thousands of workers and to pressure the Democratic Party to pay far more _____ (heedless) to workers' concerns.
5. Her well _____ (articulate) point of view has pushed me to think more openly.
6. In vain they rushed _____ (frantic) a round from place to place, trying to get any information of the lost child.
7. He is _____ (empowerment) to appoint advocates to look after the matter in the

courts and government offices.

III. Replace the italicized words or phrases with simple, everyday words.

1. ...they do enable talented but *heretofore* unacknowledged people with something to say to find an audience (　　　　)
2. ...a new *breed* of amateur has emerged (　　　　)
3. ...What accounts for this unprecedented new *surge* of citizen media? (　　　　)
4. ...or any number of *antebellum* Southern ladies... (　　　　)
5. ...but also through virtually every digital communications tool they can *get their hands on*. (　　　　)

IV. Choose the word or phrase that best completes each of the following sentences.

1. The population isn't _____ evenly across the nation but unevenly among the forty neighborhood types, with distinct socioeconomic levels, family life cycles and ethnic make-ups.
   A. attributed   B. tributed   C. distributed   D. contributed
2. Beneath his pale and coolly reserved _____ something burned and melted, hardened; he was more than excited.
   A. interior   B. inferior   C. exterior   D. better
3. The nature of the World Wide Web is unfamiliar to most people. In order to _____ this foreign environment people describe the unfamiliar in terms of the familiar.
   A. make sense of   B. make sense   C. come to sense   D. talk sense
4. The new mayor is _____ the local community to involve them in his plans for the city.
   A. reaching for   B. reaching down   C. reaching back   D. reaching out to
5. According to the statistics, volunteer applicants for Beijing Olympics had _____ competition record.
   A. crushed   B. crashed   C. smashed   D. cracked

Translation Exercises

I. Translate each of the following sentences into English, using the word or phrase given in the brackets.

1. 他费了很大功夫也没弄清楚黑板上这些符号的意义。(make sense of)

2. 在过去的十年里,社会心理学家们证明了这些冲动的普遍性以及它们何时最容易左右人的行为。(document)

Unit 11　Communication

3. 上大学之后,我一直设法自立而不求助于我的父母。(turn to)

4. 过去的十年间电信业飞速发展。即时通讯系统使世界各地任何一个有电脑能上网的人都能进行实时交流。(instantaneous)

5. 国际援助给那个遭遇了严重地震的国家带来了新的希望。(give rise to)

II. **Translate the following paragraph into English.**

　　面试是门学问,而且给人留下好的第一印象的机会不会有第二次。现代人大都着装随意,但这并不代表你面试时可以随意。外表看上去整洁而且职业化很重要,但至于你是穿套装还是穿不那么正式的服装,还要取决于公司的文化和你所应聘的职位。

III. **Translate the following paragraph into Chinese.**

　　Tens of millions of people around the world are now documenting their lives, exploring their religious and political beliefs, and engaging in public conversations on everything from poetry to classic cars to the latest advances in nanotechnology. And they do so not only through blogs, but also through virtually every digital communications tool they can get their hands on. They create and distribute their own movies, record and narrate their own audio and video podcasts, send text messages to their friends' handheld devices, and share photos via their camera phones.

Language Appreciation

I. **Read the text carefully, then pick out the sentences that you think are well-written. Pay close attention to the italicized words or phrases of the following sentences. Try to appreciate the way in which the author expresses his/her ideas. Learn how to use them in your own writing.**

1. But in terms of its enormous scale, scope, and cultural impact, *nothing in history compares to today's explosion of citizen-created media.*

2. Knowledge, *once held tightly in the hands of professionals and their institutions,* will *flow into* networks of dedicated amateurs.

II. Read aloud and recite paragraphs 11 and 14.

III. Stylistics Study

Levels of Formality
— Stylistic Consciousness (2)

Formal language often appears in official reports, business letters and regulation manuals which are used publicly for some serious purposes. Informal language, often colloquial language, is mainly used in personal or private occasions, such as casual conversations, personal letters, etc. The concept of "formality" is comparative, and mainly lies in diction.

Compare the following three sentences.

Examples: 1) *When his dad <u>died</u>, Pete had to get another job.*
2) *After his father's <u>death</u>, Peter had to change his job.*
3) *On the <u>decease</u> of his father, Mr. Brown was obliged to seek alternative employment.*

Additionally, formality can also be manifested in syntax. For example, periodic sentences tend to appear more often in formal texts while loose sentences in informal ones.

Text II

Oprah Talks to Nelson Mandela

Pre-reading Questions

1. In celebrity interviews, interviews often ask very personal questions. Do you think it is appropriate? Why do you think audiences like to hear about this type of news?
2. What techniques make an interview a successful versus an unsuccessful one? Consider question type, attitude, etc.

Unit 11 Communication

1   **Oprah:** The last time we talked, you said that if you hadn't been in prison, you wouldn't have achieved the most difficult task in life—changing yourself. How did 27 years of reflection make you a different man?

2   **Nelson:** Before I went to jail, I was active in politics as a member of South Africa's leading organization—and I was generally busy from 7 A.M. until midnight. I never had time to sit and think. As I worked, physical and mental fatigue set in and I was unable to operate to the maximum of my intellectual ability. But in a single cell in prison, I had time to think. I had a clear view of my past and present, and I found that my past left much to be desired, both in regard to my relations with other humans and in developing personal worth.

3   **Oprah:** In what way did your past leave much to be desired?

4   **Nelson:** When I reached Johannesburg in the 1940s, I was neglected by my family because I had disappointed them—I'd run away from being forced into an arranged marriage, which was a big blow to them. In Johannesburg, many people were kind to me—but when I finished my studies and qualified as a lawyer, I got busy with politics and never thought of them. It was only when I was in jail that I wondered, "What happened to so-and-so? Why didn't I go back and say thank you?" I had become very small and had not behaved like a human who appreciates hospitality and support. I decided that if I ever got out of prison, I would make it up to those people or to their children and grandchildren. That is how I was able to change my life—by knowing that if somebody does something good for you, you have to respond.

5   **Oprah:** Did you feel disconnected from the world?

6   **Nelson:** We had our ways of communicating with the outside. And though we would get the news two or three days after it had happened, we still got it. Because we became friendly with certain wardens, we'd ask them, "Can't you take us to the rubbish dump?" Newspapers were dumped there, and we'd clean them off, hide them, and take them back to our cells to read.

7   **Oprah:** You became even more disciplined in prison than you had been before, studying regularly and encouraging your colleagues to study. Why?

8   **Nelson:** No country can really develop unless its citizens are educated. Any nation that is progressive is led by people who have had the privilege of studying. I knew we could improve our lives even in jail. We could come out as different men, and we could even come out with two degrees. Educating ourselves was a way to give ourselves the most powerful weapon for freedom.

9   **Oprah:** Did you come out a wiser man?

10 **Nelson:** All I can say is that I was less foolish than I was when I went in. I equipped myself by reading literature, especially classic novels such as *The Grapes of Wrath*.

11 **Oprah:** That's one of my favorite books.

12 **Nelson:** When I closed that book, I was a different man. It enriched my powers of thinking and discipline, and my relationships. I left prison more informed than when I went in. And the more informed you are, the less arrogant and aggressive you are.

13 **Oprah:** Do you disdain arrogance?

14 **Nelson:** Of course. In my younger days, I was arrogant—jail helped me to get rid of it. I did nothing but make enemies because of my arrogance.

15 **Oprah:** What other characteristics do you abhor?

16 **Nelson:** Ignorance—and a person's inability to see what unites us instead of only those things that divide us. A good leader can engage in a debate frankly and thoroughly, knowing that at the end he and the other side must be closer, and thus emerge stronger. You don't have that idea when you are arrogant, superficial, and uninformed.

17 **Oprah:** You just want *your* point of view to prevail. But a good leader always has the intention of making peace.

18 **Nelson:** That's true. When there is danger, a good leader takes the front line; but when there is celebration, a good leader stays in the back of the room.

19 **Oprah:** What characteristics do you most admire in those you respect?

20 **Nelson:** Sometimes a leader has to criticize those with whom he works—it cannot be avoided. I like a leader who can, while pointing out a mistake, bring up the good things the other person has done. If you do that, then the person sees that you have a complete picture of him. There is nobody more dangerous than one who has been humiliated, even when you humiliate him rightly.

21 **Oprah:** As I sit here and talk with you, I find it hard to imagine that you can

be the man you are after spending all that time in a seven-by-nine-foot cell. When you went back to see the cell years later, could you believe it was that tiny?

22   **Nelson:** Back then I was used to it, and I could do all sorts of things in there, like exercise every morning and evening. But now that I'm on the outside, I don't know how we survived it—the space was so small.

23   **Oprah:** Do you believe people are good at their core?

24   **Nelson:** There is no doubt whatsoever, provided you are able to arouse the goodness inherent in every human. Those of us in the fight against apartheid changed many people who hated us because they discovered that we respected them.

25   **Oprah:** How can you respect people who oppress you?

26   **Nelson:** You must understand that individuals get caught up in the policy of their country. In prison, for instance, a warden or officer is not promoted if he doesn't follow the policy of the government—though he himself does not believe in that policy.

27   **Oprah:** At one point you were offered the chance to leave prison early if you renounced violence—and you chose not to. Did you believe that violence was a solution?

28   **Nelson:** No. When I was told, "You'll be released as soon as you renounce violence," I said, "You started violence—our violence is a defense. The methods of political action that oppressed people use are determined by the oppressor." And I didn't want to leave jail under conditions. I also wouldn't allow myself to be singled out from my colleagues.

29   **Oprah:** In 1986 you began the negotiations that led to your release. Did you really believe you would be freed?

30   **Nelson:** We always knew that one day we would be released—we just did not know when. The prison would send a warden to say to us, "Give me your names, the places you came from, and exactly where you'd go if you were released." Sometimes the wardens would tell us, "You chaps cannot be kept, because the whole world is insisting that you be released."

31   **Oprah:** Is it true that when you were freed at age 71, it was like being born again?

32   **Nelson:** Yes. When I was inside the prison, I told the wardens to come to the gate with their families because I wanted to thank them. I honestly thought

they would be the only people who would be at the gate! I had no idea that I would meet a huge crowd.

33   **Oprah:** You once told me that humility is one of the greatest qualities a leader can have. Did you come out of prison a more humble man?

34   **Nelson:** If you are humble, you are no threat to anybody. Some behave in a way that dominates others. That's a mistake. If you want the cooperation of humans around you, you must make them feel they are important—and you do that by being genuine and humble. You know that other people have qualities that may be better than your own. Let them express them.

35   **Oprah:** One of the greatest lessons your life teaches us all is the power in forgiving our oppressors. As you once told me, you made the brain dominate the blood. "How were you able to practice that principle?"

36   **Nelson:** We all struggled with it, especially since we were dealing with an enemy who was more powerful than us. But because we wanted to avoid slaughtering each other, we had to suppress our feelings. That is the only way to bring about a peaceful transformation.

37   **Oprah:** Many people can't even do that in their own families.

38   **Nelson:** True, but we must teach people that when they've been wronged, they must talk to their enemies and resolve their differences for the sake of peace.

39   **Oprah:** Now that you are in what you call the evening of your life, what do you most look forward to?

40   **Nelson:** I want to continue the work I'm doing. In some areas, poor people haven't had proper roads, electricity, water, or even toilets. But things are changing. The whole process will take many years.

41   **Oprah:** One reason I hold you and your comrades in such high reverence is that you maintained your dignity in the face of oppression. You must be proud of yourself for that.

42   **Nelson:** You are very generous, Oprah. All I can tell you is that if I am the person you say I am, I was not always that man.

43   **Oprah:** Do you fear death?

44   **Nelson:** No. Shakespeare put it very well: "Cowards die many times before their deaths; the valiant never taste of death but once. Of all the wonders that I yet have heard, it seems to me most strange that men should fear; seeing that death, a necessary end, will come when it will come." When you believe that,

you disappear under a cloud of glory. Your name lives beyond the grave—and that is my approach.

(1,653 words)

Reading Comprehension

I. Answer the following questions with the information you read from the passage.
   1. How did 27 years in jail make Nelson Mandela a different man?
   2. What influence did the book *The Grapes of Wrath* have on Nelson Mandela?
   3. What was the size of Mandela's cell and what was his life like in the cell?
   4. Did Mandela think that violence was the solution to their problem(s)? Why?
   5. How was Mandela able to practice the principle of making the brain dominate the blood?

II. Topics for discussion and reflection.
   1. In the interview, Oprah asks Mandela if he fears death. Do you? Why or why not?
   2. If violence was an option for you to get what you wanted, would you take it? Why or why not?
   3. "Violence is not the answer." How much truth do you think there is to this? When is violence acceptable?

Exercises for Integrated Skills

I. Dictation

   Listen to the following passage. The passage will be read to you four times. During the first reading, which will be read at normal speed, listen and try to understand the meaning. For the second and third readings, the passage will be read sentence by sentence, or phrase by phrase, with intervals of 15 to 20 seconds. The last reading will be done at normal speed again and during this time check your work. You will then be given 2 minutes to check through your work a second time.

II. Cloze

The sports arena, stadium, amphitheater, or __1__ is a public place. From Greece and Rome to the Superdome, venue serves as a place of __2__. Public places are essential __3__ of communication. The stadium is a place of communal activity. Professional sports __4__ in spaces that yield community affiliation and contact. Modern culture is __5__ with citizens who live their lives behind locked doors and darkened car windows, individuals who __6__ themselves from contact in public with others. __7__, the very same people shout, converse, and sing the national anthem in unison. This context has become increasingly mediated as the PA announcer supplements the images __8__ on diamond vision. Stadiums offer __9__ capacity with access ruled by barriers of financial means and distance, but the modern micro and mass media place no such __10__ on fans.

1. A. complication   B. complex   C. comprehensive   D. combination
2. A. interaction   B. intercourse   C. intermediation   D. interchange
3. A. ways   B. means   C. conveyors   D. carriers
4. A. happen   B. held   C. take place   D. played
5. A. filled   B. populated   C. packed   D. inhabited
6. A. shield   B. guard   C. keep away   D. stay away
7. A. But   B. And   C. Yet   D. Then
8. A. to appear   B. appearing   C. appeared   D. appear
9. A. endless   B. tremendous   C. enormous   D. finite
10. A. limitations   B. rules   C. boundaries   D. restraints

Oral Activities

1. Role Play: Boss and Interview Candidate.

Take notes as others are presenting and discuss what was good about the interview techniques and responding tactics. What could be improved upon? Summarize and create a top 5 Dos and Don'ts about interviewing from the interviewee's perspective.

2. Role Play: Notable Figure and Reporter.

Reporter: Interview a notable person about a sensitive or controversial topic (can be decided by teacher or student). What are some techniques you can use to help get the information you need without offending the interviewee.

Interviewee: Don't give up the information too easily. Respond naturally to the questions, with the thought of not wanting to talk too much about your situation, but also not wanting the media and audience to think ill of you and make up stories.

Afterthought: Discuss the techniques used and how certain questions made you feel as the interviewee and as the reporter.

riting Practice

Composition Writing

Some people say there's a book inside everybody; today, blogs have let the book out. As stated in the text, "Blogs help break through the anonymity and isolation of modern life." The "blog revolution" has been changing people's lives and transforming society. Write a composition of about 200 words, expressing your understanding of the blog phenomenon.

Unit 12 Nurturing

Warm-up Activities

1. What are some ways to develop a child's independence and concern for others?
2. What do you think it takes to become an Olympic athlete? What are important characteristics in a coach that can help create a successful athlete?

Text I

Take This Fish and Look at It

Pre-reading Questions

1. How would you rate your level of attention to detail? When you observe the things around you, what percentage of the details around you do you think you actually notice?
2. How can you increase your ability to notice more details when making observations?

Most of us tend to look at things without really seeing what is there. In everyday life this lack of observation may not be noticed, but in science it would be considered a serious failing. Louis Agassiz (1807–73), the distinguished Harvard professor of natural history, knew this and used to subject his students to a rigorous but useful exercise in minute observation. One of his students was Samuel Scudder, who has left us the following account.

Unit 12 Nurturing

1   It was more than fifteen years ago that I entered the laboratory of Professor Agassiz, and told him I had enrolled my name in the Scientific School as a student of natural history. He asked me a few questions about my object in coming, my antecedents generally, the mode in which I afterwards proposed to use the knowledge I might acquire, and, finally, whether I wished to study any special branch. To the latter I replied that, while I wished to be well grounded in all departments of zoology, I purposed to devote myself specially to insects.

2   "When do you wish to begin?" he asked.

3   "Now," I replied.

4   This seemed to please him, and with an energetic "Very well!" he reached from a shelf a huge jar of specimens in yellow alcohol. "Take this fish," he said, "and look at it; we call it a haemulon; by and by I will ask what you have seen."

5   With that he left me, but in a moment returned with explicit instructions as to the care of the object entrusted to me.

6   "No man is fit to be a naturalist," said he, "who does not know how to take care of specimens."

7   I was to keep the fish before me in a tin tray, and occasionally moisten the surface with alcohol from the jar, always taking care to replace the stopper tightly. Those were not the days of ground-glass stoppers and elegantly shaped exhibition jars; all the old students will recall the huge neckless glass bottles with their leaky, wax-besmeared corks, half eaten by insects, and begrimed with cellar dust. Entomology was a cleaner science than ichthyology, but the example of the Professor, who had unhesitatingly plunged to the bottom of the jar to produce the fish, was infectious; and though this alcohol had a "very ancient and fishlike smell," I really dared not show any aversion within these sacred precincts, and treated the alcohol as though it were pure water. Still I was conscious of a passing feeling of disappointment, for gazing at a fish did not commend itself to an ardent entomologist. My friends at home, too, were annoyed when they discovered that no amount of eau-de-Cologne would drown the perfume which haunted me like a shadow.

8   In ten minutes I had seen all that could be seen in that fish, and started in search of the Professor—who had, however, left the Museum; and when I

returned, after lingering over some of the odd animals stored in the upper apartment, my specimen was dry all over. I dashed the fluid over the fish as if to resuscitate the beast from a fainting fit, and looked with anxiety for a return of the normal sloppy appearance. This little excitement over, nothing was to be done but to return to a steadfast gaze at my mute companion. Half an hour passed—an hour—another hour; the fish began to look loathsome. I turned it over and around; looked it in the face-ghastly; from behind, beneath, above, sideways, at a three-quarters' view—just as ghastly. I was in despair; at an early hour I concluded that lunch was necessary; so, with infinite relief, the fish was carefully replaced in the jar, and for an hour I was free.

9   On my return, I learned that Professor Agassiz had been at the Museum, but had gone, and would not return for several hours. My fellow students were too busy to be disturbed by continued conversation. Slowly I drew forth that hideous fish, and with a feeling of desperation again looked at it. I might not use a magnifying-glass; instruments of all kinds were interdicted. My two hands, my two eyes, and the fish: it seemed a most limited field. I pushed my finger down its throat to feel how sharp the teeth were. I began to count the scales in the different rows, until I was convinced that that was nonsense. At last a happy thought struck me—I would draw the fish; and now with surprise I began to discover new features in the creature. Just then the Professor returned.

10 "That is right," said he; "a pencil is one of the best of eyes. I am glad to notice, too, that you keep your specimen wet, and your bottle corked."

11 With these encouraging words, he added: "Well, what is it like?"

12 He listened attentively to my brief rehearsal of the structure of parts whose names were still unknown to me: the fringed gill-arches and movable operculum; the pores of the head, fleshy lips and lidless eyes; the lateral line, the spinous fins and forked tail; the compressed and arched body. When I finished, he waited as if expecting more, and then, with an air of disappointment:

13 "You have not looked very carefully; why," he continued more earnestly, "you haven't even seen one of the most conspicuous features of the animal, which is as plainly before your eyes as the fish itself; look again, look again!" and he left me to my misery.

14 I was piqued; I was mortified. Still more of that wretched fish! But now I set myself to my tasks with a will, and discovered one new thing after another,

until I saw how just the Professor's criticism had been. The afternoon passed quickly; and when, towards its close, the Professor inquired:

15   "Do you see it yet?"

16   "No," I replied, "I am certain I do not, but I see how little I was before."

17   "That is next best," said he, earnestly, "but I won't hear you now; put away your fish and go home; perhaps you will be ready with a better answer in the morning. I will examine you before you look at the fish."

18   This was disconcerting. Not only must I think of my fish all night, studying, without the object before me, what this unknown but most visible feature might be; but also, without reviewing my discoveries, I must give an exact account of them the next day. I had a bad memory; so I walked home by Charles River in a distracted state, with my two perplexities.

19   The cordial greeting from the Professor the next morning was reassuring; here was a man who seemed to be quite as anxious as I that I should see for myself what he saw.

20   "Do you perhaps mean," I asked, "that the fish has symmetrical sides with paired organs?"

21   His thoroughly pleased "Of course! Of course!" repaid the wakeful hours of the previous night. After he had discoursed most happily and enthusiastically—as he always did—upon the importance of this point, I ventured to ask what I should do next.

22   "Oh, look at your fish!" he said, and left me again to my own devices. In a little more than an hour he returned, and heard my new catalogue.

23   "That is good, that is good!" he repeated; "but that is not all; go on"; and so for three long days he placed that fish before my eyes, forbidding me to look at anything else, or to use any artificial aid. "Look, look, look," was his repeated injunction.

24   This was the best entomological lesson I ever had—a lesson whose influence has extended to the details of every subsequent study; a legacy the Professor had left to me, as he has left it to many others, of inestimable value, which we could not buy, with which we cannot part.

25   A year afterward, some of us were amusing ourselves with chalking outlandish beasts on the Museum blackboard. We drew prancing starfishes; frogs in mortal combat; hydra-headed worms; stately crawfishes, standing on their

tails, bearing aloft umbrellas; and grotesque fishes with gaping mouths and staring eyes. The Professor came in shortly after, and was as amused as any at our experiments. He looked at the fishes.

26 "Haemulons, every one of them," he said; "Mr.—drew them."

27 True; and to this day, if I attempt a fish, I can draw nothing but haemulons.

28 The fourth day, a second fish of the same group was placed beside the first, and I was bidden to point out the resemblances and differences between the two; another and another followed, until the entire family lay before me, and a whole legion of jars covered the table and surrounding shelves; the odor had become a pleasant perfume; and even now, the sight of an old, six-inch, worm-eaten cork brings fragrant memories.

29 The whole group of haemulons was thus brought in review; and, whether engaged upon the dissection of the internal organs, the preparation and examination of the bony framework, or the description of the various parts, Agassiz's training in the method of observing facts and their orderly arrangement was ever accompanied by the urgent exhortation not to be content with them.

30 "Facts are stupid things," he would say, "until brought into connection with some general law."

31 At the end of eight months, it was almost with reluctance that I left these friends and turned to insects; but what I had gained by this outside experience has been of greater value than years of later investigation in my favorite groups.

By Samuel H. Scudder

(1,520 words)

Unit 12 Nurturing

Words and Expressions

enroll	/ɪnˈrəʊl/	vt.	to officially arrange to join a school, university, or course, or to arrange for someone else to do this 注册(学习),招(生),吸收(成员)
antecedent	/ˌæntɪˈsiːdənt/	n.	an event, organization, or thing that is similar to the one you have mentioned but existed earlier 先例
zoology	/zəʊˈɒlədʒɪ/	n.	the scientific study of animals and their behaviour 动物学
specimen	/ˈspesɪmən/	n.	a single example of something, often an animal or plant 标本,样本,抽样
haemulon	/ˈhiːmjʊlən/		石鲈属
explicit	/ɪkˈsplɪsɪt/	adj.	expressed in a way that is very clear and direct 清楚的,明确的
entrust	/ɪnˈtrʌst/	vt.	to make someone responsible for doing something important, or for taking care of someone 交托,委托
moisten	/ˈmɔɪsən/	vt.	to make something slightly wet (使)湿润,(使)潮湿
stopper	/ˈstɒpə/	n.	the thing that you put in the top part of a bottle to prevent whatever is inside from coming out 瓶塞
leaky	/ˈliːkɪ/	adj.	a container, roof, etc. that is leaky has a hole or crack in it so that liquid or gas passes through it 有裂缝的,漏的,有漏洞的
besmear	/bɪˈsmɪə/	vt.	to make filthy 弄脏,败坏,玷污
begrime	/bɪˈgraɪm/	vt.	to make dirty 弄脏,玷污
cellar	/ˈselə/	n.	a room under a house or other building, often used for storing things 地窖,地下储藏室
entomology	/ˌentəˈmɒlədʒɪ/	n.	the scientific study of insects 昆虫学 **entomologist** n. 昆虫学家 **entomological** adj. 昆虫学的
ichthyology	/ˌɪkθɪˈɒlədʒɪ/	n.	the branch of zoology that deals with the study of fish 鱼类学

infectious	/ɪnˈfekʃəs/	adj.	describes something that has an effect on everyone who is present and makes them want to join in 富有感染力的
aversion	/əˈvɜːʃən/	n.	a strong dislike of something or someone 反感,厌恶,讨厌
ardent	/ˈɑːdənt/	adj.	showing strong positive feelings about an activity and determination to succeed at it 热心的,强烈的
eau-de-Cologne		n.	a sweet-smelling liquid used to make you feel fresh and smell nice 古龙水,科隆香水
resuscitate	/rɪˈsʌsɪteɪt/	vt.	to make someone breathe again or become conscious after they have almost died 使苏醒,使恢复呼吸
sloppy	/ˈslɒpɪ/	adj.	wet and disgusting (令人讨厌地)湿漉漉的
steadfast	/ˈstedfɑːst/	adj.	faithful and very loyal 忠实的,忠诚的
mute	/mjuːt/	adj.	unable or unwilling to speak 缄默的,不说话的,拒绝说话的
loathsome	/ˈləʊðsəm/	adj.	very unpleasant or cruel 令人厌恶的,讨厌的
ghastly	/ˈɡɑːstlɪ/	adj.	extremely bad, shocking, or upsetting 极差的,令人震惊的,使人烦恼的
hideous	/ˈhɪdɪəs/	adj.	extremely unpleasant or ugly 极丑的,极难看的,极坏的
magnifying-glass		n.	a round piece of glass with a handle, used to make objects or print look bigger 放大镜
interdict	/ˈɪntədɪkt/	vt.	to tell someone not to do sth. 禁止(行动),禁用,限制
fringe	/frɪndʒ/	vt.	to be around the edge of something 围绕着……,成为……的边缘
gill	/ɡɪl/	n.	one of the organs on the sides of a fish through which it breathes 鱼鳃
operculum	/əˈpɜːkjʊləm/	n.	a lid or flap covering an aperture (鱼类的)鳃盖
fleshy	/ˈfleʃɪ/	adj.	having a lot of flesh 多肉的,肥胖的
lateral	/ˈlætərəl/	adj.	relating to the sides of something, or movement to the side 侧面的,横向的
spinous	/ˈspaɪnəs/	adj.	relating to, shaped like, or having a spine or spines 多刺的,刺状的

Unit 12 Nurturing

compress	/kəm'pres/	vt.	to press something or make it smaller so that it takes up less space, or to become smaller 压紧,压缩
earnest	/'ɜːnɪst/	adj.	very serious and sincere 诚恳的,认真的 **earnestly** adv. 诚恳地,认真地
conspicuous	/kən'spɪkjʊəs/	adj.	very easy to notice 显眼的,与众不同的,显著的
pique	/piːk/	vt.	to make someone feel annoyed or upset, especially by ignoring them or making them look stupid 使(某人)生气,激怒
mortify	/'mɔːtɪfaɪ/	vt.	to cause someone to feel extremely embarrassed or ashamed 使深感窘迫(丢脸)
disconcerting	/ˌdɪskən'sɜːtɪŋ/	adj.	making you feel slightly confused, embarrassed, or worried 令人略感困惑(担忧,尴尬)的
distracted	/dɪs'træktɪd/	adj.	anxious and unable to think clearly 心神不宁的,心烦意乱的,思想不集中的
perplexity	/pə'pleksətɪ/	n.	something that is complicated or difficult to understand 令人费解的事物,令人困惑的事物,复杂的事物
cordial	/'kɔːdɪəl/	n.	friendly, but formal and polite 热诚的,友好的
symmetrical	/sɪ'metrɪkəl/	adj.	having two halves that are exactly the same shape and size 对称的
discourse upon			to make a long formal speech about something, or to discuss something seriously 演讲,论述
catalogue	/'kætəlɒg/	n.	a complete list of things that you can look at, buy, or use, for example in a library or at an art show 目录
injunction	/ɪn'dʒʌŋkʃən/	n.	a piece of advice or an order from someone in authority 忠告,指令,训谕
outlandish	/aʊt'lændɪʃ/	adj.	strange and unusual 奇异的,另类的
prance	/prɑːns/	vi.	to walk or dance with high steps or large movements 昂首阔步,趾高气昂地走
mortal combat			fighting until one person kills another 殊死的战斗,你死我活的搏斗
hydra-headed		adj.	having many heads or containing many problems, difficulties, or obstacles 多头的,多问题的,多困难的

crawfish	/ˈkrɔːfɪʃ/	n.	a small animal like a lobster that lives in rivers and streams 淡水螯虾
aloft	/əˈlɒft/	adv.	high up in the air 在高处，在空中
grotesque	/grəʊˈtesk/	adj.	extremely ugly in a strange or unnatural way 极丑陋的，怪异的
dissect	/dɪˈsekt/	vt.	to cut up the body of a dead animal or person in order to study it 解剖（人或动物的尸体）**dissection** n. 解剖
exhort	/ɪgˈzɔːt/	vt.	to try very hard to persuade someone to do something 恳请，规劝 **exhortation** n. 规劝，告诫

Notes:

1. **Samuel H. Scudder (1837–1911)** was an American scientist who was educated at Williams College and Harvard University. His main scientific contributions were in the study of butterflies and orthoptera (an order of insects that includes grasshoppers and crickets). He was one of the most learned and productive entomologists of his day.

Reading Comprehension

I. **Summarize *my* procedure of discovering the nature of the fish in chronological order:**

In the morning (of the day): _____

_____

_____

In the afternoon (of the day): _____

_____

_____

The next morning: _____

Unit 12 Nurturing

II. Answer the following questions.

1. What was *I* told to do on the day that *I* entered Professor Agassiz's laboratory?
2. What was the fish like?
3. Why did *I* go to have lunch at an early hour?
4. What do the "two perplexities"(Para.18) refer to?
5. What is the most conspicuous feature of the fish according to the text?

III. Paraphrase the following sentences within the context of the reading passage.

1. (Para.5) With that he left me, but in a moment returned with explicit instructions as to the care of the object entrusted to me.
2. (Para.7) ...and though this alcohol had a "very ancient and fishlike smell," I really dared not show any aversion within these sacred precincts, and treated the alcohol as though it were pure water.
3. (Para.8) I dashed the fluid over the fish as if to resuscitate the beast from a fainting fit, and looked with anxiety for a return of the normal sloppy appearance.
4. (Para.14) I was piqued; I was mortified.
5. (Para.28) Agassiz's training in the method of observing facts and their orderly arrangement was ever accompanied by the urgent exhortation not to be content with them.

IV. Based on the text, decide whether the following statements are true or false. For false statements, write the facts in parentheses.

1. I told Professor Agassiz that I would devote myself to fish.
   (   )
2. I could not use any instruments while observing the fish.
   (   )
3. Professor Agassiz said that counting the scales of the fish was nonsense.
   (   )
4. It was troublesome for me to think of the fish all night.
   (   )
5. The author speaks highly of Professor Agassiz's training.
   (   )

Vocabulary Exercises

I. Fill in the blank in each sentence with a word or phrase from the box below. Make sure the appropriate form of the word is used.

a legion of   bid   infectious   dissection   conspicuous   interdict
mortify   prancing   antecedent   reluctance   exhortation   aloft

1. Four world championship gold medals and two World Cup overall titles gained high reputation for Bode Miller and earned him _____ fans around the world.
2. Laura was _____ to discover that her daughter had been out drinking with boys.
3. The historical _____ of the Replica Miu Miu handbags began in 1992 when the original brand was developed by Miuccia Prada.
4. No amount of government _____ will completely eliminate the problem of old people who have insufficient means to make ends meet.
5. A tireless worker with _____ enthusiasm for his subject and a loyal colleague, he was held in affectionate esteem by students and colleagues in the university.
6. His _____ to compromise is an obstacle to his political success.
7. Her first experience of _____ was so unpleasant that she changed her mind about becoming a doctor.
8. She is restlessly _____ forwards and backwards, waiting for the right moment to break out.
9. As is shown from studies, monkeys were cautious when confronted with _____ markings.
10. Modern birds use their legs to launch and their wings to stay _____. Once they're in the air, their hind limbs are essentially payload.
11. Do as you're _____ and you'll never bear blame.
12. Governments in developing countries did not have the insight to _____ overuse of chemical fertilizers.

II. Fill in the blanks with the appropriate forms of the given words.

1. The audience looked _____ (perplexity), so the speaker tried to explain the term again.
2. Michele was _____ (disconcerting) by the news that she would not be getting a promotion, because she was sure that she deserved one.
3. With French as her first language, she can approach some English words _____ (unhesitatingly), yet in a perfect BBC accent.

Unit 12 Nurturing

4. If we can find a common point for cooperation, the chance to realize world peace will be _____ (inestimable) enhanced.
5. Standing at the bus stop in the rain, she found her skirt and boots were soon _____ _____ (besmeared) with mud from passing cars.

III. Replace the italicized words or phrases with simple, everyday words.
   1. ...half eaten by insects, and *begrimed* with cellar dust. (   )
   2. ...I really dared not show any *aversion* within these sacred precincts...(   )
   3. "Look, look, look," was his repeated *injunction*. (   )
   4. ... as if to *resuscitate* the beast from a fainting fit.... (   )
   5. ...I *purposed* to devote myself specially to insects. (   )
   6. I *was piqued*; I was mortified. (   )

IV. Choose the word or phrase that best completes each of the following sentences.
   1. The two governments have agreed to engage _____ a comprehensive dialogue to resolve the problem.
      A. upon   B. at   C. with   D. for
   2. His latest novel was reported to have drawn heavily _____ his own learning experience of the 1980s.
      A. in   B. on   C. forth   D. off
   3. Language is not _____ throughout the country but falls into dialects.
      A. constant   B. uniform   C. steady   D. steadfast
   4. Generally, employees define _____ communication as "the sharing of information across the organization within departments and between departments."
      A. lateral   B. internal   C. formal   D. external
   5. According to the experiment, the students who had been asked to _____ their feelings performed much worse in the memory test than the others.
      A. repress   B. impress   C. suppress   D. compress

Translation Exercises

I. Translate each of the following sentences into English, using the word or phrase given in the brackets.
   1. 在国外工作期间,她把儿子的教育委托给了一位可信赖的家庭教师。(entrust)

   2. 我非常喜欢这种葡萄酒,希望哪天能和几位挚友一起细细品尝。(linger over)

217

3. 他的画风过于独特，根本得不到大众的认可。(commend oneself to somebody)

4. 在最后一次英国文学讲座中，李教授讲了约翰·济慈(John Keats)的诗歌风格。(discourse upon)

5. 如果想取得第一手资料，你不妨亲自去看看。(see for oneself)

6. 老师询问了那个捣乱的学生，并要求他对所发生的事情做出详细解释。(give an account of)

II. Translate the following paragraph into English.

为人父母必须付出极大代价，教养孩子需要付出耐心、爱心、智慧、勇气以及高度的幽默感。有些人就干脆决定不生孩子，因为他们不确定这样的付出值不值得，但是养育孩子意味着培养下一代并且传承我们的文化，又有什么会比这更有价值呢？

III. Translate the following paragraph into Chinese.

This was the best entomological lesson I ever had—a lesson whose influence has extended to the details of every subsequent study; a legacy the Professor had left to me, as he has left it to many others, of inestimable value, which we could not buy, with which we cannot part.

Language Appreciation

I. Read the text carefully, then pick out the sentences that you think are well-written. Pay close attention to the italicized words or phrases of the following sentences. Try to appreciate the way in which the author expresses his/her ideas. Learn how to use them in your own writing.

1. This little excitement over, *nothing* was to be done *but* to return to a steadfast gaze at my mute companion.

2. This was the best entomological lesson I ever had—*a lesson whose influence has extended to the details of every subsequent study; a legacy the Professor had left to me, as he has left it to many others, of inestimable value, which we could not buy, with which we cannot part.*

Unit 12　Nurturing

II. **Read aloud and recite paragraphs 24 and 31.**

III. **Stylistics Study**

Levels of Formality
— Stylistic Consciousness (3)

Familiar (intimate) language is used among close friends and family members during informal occasions. However, talking to unfamiliar people or people more senior in age or social position (judges, professors, supervisors, etc.) often requires a more polite usage of language.

Question:

Compare the following two sentences. Which one is familiar language and which one is polite language?

1) *Peter's old woman hit the roof when he came home with that doll from the disco.*
2) *Peter's wife was very angry when he came home with the girl from the discotheque.*

Written, formal and polite language tends to be elevated or uses more rhetorical language which often belongs in the realm of literary language so that it can convey a stronger sense of seriousness.

Text II

My Mother's Promise

Pre-reading Questions

1. What are some promises your mom made to you?
2. What is the value of a promise? What kinds of promises have you made in the past? Did you keep them?

1   The marquee was lit like a Roman candle, even in daylight. Tonight: The Irish Tenors. I stood outside New York's Madison Square Garden and just stared, almost dumbstruck. I was one of the three. Me, a farm boy from County Kilkenny, a child who some thought would never walk, let alone go as far as I had in the world.

2   I managed to find the performers' entrance to the massive building and made my way to the dressing room area. Some of the best musicians in the world had

performed at the Garden, some of the greatest athletes had competed. *Good Lord*, I thought, looking out at the empty stage, *have I come through the wrong door?*

3   I walked to the center of the stage. In a few hours I'd be singing to 15,000 people with my two singing partners, John McDermott and Anthony Kearns. I looked down at my trousers, which hid my two prosthetic legs. *Forget the odds of me singing on this stage,* I thought. *The miracle is that I can walk out here at all.*

4   From the day I was born, Mam always said, I've never been shy about expressing myself. She said I came out of the womb kicking and screaming. But there was a problem. "It's his legs," said the midwife who helped deliver me. The doctors at the Dublin hospital told my parents I had phocomelia, a deformity that affected both legs below the knee. Each shin splayed outward, was shorter than normal and each foot had just three toes.

5   My parents returned home to our farm in County Kilkenny. I was moved to Temple Street Children's Hospital in Dublin for more treatment, though there was little doctors could do. Eventually they sent me home, to our farm outside the village of Nass.

6   Life was tough. I couldn't stand, much less walk. I rarely left the farmhouse—and then only in someone's arms. Mam bundled me up whenever she took me to town, no matter the season. No one outside the family was to see my legs. Not that my family was ashamed of me. No, I was as loved as loved could be. It was just that my mother had plans for me.

7   "I don't want him to see others giving him odd looks," she told Dad. "I want him to grow up believing he has the same chance as everyone else."

8   "You can't shut him off from the world," Dad told her.

9   "The world will see him when he can walk," she answered. "And he will walk."

10   Mam dedicated herself to helping me. She tried everything to get me on my feet. She tried to tempt me with toys she'd put a little ways away from me. "Stand up and get it," she'd urge. But I couldn't. She could read the frustration in my face. And I could see it in hers. Finally, when I had grown a bit, she and

Dad took me to a prosthetics clinic in Dublin. "You're going to get new legs, today, Ronan," Dad said.

I was three. The clinicians looked me over. Prosthetics was rudimentary at best in the 1960s. They laid me down on a table, atop a large sheet of hard, white paper. One drew an outline of my body. Another measured me hip to knee, knee to ankle. Next they cast my legs in plaster of Paris, to make molds for artificial lower limbs.

I felt like a lab rat. "Mam," I asked, "why do I need these?" Around the house I had become a champion crawler, with strong shoulders and arms.

"To help you walk like everyone else," she told me.

"Will I need them the rest of my life?"

"Yes," she answered. "Yes, you will."

I wasn't sure I wanted to go through with the procedure. Change is scary, especially to a child. I didn't understand how these things would work. But Mam insisted. Dad backed her up. "It's for the best, Son," he said.

A few weeks later we returned to Dublin. My artificial limbs were ready. In the examining room, Mam closed her eyes. I knew she was praying. She always closed her eyes when she prayed. And I knew she was praying for me to walk. She prayed that every day. I closed my eyes and prayed along with her.

The clinicians entered, carrying what looked to be a pair of knee-length, ladies' lace-up platform boots. "Put these on," one of the men said, handing me a pair of leather socks. "They'll keep your feet from cutting on the rivets in the boots." Then, one at a time, he slipped my legs into the boots and laced them up. Attached to their sides were reinforced steel rods to hold the limbs in place. He lifted me off the table and placed my feet on the floor. In front of me was a pair of parallel bars.

"Grab on to the bars, little man, and place one foot in front of the other," he said.

I reached up, got a good grip and pulled myself to a standing position. "I'm standing!" I exclaimed to Mam and Dad. You have no idea what an incredible sensation that was. To this day I can remember exactly how it felt to finally stand upright in the world, to not have to crawl or be carried.

"Now, walk," the clinician told me.

I took a deep breath and shifted my weight to my left foot. Then I lifted my right foot and swung it out. It felt heavier than lead in that boot. I set it down on the shiny floor beneath me. I then did the same with the left.

23   "I'm walking!" I cried.

24   I took four glorious steps. Dad's eyes were red. Mam gripped his hand tightly and beamed with pride.

25   Back home I practiced walking with my new limbs—at first while holding on to something. Then one day, just before my fourth birthday, all on my own. "There's nothing anyone can do that you can't," Mam said. She turned to Dad. "It's time for Ronan to see the world—and for the world to see him."

26   "You and I are going to walk through town," she said, turning to me.

27   The next day Mam dressed me in red dungarees and a tartan shirt. She donned a summer dress and fixed her hair and makeup. Dad drove us to the church at the edge of town. We stepped out of the car. Mam took my hand. "Hold your head up high, now, Ronan," she said.

28   We walked 300 meters to our first stop, the post office. It was the farthest I'd walked, and I was sweating from the effort. Mam greeted the clerk. "I have Ronan here with me," she said. The lady clerk came from behind the counter to have a look at me—the Tynan that townspeople had seldom seen. She handed me a yellow lollipop. "Is this the poor little dickens?" she asked.

29   We left the post office and continued down the street, Mam's eyes gleaming with a mother's pride. She walked me into the butcher shop, then the grocery store. The heavy boots and my splayed feet gave me an unnatural gait. People stared. "I don't like this," I whispered to her.

30   "I know it's hard right now, Ronan," Mam said. "But after today these people won't focus on your legs. They'll only see your courage."

31   "Okay." We kept on even though I was in pain. At the edge of the village we ran into the parish priest. "Oh, is that the delicate little fellow?" he asked.

32   "None of my children are delicate, Father," Mam replied. "especially not this one. And he won't be little." With that, we resumed our walk.

33   That night, back on our farm, I lay exhausted and sore on my bed. I'd still be sore in the morning. It meant nothing, though, compared to what I'd done on my walk. A new chapter had begun in my life and I would never forget this day.

34   And it was true. But life was still tough. Eventually I had to have both legs amputated below the knee. I was fitted with new prostheses, but still I lived in pain.

Yet whenever that pain felt too great, I remembered that walk through Nass with Mam. Her lesson has stayed with me. I've set track and field records in the World Amputee Games.

I spent so much time in hospitals that I decided to become a doctor, and earned a medical degree.

Then I bypassed the security of a career to pursue my dream of singing. And at every step Mam's words came back to me—*Ronan, you can do anything anyone else can do*—and the faith she had in God, who would help me do it.

I've sung from the grandest stages in Europe, to music played by the world's finest musicians. But Madison Square Garden has always been the Everest of concert halls to me. That night as I walked from the wings with the Irish Tenors, Mam's words chimed in my ears. Light bulbs flashed. The crowd rose to its feet. Just before the orchestra began playing I took a deep breath. My parents weren't there—Dad has passed away and Mam was back in Ireland—but I imagined their faces beaming in the footlights. The conductor waved his baton. The orchestra started playing one of my solos—"The Town I Loved So Well." I began singing. I couldn't feel the pulse of the music in my feet, but I felt it deep in my heart, the same place where Mam's promise lived.

By Ronan Tynan
(1,612 words)

Reading Comprehension

I. **Answer the following questions with the information you read from the passage.**
   1. Who would sing at New York's Madison Square Garden that night?
   2. What is phocomelia?
   3. What was *my* mother's justification for not allowing other people to see my legs?
   4. How did Ronan Tynan get his new legs at the age of 3?
   5. How was the experience of walking through town for Tynan?

II. **Topics for discussion and reflection.**
   1. What are some ways to develop a child's independence according to the text?
   2. A parent is thought to give ultimate, unconditional love. However, someone once said that

a relationship between a parent and a child is one that only grows further and further apart. Discuss your views and thoughts on this topic.

Exercises for Integrated Skills

I. Dictation

Listen to the following passage. The passage will be read to you four times. During the first reading, which will be read at normal speed, listen and try to understand the meaning. For the second and third readings, the passage will be read sentence by sentence, or phrase by phrase, with intervals of 15 to 20 seconds. The last reading will be done at normal speed again and during this time check your work. You will then be given 2 minutes to check through your work a second time.

_____

_____

_____

_____

_____

II. Cloze

The training and environment are two crucial factors that influence the ___1___ of sport expertise. Researchers ___2___ in identifying the factors that distinguish the ___3___ from the ordinary performer have created numerous theories to explain the development of expertise. ___4___ Francis Galton wrote the phrase "nature and nurture" in 1874, scientists ___5___ this phrase to describe factors that ___6___ to promote high ___7___ of human achievement (i.e., expertise). Our current understanding of the relative ___8___ of genetic (nature) and environmental (nurture) factors suggests that a significant ___9___ of the variation among individuals can be accounted for by "heritability". ___10___ whether one completely supports this position or not, environmental factors clearly play important roles in accounting for inter-individual variation.

1. A. acquisition   B. formation   C. accomplishment   D. shaping
2. A. are interested   B. have interested   C. being interested   D. interested
3. A. peculiar   B. special   C. exceptional   D. exceeding
4. A. When   B. Since   C. From   D. After
5. A. use   B. have used   C. using   D. used
6. A. interact   B. influence   C. affect   D. interplay

7. A. performance	B. levels	C. qualities	D. grades
8. A. promotion	B. distribution	C. contribution	D. attribution
9. A. fraction	B. limitation	C. division	D. portion
10. A. Regardless of	B. Despite	C. However	D. In spite of

Oral Activities

1. Some people say that marriage is the ultimate "promise." If that is the case, why is the divorce rate so high in today's society?
2. Think about some successful individuals in your life or in history or in the world today. What "habits" do you think they share/have? Why would this allow them to be successful?

Writing Practice

Composition Writing

Early childhood education has drawn more and more attention from parents. In your opinion, which is the better way for parents to nurture their kids for success in life: developing a spirit of competitiveness or cooperation? Write a composition of about 200 words to support your opinion.

References

Anthony, D. W. J. (1968) Sport and Physical Education as a Means of Aesthetic Education, *Physical Education*, 60 (179), pp. 1–6. Retrieved December 12th, 2009, from www.la84foundation.org/OlympicInformationCenter/.../1969/.../ore171.pdf

Armstrong, Lance & Jenkins, Sally. (2000) *It's Not About the Bike: My Journey Back to Life*. New York: G. P. Putnam's Sons.

Briggs, Rachel; McCarthy, Helen & Zorbas, Alexis. (2004) *16 Days: The Role of the Olympic Truce in the Toolkit for Peace*. London: Demos.

Faust, Drew (2008) "Illuminating One's Bright Virtue": Higher Education in a Changing World. Retrieved April 16th, 2008, from http://www.president.harvard.edu/speeches/ faust/080326_beida.php

Haapoja, Heather. (2005) The Stress Watchers Diet. Retrieved January 4th, 2010, from http://www.associatedcontent.com/article/1238/the_stress_watchers_diet.html

Hemingway, Ernest. (1952) *The Old Man and the Sea*. London: Jonathan Cape.

Henry, O. (2000) *Whirligigs*. New York: Bantam Doubleday Dell Publishing Group.

Hood, Leroy. (2009) A Doctor's Vision of the Future of Medicine. *Newsweek*. Retrieved July 7th, 2009, from http://www.newsweek.com/id/204227

Huxley A. (2001) *Aldous Huxley Complete Essays: Volume III, 1930–1935*, in Robert Baker and James Sexton (Eds.). Chicago: Dee.

Kline, David; Burstein, Dan & Keijzer, Arne De. (Eds) (2005) *Blog! How the Newest Media Revolution Is Changing Politics, Business, and Culture*. New York: CDS Books.

King, Martin Luther. (1964) Acceptance Speech. Retrieved October 3rd, 2009, from http://nobelprize.org/nobel_prizes/peace/laureates/1964/king-acceptance.html

Manore, Melinda; Meyer, Nanna L.& Thompson Janice. (2009) *Sport Nutrition for Health and Performance* (2nd ed.) Champaign, Illinois: Human Kinetics.

James, Muriel & Jongeward, Dorothy. (1996) *Born to Win*. Boston: Addison Wesley Publishing Company.

Noble, Thomas F.X. etc. (1998) *Western Civilization: Beyond Boundaries* (2nd edition) Boston: Houghton Mifflin Company.

Reid, Stephen and Reid, Stephen P. (2007) *The Prentice Hall Guide for College Writers* (8th ed.). Boston: Pearson Education.

Sack, Allan. & Yourman, Jack. (1984) *The Sack-Yourman Developmental Speed Reading Course* (5th edition). Baltimore, Maryland: College Skills Center.

Shivers, Jay S. & Lisle, Lee J. (1997) *The Story of Leisure: Context, Concepts, and Current*

References

Controversy. Champaign, Illinois: Human Kinetics.

Smith, Logan Pearsall and Santayana, George. (1922) *Little Essays, Drawn from the Writings of George Santayana.* New York: Scribner's sons.

The Oprah Magazine. (April, 2001) Retrieved September 16th, 2009, from http://www.oprah.com/article/omagazine/omag_200104_ocut/10

Topping, Seymour. (1999) Joseph Pulitzer and the Pulitzer Prizes. Retrieved August 14th, 2009, from http://beijing.usembassy-china.org.cn/uploads/.../joseph_pulitzer.pdf.

Tynan, Ronan. (2010) My Mother's Promise. *Guidposts.* Retrieved January 10th, 2010, from http://www.guideposts.com/story/ronan-tynan-irish-tenor?page=0%2C0

Whitehead, Alfred North.(1929) *The Aims of Education and Other Essays.* New York: Macmillan.

Williams, Melvin H. (1989) *Beyond Training: How Athletes Enhance Performance Legally and Illegally.* Champaign, Illinois: Leisure Press.

侯维瑞. (2008)《文学文体学》. 上海:上海外语教育出版社.

林语堂. (1998)《生活的艺术》. 北京:外语教学与研究出版社.

钱瑗. (2006)《实用英语文体学》. 北京:外语教学与研究出版社.

秦秀白. (1986)《英语文体学入门》. 长沙:湖南教育出版社.

王佐良,丁往道. (2004)《英语文体学引论》. 北京:外语教学与研究出版社.